Fact and Meaning

PHILOSOPHICAL THEORY

SERIES EDITORS
John McDowell, Philip Pettit and Crispin Wright

For Truth in Semantics
Anthony Appiah

The Dynamics of Belief: A Normative Logic
Peter Forrest

Abstract Objects
Bob Hale

Fact and Meaning
Jane Heal

Conditionals
Frank Jackson

Reality and Representation
David Papineau

Facts and the Function of Truth
Huw Price

Moral Dilemmas
Walter Sinnott-Armstrong

Fact and Meaning
Quine and Wittgenstein on Philosophy of Language

JANE HEAL

Basil Blackwell

Copyright © Jane Heal 1989

First published 1989

Basil Blackwell Ltd
108 Cowley Road, Oxford, OX4 1JF, UK

Basil Blackwell Inc.
432 Park Avenue South, Suite 1503
New York, NY 10016, USA

British Library Cataloguing in Publication Data
A CIP catalogue record for this book is available
from the British Library.

Library of Congress Cataloging in Publication Data

Heal, Jane.
    Fact and meaning: Quine and Wittgenstein on philosophy of
language / Jane Heal.
        p.   cm.   — (Philosophical theory)
    Bibliography: p.
    Includes index.
    ISBN 0–631–14591–5
    1. Languages—Philosophy.   2. Quine, W. V. (Willard Van Orman)–
–Contributions in philosophy of language.   3. Wittgenstein, Ludwig,
1889–1951—Contributions in philosophy of language.   I.   Title.
II. Series.
P106.H355   1989
149′.94—dc19   88–7890
                                                                              CIP

Typeset in 11 on 13 pt Baskerville
by Vera-Reyes, Inc.
Printed in Great Britain at
The Camelot Press Ltd, Southampton

Contents

Preface   vii

1 Introduction   1

2 Varieties of Realism   11
  2.1 Minimal Realism   11
  2.2 Reflecting on Minimal Realism   21
  2.3 Realism, Idealism and Empiricism   25
  2.4 Realism, Relativism and Intersubjectivity   28

3 Instrumentalism and Meaning Scepticism   35
  3.1 Quine's Arguments for the Indeterminacy of Translation   35
  3.2 Setting up a Predictive Sentence Machine   40
  3.3 Indeterminacy of Function and Meaning   45
  3.4 Instrumentalism and the Revisability of Logic   55

4 Quine's Naturalized Empiricism   60
  4.1 Quine's Epistemology   60
  4.2 Ontological Relativity and Disquotation   70
  4.3 Quine's Version of Realism   75
  4.4 Should Empiricism be Naturalized?   82

5 The Mona Lisa Mosaic   86
  5.1 Semantic Holism   86
  5.2 Holism and Indeterminacy: the Mosaic Analogy   92
  5.3 Holism, Indeterminacy and Language   98
  5.4 Can We Restore Determinacy?   102

6 The Slide into the Abyss 112
  6.1 The Incompatibility of Realism and Meaning
    Scepticism 112
  6.2 Thoroughgoing Pragmatism 121
  6.3 Wittgenstein and Pragmatism 129
  6.4 Empiricism and Platonism 134

7 The Dissolving Mirror 143
  7.1 Wittgenstein's Hostility to Mirroring Realism 143
  7.2 Explanation and the Absolute Conception 149
  7.3 Kripke and Norms 160

8 Interpretations and Misinterpretations 167
  8.1 Speech Acts and Language Games 167
  8.2 Wittgenstein and Anti-Realism 178

9 Interests, Activities and Meanings 192
  9.1 Proof and New Concepts 192
  9.2 Conceptual Change and Determinacy of Sense 196
  9.3 Other Forms of Life? 206
  9.4 Modal Realism 210
  9.5 Facts about Meaning 216

Notes 229
Bibliography 240
Index 245

Preface

The aim of this book is to formulate a view of some very wide-ranging themes about which an enormous amount has been written, and it would be absurd to claim any kind of comprehensiveness or finality for this treatment of them. Philosophical discussion forms a kaleidoscopically changing scene. New, or seemingly new, pieces are constantly emerging into view and new juxtapositions of old pieces reveal themselves. I hope that I have detected and described the salient features of some recurrent and significant patterns – but it may be that I have only provided a muddled account of some temporary configuration. In any case it is certain that other interesting arrangements are possible, other connections can be made and other themes justifiably brought to prominence. I hope that this does not provide an excuse for sloppiness or for failing to notice matters which need discussion. But it goes some way to explain why a great amount of excellent work goes undiscussed here.

I have tried to acknowledge the main sources of and influences on my views; but I am far from sure that I have identified and remembered all of them, since philosophical views develop in such devious ways and over such a length of time. I have several times had the disconcerting experience of writing down some thought I took to be new and then discovering the very same idea on looking through old notes of my own. If in this way I can mislay and seemingly re-invent my own ideas, it is surely possible to do it to those of others as well and I am certain that many cases of such borrowing exist in the following pages. To all those whose ideas I have thus appropriated without acknowledgement, I apologize.

The references in the Notes section are given in an abbreviated and informal fashion. In connection with Wittgenstein's works, numbers refer to sections, except for *Philosophical Investigations* Part II , where numbers refer to pages. Full details of the works cited are to be found in the bibliography.

I am conscious of a debt to many friends and colleagues who are not explicitly mentioned in the book and with whom I have discussed these matters. I would like to record in particular my gratitude to Geoffrey Midgley, conversations with whom over many years have much enlivened and enriched my understanding of Wittgenstein. I would also like to thank Crispin Wright who encouraged me to undertake this project in the first place and whose acute comments on an earlier draft saved me from many blunders.

St John's College
Cambridge

1

Introduction

When we make remarks which attribute content or significance to things – for example when we say what a sentence means or what a person's thought is – should the claims we make be treated as factual? The aim of this book is to clarify what this question means and to examine some possible answers to it.

It proceeds primarily by consideration of what Quine and Wittgenstein say, or have been thought to say, about the matter. Some have supposed that their views are importantly similar. Quine himself triggers this comparison when he quotes with approval Wittgenstein's dictum 'Understanding a sentence means understanding a language', and comments in a footnote 'Perhaps the doctrine of indeterminacy of translation will have little air of paradox for readers familiar with Wittgenstein's latter-day remarks on meaning.'[1] Others also have claimed to find significant resemblances.[2] But are the Quinean and Wittgensteinian outlooks really alike?

It is certainly very plausible to hold that there are negative views which are shared by Quine and Wittgenstein. Both are hostile to what we may label 'Platonism' – that is, to the idea that there are concepts or meanings existing fully formed and determinate in some crystalline realm. They are hostile also to a conception of philosophy which is the natural companion of this – namely the view that philosophers should spend their time analysing concepts and laying out the connections existing in the Platonic realm. There is also another negative thesis which it seems highly plausible to hold that they share, although discussion explicitly directed to the issue does not figure prominently in the writings of either. This is scepticism about that strategy in philosophy of mind and semantics which we may call reductive materialism, of which functionalism in its many varieties is the current favoured representative. It is characteristic of this strategy to take it that psychological and semantic concepts are particular cases of the kind of concepts used in the natural sciences. Given this framework, functionalism proposes to elucidate psychological notions using centrally such ideas as causation, mechanism and law. Both Quine and Wittgenstein seem to think that this sort of approach underestimates the differences between the concepts of the natural sciences and those of psychology and semantics – differences in the kinds of explanations we give by their use and the methodology of establishing claims couched in their terms.

This leads us to remark upon another and more positive point of resemblance – the one Quine draws attention to in the quotation he cites. Both Quine and Wittgenstein lay stress on what we might call 'holistic considerations', that is on the idea that items are meaningful only if they play a role in some complex structure and that their meaning is bound up with the whole operation of the structure.

And, to note one more apparent similarity, it is easy enough to read some of the epistemological remarks in *On Certainty* (for example, the image of the river and its shifting banks)[3] as expressing a fallibilism and pragmatism similar to those famously espoused by Quine in 'Two Dogmas of Empiricism'.[4]

Pursuit of these lines of thought suggests an interpretation of both authors in which they are revealed as sceptics about meaning, on grounds having something to do with inextricable links between holism, pragmatism and the idea of meaning.

But before we rush to elaborate this picture we should set against the striking similarities (or seeming similarities) some equally striking differences. We find in Quine explicit statements to the effect that there is no fact of the matter where meaning is concerned. We have the use by him of disparaging epithets about meaning and the intensional and, in contrast, laudatory remarks about the extensional and scientific; philosophy is presented as study of the methodology of science and moreover as continuous with science itself.[5]

All this is totally absent from Wittgenstein. He may attack Platonism but he does not make any overtly sceptical remarks about meaning. And, for him, science does not play any central standard-setting role for intellectual enterprises. Wittgenstein's concerns with meaning, if we take that notion narrowly, link up with concerns about meaning as we might understand it more broadly – as significance, importance or value. A recent study proposes that we read the *Philosophical Investigations* as primarily a work on ethics.[6] This suggestion may not be totally persuasive but it is by no means absurd – as it surely would be if offered about *Word and Object*.

It may be that these are differences merely of tone and context. Perhaps the views of both Quine and Wittgenstein about meaning are sceptical for similar reasons and they differ only in their response to this insight. But on the other hand it may be that the differences we have noted connect with differences about the nature of the 'holism', which each can be said to endorse, and indeed about the conception each has of what it is to be 'factual'. The view I shall endeavour to defend is this second one. I shall argue that although there are some genuine resemblances, these occur in the contexts of radically different fundamental pictures of what it would be like to understand meaning. And the most important outcome of these different approaches is that Wittgenstein is not a sceptic or non-realist about meaning whereas Quine is.

What has been said so far may suggest that the book is primarily exegetical. This would however be a misleading impression. What I actually have to offer is somewhat uneasily balanced between exegesis and freestanding discussion of the issues. I do not say enough to defend fully the claims I advance about how to read Quine or Wittgenstein. That would require more textual citation and canvassing of rival readings than is included here. But perhaps I do not say enough either about the opposed theories I discuss to make their viability or otherwise apparent. I can only hope that I have said enough to suggest that both interpretations and evaluations have some interest and plausibility.

The shape of the discussion and its main themes are as follows. Chapter 2 considers various senses we may give to the word 'realism'. We start with what I label 'minimal realism', which is presented as an interlocked structure of comparatively uncontentious claims, about non-contradiction and epistemological independence, which are involved in being a realist. I then introduce the idea of trying to understand or explain this minimal realism. Eventually I shall recommend a *quietist* response to the challenge, conforming to the Wittgensteinian injunction to be content with description and with assembling reminders. But to see why this is attractive we need first to allow free rein to the impulse to seek for more positive seeming accounts. One such attempt at justification may proceed *pragmatically*, by remarking on the convenience, serviceability etc., of minimal realism. Another will call upon the doctrine of *mirroring realism*. This is a metaphysically ambitious view which may be summarized as follows: there is a way that the world is, independent of any observer; and in some, but only some, of our judgements we succeed in describing the world as it thus is, in itself. Chapter 2 suggests further that some variety of empiricism will be a natural outcome of accepting mirroring realism, given commitment to a naturalistic account of concept acquisition. If, moreover, we demand foundational validation of at least some concepts and exercises of them, we shall end up in sense-datum empiricism.

Chapters 3 and 4 take such an empiricism as a starting point for understanding Quine. Chapter 3 argues that instrumentalism will be the natural construal of those sentences which do not record or predict our sense data and that the idea that there are no facts about the meanings of instrumentally construed utterances can be made plausible on very Quinean-sounding grounds. Chapter 4 then attempts to meet the objection that this instrumentalist talk grossly misrepresents Quine, who professes to be a physicalist and scientific realist. I suggest that we can make a great deal of sense of Quine by supposing him to be, in truth, fundamentally an instrumentalist (albeit a 'naturalized' one) and that both his realism and his physicalism are, when considered in the light of his disquotational theory of truth and his doctrine of ontological relativity, a good deal less robust than some have supposed.

Mirroring realism in its simplest empiricist form is, on this interpretation, at the root of the Quinean view. This is not to say that Quine ends up with any straightforward realism, let alone a sense-datum view. He does not. And when, in section 4.3, I unpack his account of the activities we might label 'describing the world as it is in itself', it is a strange one, which no more commonsensical mirroring realist would be happy to accept. But empiricist mirroring realism nevertheless has the crucial role of providing Quine with his conception of what meaning is like, if there is any.

The upshot of this early phase of the argument might well be that is not particularly surprising that we get sceptical conclusions out when we feed in empiricist premises about limitations on the concepts and knowledge that people can acquire. Moreover it seems far from mandatory to accept the premises in the Quinean form. So realism about meaning, if assailed only on the basis allowed in chapters 3 and 4, will not be seen as under serious threat. But stronger attacks are in prospect.

The theme of 'holism' surfaces briefly, in chapter 3, but only in the form of remarking on the impossibility of understanding in isolation the function of the elements of the instrumentalist's theories. In chapter 5 another sort of holism comes to prominence, in considering which I abandon (or seem to abandon) the whole empiricist and mirroring realist line of thought and move to consider a less controversially based, and consequently more powerful, attack on realism about meaning.

This attack starts from the claim of semantic holism, namely the view that items with representational roles, whether they are sentences in a language or elements in a picture, have the significance they do in virtue of their placement in a suitable assemblage of similar representational items. Semantic holism is a different thesis from that of epistemological holism and needs to be clearly distinguished from it (as it is not by Quine). They are not, however, incompatible and chapter 5 argues that semantic holism, in tandem with a comparatively mild and uncontroversial form of epistemological holism, delivers the Quinean-sounding conclusion of indeterminacy of meaning. Hence (following my account of what is involved in minimal realism) I have an argument against a realistic construal of our talk about meaning.

The picture presented in this discussion might be thought to be latent in much of what Quine says but prevented from full emergence by his residual strong attachment to simple empiricism. It has, I would suggest, a good deal in common with Davidson's outlook – although Davidson's anti-factualist conclusions about meaning are not as strong as the ones I endeavour to extract from the premises.

The question now is whether the resulting theory is acceptable; and in chapter 6 we discover that trouble lurks. The position of chapter 5 purported to be realist about things other than meanings, for example, material objects. But in chapter 6 non-realism about meaning is argued to be incompatible with realism about anything at all. How, then, are we to account for the appearances of realism at various points in our linguistic practices? We are here led to consider at last that other strategy, mentioned in chapter 2, for justifying our minimal realist practices – namely a thoroughgoing pragmatism. This seems to be the direction in which our considerations are tending. (Many have thought that Quine, when we have discounted in his views the remnants of the empiricist notion of the 'given', suggests such an outlook.) But what we find on closer inspection is that pragmatism does not, after all, offer a stable resting place since it is itself incoherent.

The final section of chapter 6 suggests that mirroring realism, although not explicitly invoked in the arguments of chapter 5, nevertheless has an important part in making them seem plausible, It does this by presenting as natural and inevitable certain modal and epistemological assumptions which do play an important role in the arguments.

The claim then, at this stage of the discussion, is that a certain combination of views will land us in a morass. One element is mirroring realism and another is the idea that semantic holism commits us to the view that there is an important difference between the workings of semantic concepts and those of natural science. There are then at least two lines of enquiry we may pursue in endeavouring to extract ourselves from the difficulties. Indeed there are many more, since the conclusion that we are in a morass has been derived through an intricate collection of moves, concerning what I claim to be the implications of certain leading ideas and the independent plausibility of some extra premises which are required. But the lines to be mentioned are those which a good number of philosophers have in fact chosen to follow.

The first is to challenge the second of the two elements men-

tioned above (which I remarked earlier was a view plausibly held
in common by Quine and Wittgenstein) namely accepting the
existence of a radical difference between the concepts of natural
science and those of psychology and semantics. This challenge may
come to seem very plausible: Suppose one thinks that the world
revealed by the natural sciences is certainly real and also that
Cartesian dualism will not do; the material world, then, is all there
is. What will one do, confronted with the argument of chapter 6 –
that realism about the material is incompatible with non-realism
about meaning? Clearly one will make every attempt to arrive at a
view on which statements about meaning can be realistically
construed. But given the imagined assumptions about what is real,
this involves trying to assert that statements about meanings
describe, or are true in virtue of, facts discovered in the non-human
sciences. (Many other factors push us in the same direction, for
example, a desire to assimilate all explanation to the same broadly
causal pattern.) One's effort then will be directed to defending
some broadly materialist theory of mind (most plausibly this will
be a form of functionalism) and finding some flaw in the considerations, about semantic holism and the like, which seemed to lead to
indeterminacy and non-realism about meaning.

There are many difficulties in this materialist and functionalist
programme in the philosophy of mind. Equally, we must note,
there are many ingenious theories which aim to overcome these
difficulties. But the defensibility of these theories is a matter which
I shall not discuss in detail. Instead I shall pursue the second line of
enquiry to be described below. There is thus at this point a great
gap in my argument, if one were to regard it as attempting some
kind of demonstration of the likely correctness of a Wittgensteinian
outlook. Philosophers sympathetic to the functionalist view of mind
and meaning may nevertheless find something of interest in the
later stages of the discussion, if only of an exegetical character.

The first line, just discussed, leaves largely unexamined the
issues of what 'realism' amounts to (although it probably has an
inexplicit commitment to some version of the mirroring view) and
tries by ingenious manoeuvres to persuade itself that psychological
and semantic notions fit into some (as it seems to any exponent)
quite commonsensical notion of 'reality'. The second line of

thought, however, explores the idea that the problems exposed by chapter 6 cannot be handled this way but require a more drastic move – namely a reappraisal of the mirroring realist idea. This is the thread which is pursued through chapters 7, 8 and 9. The interest of proceeding in this way is that it offers the best chance of finding the interesting points of contrast between Quine and Wittgenstein. If Wittgenstein's views are importantly different from Quine's, in that Wittgenstein is a realist about meaning where Quine is not, the difference certainly does not lie in Wittgenstein's greater sympathy to functionalism. My suggestion is rather that we should conceive Wittgenstein's outlook as even more absolutely holistic than Quine's and as involving a rejection of the whole mirroring realist (and relatedly empiricist) manner of conceiving of meaning.

Chapter 7, then, starts by trying to make plausible the idea that Wittgenstein is hostile to mirroring realism. The grounds for this may be sketched as follows. Semantic holism insists that in understanding a person's claims about the world we have to place them in an extensive web of other judgements. But what if this web is not the whole story? What if to understand a person's thoughts and concepts we require also to place them in the context of a life, with its characteristic interests and activities? What if the idea of a purely cognitive response to a pre-sliced world is unintelligible? The outcome of these suspicions is the idea that we cannot explain or justify our concepts in the way mirroring realism desires, by pointing to the world whose nature forces these concepts on us for its correct description. What we can do instead is to describe how possession of our concepts interlocks with our interests and characteristic activities to constitute our form of life. Chapter 7 attempts also to link these thoughts with the so-called 'rule following considerations'.

The later parts of chapter 7 and all of chapter 8 are concerned with exploring some implications of this reading of Wittgenstein – in part by contrasting the interpretation I would like to recommend with those offered by others, notably Kripke, Dummett and Wright. I consider also a counter-attack on behalf of a sophisticated version of mirroring realism which is mounted by Bernard Williams.

Chapter 9 explores some elements in Wittgenstein's views on the philosophy of mathematics and uses this example to try to clarify his views on necessity and possibility and on other 'forms of life'. The last section of chapter 9 tries to assemble the various clues we have been offered to show finally how and in what sense realism about meaning can be defended.

In the terms of the original three-fold distinction of chapter 2 – pragmatism, mirroring realism and quietism – the outcome is a justification of the quietist approach to these matters. The difficulty that many have had in understanding Wittgenstein is that of seeing how rejection of mirroring realism can avoid bringing with it something in the relativist or pragmatist, and so non-realist, line. The constant temptation is to construe Wittgenstein's remarks against the metaphysical pretensions of the mirroring conception as some form of scepticism. I hope to have suggested why this is a misconstruction and thus to have vindicated the claim that his outlook on meaning is significantly different from that of Quine.

Why, one might ask, is this whole question about the 'reality' of meaning or the 'factuality' of meaning statements, of importance? At the extreme risk of vagueness and portentousness, something needs to be said about this. In part the answer is that consideration of what the question could mean, and how one could defend any particular view, is part of the modern phase of a long-running attempt by human beings to arrive at some satisfactory conception of themselves and their relations to their world. The reflective self-consciousness which leads to this philosophical project is an important human characteristic. But one can add also that the question is important because the notion of 'reality' is itself a weighted notion. There are strong links between what is real, what is worth attending to and what deserves respect. The claim that something we had thought real is not real (however we hedge about that claim or attempt to soften its impact) will almost inevitably be seen as an attempt at downgrading or debunking. The suspicion that it might be true that there are no facts about meaning can hardly do other than give us a curious sinking or dwindling feeling. However little we understand the denial of facts about meaning, the threat implicit in it seems to be that of our futility.

One thing which is at issue, then, in the question of realism about meaning (as with the closely related topic of ethical realism) is how much confidence and what kind of confidence we can have in our various human enterprises and modes of thought. Whatever the details of the fully articulated picture, it is clear that a Wittgensteinian will stand opposed to the view in which the enterprise of natural science acquires some kind of pre-eminence. He or she will want to remark that the construction of scientific theories is only one human project among many and that the (undoubted) value and validity it has should not be seen as undermining (indeed probably cannot be made intelligible without) the equal, if different, value and validity of other projects.

Something like this would be common ground among many (if not all) commentators on Wittgenstein. But it seems to me important also to emphasize that, on the view I would like to recommend, no easy endorsements or condemnations are to be had. We do not arrive at an immovably conservative viewpoint where we see that there could be no basis for criticism of or alteration to any of our 'language games'. We do not discover, for example, that the idea of enriching, altering or extending the 'psychological language game' in the light of investigations in cognitive psychology, formal semantics or artificial intelligence must be rejected as completely misguided. Wittgenstein remarks that philosophy leaves everything as it is. And one of the things which is left the same is the practice of applying ideas from one area of thought to another, of seeking parallels, of perceiving tensions and trying to resolve them. It may be that, after working through the Wittgensteinian lines of thought, we shall have a subtly altered sense of what kinds of endeavours on these lines will be fruitful or of how to describe some projects. But the proof of the pudding is in the eating, and Wittgenstein is not in the business of trying to prevent the cooking of new puddings or of predicting what all possible future puddings will taste like.

2

Varieties of Realism

2.1 MINIMAL REALISM

There are a variety of ways in which we talk about the meaning or content of items. We make remarks like 'John said that the train was late', or 'Mary has learned that there is a planet beyond Pluto', or '"Es regnet" means in German that it is raining'. Here we ascribe meaning or content to something, an utterance, psychological state or sentence type. On other occasions we speak of people knowing or not knowing the meaning of certain words or utterances. We say that we ourselves had not understood something and then suddenly saw what it meant. We report that two things (words, sentences, remarks) mean the same.

The question I want to address is whether in doing all or any of these things we are making statements. In other words (or words which I shall take to be equivalent) I shall ask whether there are facts about meanings, and whether we should be realists about meaning.

A number of important questions can be posed about the relations between thought and language and thus about the connections between ascriptions of content to linguistic and to non-linguistic items. But that there are close links seems evident. And it would be strange if content ascriptions for linguistic expressions could be defended as factual while those concerning thoughts could not, or vice versa. Hence I shall, in what follows, talk indifferently of thoughts, remarks, judgements, sentences etc., except in those contexts where attention to type/token or vehicle/meaning distinctions is demanded.

Once we have posed our initial question, further questions

immediately present themselves. What is it to be a realist, either in general or about some specific subject matter? And what is it to be right in being a realist? The exploration of various possible answers to these questions, their motivations and ramifications, will occupy much of this book. Let us start obliquely by making some observations, the acknowledgement of which would, I think, be common ground to those debating these issues.[1] In accordance with the policy announced in the last paragraph, I shall present the matter via discussion of language, although it could equally be presented in terms of the psychological states which are expressed by utterances (except for some complications which I shall mention later).

If we consider a particular, possible, move in language we find it very natural to say that in a large number of cases there are one or more other individually possible moves which are incompatible with it. By this I do not mean that it is impossible (e.g. physically) to do both moves but rather that we can make no sense of someone who makes the given move and also one of the set of incompatibles. The doing of the latter stultifies or makes nonsense of the former and the whole linguistic episode is one to which the hearer will be at a loss to respond. For example if I say 'Go away' and then (in the same breath and to the same person) 'Don't go away', the hearer will be bemused. Or if I say 'My new coat is bright red all over. And also it is deep black' my audience will not know what to make of it.

It is not clear that all classes of utterances have incompatibles of this kind. For example optatives ('Would that so and so' or 'How I wish . . .') may be imagined not to have incompatibles. Contradictory wishes may not be self-stultifying but merely unfortunate for their subject. But with intentions and beliefs (and their linguistic relatives, indicatives and imperatives) the notion is very much at home. This contrast between desires and these other intentional psychological states is perhaps connected with the fact that our desires are (on some conceptions at least) merely supplied to us as raw material, while for our intentions and beliefs we take some kind of responsibility; we regard their formation as subject to rational control and scrutiny which it is our business to apply.

The notion of incompatibility here invoked is not entirely perspicuous. It depends upon that of stultifying oneself and is only as clear as that is. Let us consider a few more examples to help get the idea in focus. If someone says 'This is a lemon' and also 'This is sweet' we may find it bizarre. But he does not stultify himself. We may easily suppose that he has strange beliefs about lemons (while still understanding 'lemon' quite adequately) or we may suppose that what is in question is an unusual lemon. We certainly do not have to entertain the suspicion that something has gone radically wrong with his thinking. What if someone says 'This is red – but it is sort of orange too'? This may again cause bewilderment for an instant. But a way of removing it is not far to seek – what she is looking at is a borderline case. Thus 'This is red' and 'This is orange' are not incompatibles.[2]

Here are two cases where we have, by various moves, explained prima facie strange remarks. And one might wonder whether these sorts of moves, or analogous ones, might not lead us to withdraw other judgements of self-stultification. There might be suspicion that the notion is not a particularly robust or fundamental one but merely reflects some superficial feature of our imaginations, of the familiarity of various situations or some other contingency of our actual experience.

Now it is certainly true that we need not be totally nonplussed by incidents such as those I mentioned earlier, e.g. someone saying both 'Go' and 'Don't go'. We have a variety of labels and techniques for assimilating and dealing with them. We may, prosaically, diagnose a slip of the tongue or look for indexical features of the utterances which would assign them to different types from those which we first assumed; more excitingly, we may discern deep psychological ambivalences or metaphorical significance.

But these moves are unlike the ones we made in response to the lemon or red/orange examples. They do not leave the full force of the original remark unaffected. In various ways they lead us to distance the speaker from the utterance produced. The doubter about incompatibility is seeking something stronger than this. His view will be that the notion of incompatibility, at least as I have introduced it, smacks strongly of some suspect conceptual/non-conceptual or analytic/synthetic distinction. His suggestion will be that there is no combination of linguistic moves which is to be ruled out as senseless. The point is not just that we might get muddled and suppose something made sense when it did not, or vice versa. The suggestion is rather that the distinction itself involves the imposition of a two-fold division on what is really a continuum; moreover, the suggestion continues, this continuum is not one with respect to something in the same conceptual area as the suspect distinction (e.g. making more or less sense, where the extremes would be close relatives of the original concepts) but with respect to something of a different kind (e.g. familiarity or unfamiliarity).

This Quinean style of challenge introduces something of import- ance to which we shall need to return. The issues it raises will be discussed further in section 6.2. But for the moment we need note only two things, both of which the doubter should be happy to concede. The first is that, however fundamental we suppose it and whatever its underpinnings, some such notion as that of incompati- bility is operable in connection with our thoughts and utterances. The second is that it is bound up with realism in the way to be sketched in the remainder of this section. Our construal of incom- patibility will thus feed back into our construal of realism.

Suppose we accept then that some moves are incompatible, however this is to be elucidated. We may move then to remark another fact: it is not always the case that of two incompatible linguistic moves one must be preferable to or more defensible than the other. For example, if my child asks me 'What colour shall I paint this dinosaur?' I may answer either 'Paint it green' or 'Paint it orange', and it is surely possible that no fault should exist in either answer. This does not mean that I can with impunity do both. If I did then then each would have a fault, namely that it is stultified by the other. It means only that if I do either one, and taking into account all circumstances (except whether or not I have done the other) there is no fault to be found in that move. It is, of course possible that there should be some reason, in the paint available or the existing aesthetic state of the picture, for giving one answer rather than the other. Choice between incompatible alter- natives is far from generally arbitrary. But it is no part of our understanding of what it is to answer such a question that there *must* be some ground, even if unknown to us, for preferring one to the other. We are not speaking here merely of the two moves being equally rationally defensible from some limited state of knowledge, but rather of there being no shadow of criticism to be levelled at either from any being or hypothetical being however knowledgeable.

On the other hand, in some areas of language use we take it that of two incompatible moves, if either is in order, one must be preferable to the other; we do not, in the way that we treat these moves, allow that both could be totally and in all respects without fault. For example, it cannot be that making the linguistic move of saying 'We've just missed the bus' is completely in order in all respects and also that the incompatible 'We have not missed the bus' is also fully in order. It may be that, given a few difficult-to-interpret glimpses of traffic passing and the unreliable state of our watches, both remarks are rationally defensible. But they cannot both be true. One of them at least must have something serious to be laid against it. (Perhaps both have something unfortunate about them in that there is no bus on that route.)

Let me, for the sake of having a label, call this idea that two incompatibles cannot both be fully acceptable 'the principle of non-contradiction'. There is a risk in this label, since it might be taken to mean simply the idea that one should not utter incompatibles. But I hope that, with this explicit warning, we can remember that it has a stronger content.

The relevance of this to realism is as follows. It would, I think, be agreed on all hands that if some sentences are treated by us in the first way and not the second, i.e. as *not* subject to the principle of non-contradiction, then those sentences can have no claim to a fact-stating role. Whatever useful function they have it is not that of describing the real. Imperatives would be a clear example of something in this category.[3] So for some utterances to be rightly construed as realistically intended statements about some subject matter it is required that those utterances be made in a way which acknowledges the principle of non-contradiction. (Let me stress that we are not at the moment talking about the correctness of realism but only about what it is to intend some utterance realistically.)

'Acknowledging the principle of non-contradiction' in the relevant sense does not mean merely having a poor opinion of an utterance which is incompatible with that which one chooses to make oneself. For example, it is characteristic of moral dispute (perhaps essential to its being moral) that one has a poor opinion of someone who differs from oneself. Hence, in a derived sense, one will have a poor opinion of those of his or her utterances which embody the opposed moral view; one thinks them expressions of wickedness, bad character or whatever. But remarking on this fact is not enough to show that we are all, in virtue of exhibiting this pattern of reaction, moral realists in the minimal sense. To be a moral realist a person must in addition take it that one or other of the opposed judgements is at fault; and it will be at fault by standards grasp of which is involved in grasp of proper use of the term. That is to say that the moral realist thinks that there is such a thing as a shared grasp of a standard for correct use of the moral term and that one or other of the disputants will be, even if unwittingly, violating a rule he or she aims to follow. (This is not to say that the dispute must be taken to be resoluble. See the remarks below on convergence.) The moral non-realist supposes, by contrast, that whatever grasping the rule for employment of a moral term amounts to, it cannot have this shape.

Let us move on to consider a second observation about realism which would, I think, be common ground. It concerns the existence of a connection between the ideas of 'realism' and 'mind independence'. The absolutely minimal version of this is the claim that if I am a realist about, for example, the existence of marigolds in my flower bed, then I take it that the existence of those marigolds is not constituted by my thinking or sincerely saying that they are there. When I think about the marigolds my thought is about some state of affairs other than itself. And the mere existence and nature of my thought does not constitute the existence of what it is a thought about, i.e. does not make the thought correct.

To say this is very far from saying that if I am a realist I must also accept various sceptical theses about my realistically intended thoughts. It does not imply that I must acknowledge some doubt about the truth of every belief of mine, let alone that I suppose it possible that they could all be false together. It does not show that we must be able to make sense of the idea of us agreeing on some complete and ideally well established theory which is nevertheless false. Also it does not rule out (at least not without a few more moves) the possibility of Cartesian direct and infallible access to certain items. It insists only that if one is a realist one admits that 'What do you think?' and 'Are things like that?' are different questions.[4]

I have presented these two, as I would claim, generally agreed observations about realism, namely its link with non-contradiction and its link with mind independence, as though they had no connection. But in fact the second is a consequence of the first. Suppose I have two remarks that I can make, e.g. 'This is a melon' and 'This is not a melon'. They are incompatible and I treat them realistically, that is as subject to the principle of non-contradiction. Remember that the incompatibility of which we speak is not a matter of the impossibility of my in fact thinking both 'This is a melon' and 'This is not a melon' or of my sincerely uttering both sentences. It is admitted that this might by mischance or muddle come about. But now let us suppose that it has come about and let us suppose also that my thinking or sincerely asserting *ipso facto* constitutes the thinking or asserting as correct. What we have described is a case where each thought or remark is, barring the presence of the other, fully correct. We have thus contradicted the initial assumption that the incompatibles were of the type where both could not be fully defensible.

There are some difficult points that I have skated over in the remarks above. The physical possibility of my uttering both 'This is a melon' and 'This is not a melon' is much clearer than is the possibility of my thinking both that something is a melon and that it is not a melon. The vehicle/content distinction does need some attention at this point. There are problems about attribution of contradictory thoughts – problems which connect with how we stultify ourselves and what it is that we prevent happening, when we make incompatible moves. One thing that we prevent is the smooth development of action and conversation, because others (and we ourselves) will be at a loss to 'see what we mean'. And we may stultify ourselves so severely that people begin to think that we do not mean or think anything at all. But I take it to be obvious that all of us do have at least some contradictory thoughts – whatever this amounts to – and, hence, that it absurd to try to fault the claim that the first uncontentious observation about realism implies the second by making out that we are always perfectly consistent.

The considerations above indicated a connection between minimal epistemological independence and the principle of non-contradiction. But a version of the 'mind independence' idea is already embedded in the very notion that certain moves are risky, even without advancing as far as the distinction between 'realistically' construed utterances or thoughts and others. If we consider imperatives, for example (or the stance towards the actions and intentions of others which they manifest), then it is clear that we do not suppose the merely sincerely and wholeheartedly issuing a command or request makes it immune from criticism. As the utterer, I may myself, in the light of information gathered later, come to think of it as a stupid command or request. And if, on the contrary, my uttering it constituted it immune from all criticism then it becomes quite opaque how it could be incompatible with any other. It becomes difficult also to see how it could have any significance beyond itself, and how issuing it or not issuing it could be a matter of importance.

So the idea of an item which does not carry with it the guarantee of its own correctness, the idea of an item which has incompatibles and which is such that it might have been better to have produced one of the incompatibles, all this is not as such the idea of a realistically meant statement or judgement. Rather the externally underpinned correctness is *truth* and the items in question are realistically meant *judgements* when the principle of non-contradiction is added. When the moves in question are seen as (always and of their nature, rather than occasionally because of contingent circumstances) such that full correctness of one rules out that of another, then the idea of their being made correct by the state of an independent reality, and the idea of their being aimed at a description of that reality, will be available.

A third observation about realism – which is again a consequence of the first – is that taking a realistic stance towards some subject matter involves supposing that when people differ about which one of a set of incompatible moves should be made, further investigation will produce *either* agreement on the question *or* recognition by both parties that no firm judgement should be made. A realist cannot, in other words, accept of some realistically construed area of language that people can justifiably persist in confident but incompatible moves within it. This is not to say that the realist may always hope for convergence of judgement. And he may tolerate continued disagreement where neither party is confident and recognizes the strength of the other's case. But he cannot make sense of a continued, clash of justifiedly confident claims which is irresoluble in principle.

A *reductio* may make this clearer. Imagine that you and I both take ourselves to have a realistic understanding of the remarks 'There are marigolds in that flower bed' and 'There are no marigolds in that flower bed'; imagine also that we accept the same linguistic system – we operate according to the same standards and accept the same constraints in assessing the remarks. (This sameness of language is a trivial condition of the convergence question arising at all in an interesting form.) Suppose further that we disagree on whether there are marigolds in that flower bed. Can we in these circumstances make sense of the idea that we also take it as a perfectly acceptable outcome that this disagreement should persist through all possible future investigation, even though each of us fully acknowledges the legitimacy of the grounds that the other has for his or her continued confident claim? This seems unintelligible (in the realist framework) because it amounts either to the acknowledgement that standards for assessing these linguistic moves provide contradictory and so incoherent guidance, or to admitting that the standards are really of the non-realist form.

So the realist thinks that there is defensible hope of convergence – in the somewhat limited sense that if a verdict on the matter is reached at all it will, with enough open mindedness and in favourable conditions of investigation, be the same verdict. But this does not commit him to thinking that every question which is realistically construed, and rightly so construed, is in fact resoluble, even 'in principle'.

Let us return now to the starting point of these reflections, namely the idea that two elements are essential to the minimal form of realism, the recognition of incompatibles within our linguistic or conceptual system and, if that is granted, the acceptance that some at least of these incompatibilities are subject to the principle of non-contradiction.

A possible strategy for undermining realism – a powerful one because it invokes such an uncontentious framework – becomes apparent at this point. It is to try to show that (contrary to what one might at first have assumed) some set of linguistic moves is performed by us in a way which does not and could not acknowledge the principle of non-contradiction. Consider for example the familiar case of secondary qualities. One could argue thus: the sentences 'This is hot' and 'This is cold' are incompatible; but the standards and rules for their use are also such that it could, in the familiar case of the warm water which feels differently to the two hands, be fully in order for me to say 'This is hot' and equally fully in order for me to say 'This is cold'; hence realism here is inappropriate.

The realist can of course fight back. He may deny that 'This is hot' is a complete sentence; it needs supplementation by an extra relational term like 'to my right hand'. Or perhaps some mention of 'normal conditions' should be built in. These moves the realist will defend as being not merely arbitrary stipulations, designed *ad hoc* to preserve the practice of non-contradiction, but as being required for the more accurate representation of the real item which we were talking about all along.

There is thus an important difference between cases where we acquiesce easily in the failure of non-contradiction when it is pointed out to us (imperatives, for example) and cases where discovery of such apparent failure makes us, at least initially, uneasy (temperature, for example). To make a denial of realism plausible in the latter sort of case one must show that there are no repairs (introduction of extra terms or the like) which are non-arbitrarily motivated and which restore obedience to the principle of non-contradiction. One needs to show also that this failure does not matter, that no fundamental interest or practice of ours is threatened. In showing this one will allay the uneasiness and demonstrate that the realist images or impulses which motivated it were the upshot of illusion or muddle. This is, in a nutshell, the strategy which we may see some meaning-sceptics (e.g. Quine) pursuing. We shall see how the arguments might go in chapters 3, 4 and 5.

It may seem to some that the invocation of notions like 'linguistic rule', 'standards of appraisal' and the like which occurs in the above discussion is question-begging. Some sceptical views about meaning and realism make play with the idea that there is no sense to be found in the idea that anyone follows any particular linguistic rule or acknowledges any standard in what he or she does. So we might seem to be setting off in the wrong style. But this would be unfair. The arguments of the meaning sceptics, whom we shall consider, themselves implicitly invoke considerations about rules, standards and so forth. They ask us to reflect how we would establish claims about meaning and when it is correct to make them. It may be that the arguments are intended to have the form of a *reductio*.[5] But reflection on the method of proceeding strongly suggests that, if we are to establish anything about the different statuses or logical shapes of the concepts we use (physical, psychological, semantic, etc.) we have nowhere else to start except with some ideas about our thoughts or remarks and what we suppose to make some more correct or defensible than others.

2.2 REFLECTING ON MINIMAL REALISM

We have, then, certain areas of language in which we (at least seem to) recognize the existence of incompatibles and the impossibility of their being equally and fully correct, where we hope for ultimate agreement in verdict and where we recognize a potential gap between our taking some remark to be correct and its being so. These are descriptive claims. Let us for convenience call what they describe 'our realist practices'. I believe there would be general agreement that going along with such practices about a particular set of remarks (i.e. not supposing the practices open to serious criticism, not abandoning them) is a necessary condition for being a realist about the subject matter of those remarks.

But can we say anything further? What are we to make of the fact that this is how we carry on, that we have these realist practices? Can we *explain* why we think and speak in ways which fit that description? And is that explanation such as to *justify* our so doing? If so, does it justify it in every case or might it give grounds for criticism or reappraisal in connection with some sorts of subject matter?

One line of thought, which I shall call pragmatism, supposes that it is possible to explain and thereby justify our realistic practices, in fact every aspect of them (e.g. the facts that we recognize incompatibles at all, that we operate the law of non-contradiction, that we do so in certain particular areas, etc.) by pointing out that the policy of adopting these practices is advantageous to us; it helps us to organize and anticipate experience, live satisfactory lives and so forth. Our way of carrying on is seen as the outcome of some decision which can be defended in the way appropriate to decisions. There is on this view no more to being a realist than recognizing the usefulness of realist practices.

It is important however to realize that this is not the only form which an explanatory or justificatory enterprise could take. The way we find it natural to speak of 'rules' or 'practices' in these contexts, together with the fact that I have talked of language rather than thought, may encourage us into an unexamined assumption that any explanation and justification there was had to be of the kind suitable for actions.

But reflection shows that this is in tension with some other natural ways of taking the matter. Realism may also, it seems, be explained and justified in the way appropriate to an *opinion*. The question here would not be whether it is practically advantageous to think or talk in a certain way but whether we think truly in taking it that the world has such and such features.

There may seem to be a smack of circularity or question-begging in this approach. It is the status of the idea of 'truth' which is under scrutiny and we are told to settle the question by asking whether certain things are true. We thus continue to use our to-be-elucidated notion in our enquiry. But a realist of a non-pragmatist character will not be bounced into supposing that every notion needs underpinning by some reductive or foundationalist manoeuvres. Moreover he may counter-attack by remarking that the pragmatist cannot himself do without the non-pragmatist notion of truth he attempts to discredit.

For a realist of this stamp, a realist-seeming practice which is underpinned only by practical considerations will be merely pseudo-realist. Someone adopting it for these practical reasons has no right to call himself a realist about the subject matter of which he professes to speak. Moreover the sham nature of his so-called 'realism' is liable to show up in certain extreme circumstances, even if this is not apparent on the surface of everyday discourse. The pragmatist may respond either by suggesting that at a certain fundamental level the distinction between opinion and decision becomes blurred, or by attempting to discredit the non-pragmatist's proposed notion of truth. For the moment we need note only that there are two stances to our realist practices, one of which takes it that they need pragmatic elucidation, the other of which rejects that strategy as inappropriate.

One version of the second stance, an extremely powerful and attractive line of thought, starts with the idea of an independent world with a determinate character or nature, a nature which is fixed quite indepedently of us. We, on this view, are (at least part of the time) trying to get an accurate, unbiased and uncontaminated view of what this independent world is like in itself. The general character of our intellectual practices, e.g. the important role of the principle of non-contradiction, is bound up with the fact that it is a *determinate* world we have to deal with. The particular features of our practices – e.g. realist ways of carrying on about material objects, the past, values or whatever – are to be explained (at least in some cases) by saying that our intellectual life contains them because we believe that possession of those concepts and use of them in that way is the response demanded by the actual nature of the world; these features of our thought are as they are because we suppose they need to be that way for us to think about and describe the world as it is in itself.

If this is the kind of description we give of our practices, then the important questions to ask in probing our realism will be 'Is there indeed a world independent of us, with a nature of its own?' And 'In which of our judgements do we succeed in representing that nature accurately?' To answer affirmatively to the first question is to be what I shall call a 'mirroring realist' (borrowing a useful term from Rorty).[6] And for such a realist the second question will seem pressing. He supposes that some of our thinking and speaking does get to grips with the world as it actually is while other elements of it may fail to do so because influenced and partially determined by our interests, sensory faculties, affective natures and so forth. A crucial matter is then how we are to sort out our concepts into those which do represent the world as it is in itself and those which do not.

We may say, then, that this mirroring perspective on our realistic practices adds to the *epistemological* independence emphasized in minimal realism the extremely important extra element of *conceptual* independence. It is not only our individual judgements which are answerable to something other than themselves for their truth or falsity; the very concepts in terms of which they are couched must also (if the judgements are to be of the real) answer to something 'out there' and independent of us.

Both pragmatism and mirroring realism are agreed in supposing that explanation and justification of our realist practices are called for, although they differ in the resources they call upon for the explanation and justification. But a third important view rejects this assumption. I shall call this position 'quietist' realism. On this view we can make nothing of the question 'Is so and so really the case?', beyond a request to examine again our particular grounds for affirming so and so, to see whether we still wish to do so in a wholehearted fashion. If we find on reflection that we can make nothing of not continuing to operate our existing realist style of linguistic practice with respect to 'so and so'-type utterances, and that we see good reason to affirm this particular sentence, then that is enough to say 'Yes, so and so *is* really the case'.

Quietist realism finds both pragmatist and mirroring realist attempts at justification of linguistic practice misguided. It denies that we can make any sense of the choice that the pragmatist supposes us to make and denies also that the idea of a, so to speak, pre-sliced world makes sense. It invites us instead to become aware of the interlocking complexities of our thought and action and to become aware also of how little sense or use we can make of the idea of (certain sorts of) things being otherwise.

The discussions of this book have to do with the virtues and failings of these approaches to what 'realism' is and with the implications of each for the factual or non-factual status of our remarks about meaning.

Given that there are (at least) two subjects of prima facie realist discourse – namely *meanings* (people, their thoughts, actions, speech etc.) and *the rest* (paradigmatically space, time, stuff etc., as dealt with in the natural sciences) – we have at least four different possible positions. They are as follows:

1 We should be realist about both meanings and the rest.
2 We should be realist about the rest but not about meanings.
3 We should be realist about meanings but not about the rest.
4 We should be realist about neither.

Each of these positions will, of course, be interpreted differently, depending on what variety of 'realism' we have in mind.

The two possibilities we shall be mainly concerned with are (1) and (2), although (4) will also make an appearance. But there are complications in the form of the existence of some hybrids and it is to the tracing of the development of one of these that we will turn in the next chapter. This is partly because it seems to be one way into an intelligible reading of Quine's difficult pronouncements on these matters and partly because it allows the introduction of some notions, such as 'holism', the later development of which will prove important. But before we turn to that we will, in the final two sections of this chapter, consider first the connection between realism in the sense in which I have been speaking of it and other outlooks to which the label is applied, and, secondly, some of the ramifying connections between the notion of realism and the ideas of cultural relativism.

2.3 REALISM, IDEALISM AND EMPIRICISM

As I shall use the term 'realism' it will mean, first, the commitments embodied in minimal realism and, second, whatever further moves (e.g. of a pragmatist, mirroring or quietist kind) are at issue in some particular attempt to understand minimal realism. But the term 'realism' is used in a variety of other ways too.

The question of whether we should be realists about some class of entities is sometimes taken as the question of whether or not statements about them can be reduced to sets of statements about some other class of entity. If the statements can be reduced then the supposed entities are not real; if they cannot then the entities are real. This debate is one which, as sketched, proceeds on the agreed assumption that both types of statement in question are factual. If, of course, that itself is in dispute – i.e. if there is a debate over the 'realistic' construal of one of the sorts of statement – then the demonstration of a reduction may be a way of preserving rather than undermining the 'realistic' status of the suspect statement and saving it from relegation to the realm of the instrumental or emotive.

A second sense in which 'realism' is used, which is not directly our concern, is as a label for commitment to the idea of 'verification transcendent truth'. There may indeed be connections between views of this shape and some of the views I label 'realism'. But whether this is so is something for further discussion and its-truth is not built into our meanings for the term 'realism'. (There is a brief discussion of some of these matters in section 8.2.)

In yet a third usage, 'realism' is opposed to 'idealism', in the sense of the view that nothing exists other than minds and their states. But rejection of this 'idealist' metaphysics is not required (or at least not without further argument) by realism in the senses that interest us. It might, for example, be possible to be an idealist, in the sense of affirming that all that fundamentally exists is states of consciousness, while being a thoroughgoing realist of the mirroring kind. This may seem an odd claim. The view that what exists are states of consciousness might seem to commit us to a denial of any of our sorts of realism because it is definitive of consciousness that one cannot be mistaken about what is going on in it. So we might seem to have a case where thinking that something was so constituted its being so and thus have a case violating the mind independence element of minimal realism. But this is too hasty. That I have infallible knowledge of my states of consciousness does not entail that my thinking that I am, for example, in pain, *makes* it the case that I am in pain or *constitutes* my being in pain. We might explain the infallibility in terms of the 'closeness' of the item to me and the consequent 'clarity' and 'directness' of my awareness of it. Indeed this is exactly the form that mirroring realism takes, when combined with certain further assumptions. Let us consider how this comes about.

Suppose that one is convinced of the mirroring realist general conception and also one is convinced that certain of our concepts are genuinely reality-representing. What account might one give of how we acquired the approved concepts? How can we certify them as ones fit for accurate representation of the world as it is in itself? And how do we justify the claim that any particular exercise of them is right? One might appeal to a benevolent and truthful God in answer to all three questions. One might take it that he had endowed us with mental capacities suitable for judging the world he has put us in, that reflection on his nature shows that he has done this and that those exercises of concepts which seem natural, indeed compelling, to us must consequently yield truth.[7]

But what if a theologically based epistemology does not appeal? A plausible move is surely to say that we acquired the right concepts for judging the world by interaction with the world itself, that the world reveals its nature to, or enforces awareness of its nature upon, the enquiring mind.

A philosopher with this naturalistic and empiricist outlook might approach the other two problems with the assumption that the questions have to be dealt with on an individual, judgement by judgement, basis – or at least that it is important to be able to answer them in such a way in at least some cases. This assumption might well be grounded in the immensely attractive idea that epistemology needs some certainties on which to found enquiry. So the idea is that we are to be able to get assurance that in thinking as we do on some particular occasion we are both exercising a reality representing concept and also doing so correctly. What would the world have to be like if this sort of assurance were to be forth-coming? The answer is (very plausibly) that it would have to contain some 'ideas' or 'sense data' – i.e. some things which present themselves to a sentient being in such a way, so clearly and directly, that he or she cannot but grasp both their nature and their existence.

It is this view, this radically empiricist and idealist version of mirroring realism, which we shall consider in the next chapter. (There are other, non-atomist and non-sensory versions of mirroring realism. Discussion of them will be postponed until section 7.2.) But before turning to that we need to remark on some potentially confusing variant uses of 'idealism'.

As I have just sketched it, 'idealism' is the thesis that nothing exists other than states of consciousness. But the label may also be used for the view that the epistemological independence element of minimal realism fails, i.e. for the view that (in general or for some particular sort of judgement) thinking it so constitutes its being so. This second sort of idealism is distinct from the first. One might plausibly argue that if we reject minimal realism everywhere then we must accept that all that exists are states of mind. The idea would be that everything required for any judgement's being correct is given in the fact that it occurs. (Whether this is a coherent view is not at all clear. There is extreme difficulty in saying what the content of any judgement is. But these difficulties need not concern us.) But the converse implication, from acceptance of metaphysical idealism to denial of minimal realism, does not obtain, as I remarked above. Hence the distinctness of the theses.

There is also a third sense of 'idealism'. This is that in which it is used as a label for any position not of the *mirroring* realist kind, i.e. for any position which sees our concepts as somehow dependent upon us.[8] The use of the term in this way hints at the idea that we cannot allow our concepts to be dependent upon us without also allowing acceptance of the view that the truth or falsity of judgements exercising those concepts is dependent upon us. If this were so then there would be no separating minimal realism from mirroring realism. This is an extremely important issue and we shall return to it, especially in section 7.2, and section 8.1.

2.4 REALISM, RELATIVISM AND INTERSUBJECTIVITY

I have, in the first section of the chapter, presented those features of realism which I wished to stress – for example, acknowledgement of the centrality of non-contradiction – mainly from the standpoint of one imagined judger. I stressed cases (that of imperatives or the two hands in warm water) where one person might (so it seems) find him or herself in a position defensibly to make either of two incompatible linguistic moves. But it would have been equally natural, and perhaps equally persuasive, to have made the point by using the idea that two speakers of the one language might recognize that they conflict in the linguistic moves they made (I say 'Go', you say 'Don't go', or I say 'It's hot' and you say 'It's cold') without either needing to acknowledge that one or other must be in error. One would say that where this could be made out to be the correct description of the situation, there the speakers would acknowledge that their utterances were not realistically intended. (We have already seen considerations like these at work in the reflections on the notion of convergence.)

The assumption which underlies this multi-person way of presenting the issue is that, for the moves in question, the identity of the speaker does not affect the question of whether the moves are 'incompatible' in the relevant sense. If I make a certain move (for example saying 'Go') then the fact that it is another person who produces the 'Don't go' does not *ipso facto* turn that token into one of a type compatible with my original utterance. (Note that what it is for utterances to be incompatible is still to be explained in terms of how one speaker would stultify him or herself by producing both.) But the recognition that I am not the only person capable of making a given linguistic move – that other can do *the same* as me in the relevant sense of 'the same' – may make it easier for anti-realist arguments to get off the ground, because the circumstances which justify the conflicting utterances can now be distributed around among different persons.

We have so far imagined one language spoken by one or more persons, and the question has been how certain intra-linguistic features (the structure of the rules which we recognize as governing the various aspects of correctness of utterances) connect with how parts of the language should or should not be realistically understood. But the question of 'realism' is often raised in the context of comparison between languages and cultures. Is this inter-linguistic issue quite a different one? The suggestion I wish to make is that it is not.

'Cultural relativists' – to put the case crudely – can be seen as drawing our attention to the existence of very widely differing 'conceptual schemes' (which are often said to be 'incommensurable') and using their existence to unsettle our previous realist confidence. We are invited to acknowledge that each culture has its acceptable collection of utterances (or practices of utterance-making) which it is entitled to go on using. But we should (it is said) recognize that the making of these utterances is not to be construed as the description of how things are independent of people; rather they are moves in complex social rituals, constitutive of various distinctive ways of life.

But how are we to be motivated to make this move? The relativist supposes that we find ourselves in a situation where several conditions are simultaneously fulfilled. The first is that we have come to understand what it is that some persons in another culture say. The second is that we see that saying what they say is incompatible with saying what we say. (This is clearly important. That what they say is *different* from what we have hitherto said and so cannot be translated into our familiar language is itself no bar to simply adding their remarks to our stock of truths. The supposed incompatibility is what blocks this move.) The third condition is that we see that there is no way of removing the incompatibility by adding in extra relational terms or the like, and thus no way of revealing their and our utterances as, at bottom, complementary parts of a unified account of what there is. The fourth and final condition is the most crucial. It is that we admit that there are and could be no grounds for saying that one set of remarks is right and the other wrong. It is at least part of the role of the idea of incommensurability in these discussions to provide support for this last claim. The fact that the other way of looking at things is incommensurable with ours is supposed to show that our familiar standards of assessment get no grip on their remarks and practices. Hence we are (it is said) in no position to condemn them. Indeed, in understanding the remarks (as we have been admitted to do) we presumably grasp what would make them correct. And we see that their justifying conditions are indeed fulfilled.

What are we to make of the idea of such a situation? The question now is not whether it is coherent or whether some particular case ought to be seen as satisfying the conditions. The questions are what the logical structure of such a case would be if it were demonstrated to exist, and what it would have to do with realism. My contention is that the structure is the same as that found in our previous intra-linguistic examples, such as that of 'hot' and 'cold', and that the threat to realism comes from the same source. By imagining ourselves as understanding but unable to fault the alien but incompatible remarks, we have, in effect, imagined ourselves in possession of an extended language, built from the amalgamation of ours and theirs, in which the intra-linguistic, realism-threatening, pattern is repeated. The idea of 'incommensurability' here plays another of its roles, namely that of providing a parallel to the logical relation of incompatible determinables of a determinate in the more domestic, intra-linguistic case. We have in both cases prima facie characterizations which are in some logical relation in as much as they exclude one another (they are incompatible if both are affirmed); but the logical relation cannot be explained through the content of one characterization being derived from that of the other by rearrangement of elements and/or the addition of negation.

But what of a potential threat to realism arising from the idea of mutually inaccessible 'conceptual schemes'? Does this also have the same structure? To say so might seem strange since *ex hypothesi* it seems it will be improper, even by extension, to regard this as a case of an intra-linguistic situation. Yet nevertheless it is illuminating to regard the possibility as a kind of limiting case of the same structure.

Let us first try to be clear what we are to consider. Imagine that we can make sense of there being a set of concepts in terms of which judgements can be made which are, of their nature, incomprehensible to any thinker able to employ our concepts and such also that the inaccessibility of our concepts is guaranteed to any thinker capable of using the others. Now the question is: if there were such another conceptual scheme, would that undermine the realistic status of our judgements?

One might urge that it did not. Perhaps we could imagine that there is, interpenetrating with our real world, another equally real but quite independent world and that users of the two schemes are thus responding to the two separate aspects of what there is. I do not wish to say that this is something which is instantly to be ruled out. One can have all kinds of philosophical (or science fiction) fun with such a hypothesis. But it is not clear that it is in fact compatible with the imagined conditions. It seems plausible that the idea of the two accounts' being complementary would need to be explained in terms of a God's eye viewpoint from which their dovetailing is apparent. But the idea that there is such a viewpoint contradicts the claim that capacity to use the concepts of one scheme excludes capacity to use the concepts of the other. If God is to be allowed to violate this restriction it becomes opaque why we should be supposed to be subject to it.

However this may be, there is a version of the 'totally different conceptual schemes' idea on which the two schemes are taken to be incompatible in the same way as the different but mutually comprehensible schemes were in the earlier example. If two judgements, taken from the two schemes, are psychologically incompatible, in the sense that entertaining one excludes so much as comprehending the other, they will be *a fortiori* also logically incompatible; were someone (*per impossibile*) to make both judgements, the result would be hopeless confusion, fragmentation of mind and, so, self-stultification.

If this is admitted to be an intelligible way of conceiving the matter then we do have a skeletal version of our original intralinguistic argument against realism. To be sure, the alternative judgements appear merely as what is imagined to occupy a box labelled 'the other way of thinking'. But their appearance within our language, even in this sketchy fashion, is enough to prevent our judgements from satisfying the law of non-contradiction. Our judgements have been supplied with incompatibles which, *ex hypothesi*, are as acceptable as themselves.

We see then that some ways of taking seriously the idea of different conceptual schemes – 'taking seriously', for example, in the sense of actually affirming their existence or possible existence – is liable to result in the rejection of minimal realism. It may seem from this that mirroring realism has acquired a powerful argument in its support. It may seem to be the only metaphysical outlook which, with its stress on the one right set of concepts, can save us from falling into conceptual relativism and the abandonment of any realism at all. But I hope to suggest later (especially in section 9.3) that this is not so. In order to avoid affirming that there are two conceptual schemes we do not have to insist baldly that there is only one, nor yet do we have to underpin the concepts exercised in the judgements we wish to interpret realistically by appealing to a classification scheme built into Nature.[9]

Another line of thought leading to the claim of a link between minimal and mirroring realism starts from reflections on the idea of intersubjectivity. If I suppose that (some of) my judgements are of their nature intelligible only to me, I credit myself to that extent with a private conceptual scheme. I think of myself as confronted with some aspect of what is real which is nevertheless in principle not even thinkable by (let alone epistemologically accessible to) any other person. But as we have just seen, this view is of doubtful coherence. In making the imagined subject matter of my judgements in principle unintelligible to anyone else, while at the same time remaining non-solipsistic, I supply my thoughts with incompatible rivals (namely those accounts of the real offered by other people in which my private objects do not figure) with which I can find no fault. Hence I seem to lose the right to be a minimal realist about my private objects.[10]

Perhaps, then, in thinking of the subject matter of a realistically intended judgement as independent of my thought about it I necessarily think of it as something intelligible to other thinkers? ('Intelligibility' and its relation to contingent limitations of intellect and also its relations to epistemological access need clarification, but we need not trouble with this for our present purposes.) If this is so then a tempting extension is to argue that I need to think of the real as that which is intelligible to (the idea of which is accessible to) *any thinker whatsoever*. And what sense can we make of this idea except by adopting the mirroring realist notion of the world?

Again I wish to suggest that this is too hasty. That any realistically intended thought must be imagined to be something which is capable of being shared by another person is one thing. To grasp this idea we need only the conception of there being other people, a concept with which it is hardly extravagant to credit ourselves. The other move, however, requires that we make sense of the idea of 'all other possible thinkers', and it is much less clear that this is a notion we can claim to be in firm control of.

Some of these issues will surface again in later chapters, especially section 7.2. But to start, we shall explore what happens when we adopt mirroring realism and also, persuaded by the arguments sketched above in section 2.3, we adopt it in the form of bold and simple sense datum empiricism.

3

Instrumentalism and Meaning Scepticism

3.1 QUINE'S ARGUMENTS FOR THE INDETERMINACY OF TRANSLATION

What is the root of Quine's scepticism about meaning? Why does he claim that there are no facts of the matter about what our sentences (other than observation sentences) mean? In this and the following chapter I shall defend the idea that the appeal of mirroring realism plays an important role in his outlook. It does so via its tendency to generate a 'direct confrontation' empiricist view and via the tendency of that view in turn to lead to instrumental construals of judgements which cannot be fitted into the direct confrontation account.

However, in trying to understand Quine's highly paradoxical views on meaning, we should surely start with something else which Quine stresses again and again, namely his naturalism. He rejects the idea of a 'first philosophy'; he does not think that we are supplied a priori with definite principles about the nature of the world, ourselves or meaning.[1] Philosophers cannot claim access to some special body of truths about knowledge (how it is to be acquired, how certified etc.) in the light of which they are entitled to lay down the law to other investigators. Philosophy may have its own subject matter – the most general features of the world and of our knowledge of it. But its concerns are continuous with those of other disciplines such as physics or psychology and it does not have any special methodology. Any thoughts that philosophy comes up with are to be judged in the same way as other claims, for example by how well they fit in with other beliefs we hold firmly and by whether they link matters in an illuminating way. And philosophy, in setting out to offer ideas about meaning, knowledge or what not, does not put aside other kinds of knowledge, seeking firm and independent foundations quite apart from commonsense and science. On the contrary, what it does is accept our world picture as a going concern. It is by reflecting on that picture, taken as mainly correct, by noticing general features discernible in it and implications latent in it, that the philospher makes his contribution.

Quine's thoughts about meaning are therefore to be seen as underpinned in the way appropriate to this conception of philosophy. They are supposed to arise from commonsense truths, or from scientific claims which are so well attested as to have the same status.

Now Quine also claims to be a physicalist.[2] And some have seen this as playing a very important role in his discussion of meaning. By Quine's own pronouncements, this in some sense must surely be right. Yet it is not entirely clear what this physicalism amounts to. We may take it in a somewhat uninteresting formal way and also as a more substantive thesis.

The former reading arises from Quine's view that it is built into the aims of physics 'to find a minimum catalogue of states – elementary states let us call them – such that there is no change without change in respect of them'.[3] And he also says 'If the physicist suspected there was any event that did not consist in a redistribution of the elementary states allowed for by his physical theory, he would seek a way of supplementing his theory. Full coverage is the very business of physics and only of physics.'[4] Being a physicalist in the sense indicated here is, for all we have yet seen, consistent with believing that having meaning is an intrinsic and fundamental property of some items and that its possession appears among the elementary states.

Physicalism in the more substantial sense involves commitment to some particular view about what these elementary states are like. We might take it, rather crudely, to be the view that only material (solid, extended) things existed and that their only properties are mass, velocity, electric charge and the like. More subtly, we could characterize physicalism as starting from the idea that medium-size material objects are the paradigm or central case of the real;

then the physicalist's commitment is to the idea that whatever is spoken of in the best current theory needed to explain the behaviour of such objects is all that is needed for the elementary states. It will be taken for granted (and rightly so given the current state of physics) that such a theory would not invoke the mental or the intentional in its fundamental vocabulary. This sort of physicalism does not directly rule out the notion that some items have meaning. But it requires that minds and meanings, if they exist, are to be seen as in some way derived from or constructed out of assemblages of inaminate and non-intentional items.

Quine in his commitment to physicalism endorses both the formal version and the subtler of the substantive versions.[5] And given his views about the analytic and synthetic, it would be silly to charge him with equivocation. The view is that if we reflect philosophically we can, early and easily, see the appropriateness of some such thesis as the first, thin, physicalist one, but that further exploration of our world view will soon lead us to flesh this out in the more substantive way.

The interesting question however is whether in understanding Quine's views about meaning we need to take the substantive physicalism as a premise or whether something weaker will do.

Let us leave this tricky question for the moment and look at his central argument for the indeterminacy of translation (and hence for the lack of any fact of the matter about meaning) as it is presented in 'On the Reasons for the Indeterminacy of Translation' and other places in Quine's later writings. (It seems best to concentrate on this paper, since Quine explicitly remarks that it is more fundamental to his thought than the argument presented in chapter 2 of *Word and Object*.)[6]

The line of thought may be presented as follows:

1 Observation sentences have determinate meanings; there is no difficulty in establishing which sets of stimulations in the world they are responses to; and in virtue of this detectable correlation each one will have its own distinct, identifiable (stimulus) meaning.[7] But:

2 Observations underdetermine theory; even given the truth of

all possible observation sentences, there may well be two or more theories which are at odds with each other but consistent with all the data. And:

3 In considering what meaning to assign to theoretical sentences, the facts about the meanings of observation sentences are the only thing that could be relevant. So:

4 A scientist speaking another language, whose observations have been translated and entirely agree with ours, can be held to accept any of the incompatible theories which systematize those data, consistently with all his or her patterns of linguistic behaviour. Therefore:

5 As far as this scientist's theoretical sentences are concerned there is no fact of the matter as to which of the opposed theories they express and hence as to what meaning they have.

It is unclear, looking at this, whether or not a substantive physicalist assumption is doing important work. It may seem that it is, and that there is a gap in the argument between (4) and (5) which it is required to bridge. On this view we would read 'relevant' in (3) as solely an epistemological notion. Then we will suppose that it is essential to an explicit account of the Quinean strategy to spell out the thought that we are not allowed to postulate special *sui generis* intrinsically intentional states to provide ontologically for facts of the matter about theoretical meanings, left epistemologically unfixed by the data. Such things, we say, violate our commitment to physicalism – namely 'physicalism' taken in a substantive sense.

Many have thought that this is the right way to read the argument. But it is worth remarking that substantive physicalism does not appear as a premise in 'On the Reasons for Indeterminacy of Translation', nor does Quine examine anti-dualist arguments in detail anywhere in his writings. It may be that he takes them as so obviously correct as to be hardly worth setting out.

But there is another way of understanding matters which does not require us to saddle him with assumption. It would stem from taking 'relevant' in (3) in a constitutive and not merely epistemological sense. On this view Quine would be inviting us to agree that the only way theoretical sentences could acquire and maintain a meaning is via determinate linkages with observational sentences. And indeed he does say things like this. For example, 'It is evident that these further linguistic structures [i.e. theoretical sentences] are based, however precariously, on the observational vocabulary that was learned by direct confrontation and simple conditioning.'[8] And 'The sort of meaning that is basic to translation and to the learning of ones own language is necessarily empirical meaning and nothing more . . . Language is socially inculcated and controlled; the inculcation and control turn strictly on the keying of sentences to shared stimulations . . . Surely one has no choice but to be an empiricist so far as one's theory of meaning is concerned.'[9] The notions of being 'based', 'inculcated', 'controlled' and 'keyed' which are here invoked seem to have a constitutive rather than an epistemological flavour.

In offering his account of our coming to have our theoretical sentences, Quine is indeed relying on parts of our general picture of the world, parts which he takes to be solidly established. He is thinking of very generally accepted facts about the physiology of perception, about natural selection and the like. (We shall discuss this at greater length in section 4.1.) So this view about meaning is not (he thinks) a reprehensible deliverance of some first philosophy. But what is interesting is that the required parts of the world view can be spelt out without explicit commitment to a fully fledged, anti-intentionalist version of physicalism.

The outcome of these reflections is as follows. It is a hypothesis worth consideration that it is the constitutive connection between the meanings of theoretical sentences and the observation sentences through which they are taught, which is central to Quine's argument. The claim that there is such a connection springs from premises Quine believes himself entitled to because of his naturalism. If this is so, then the increasingly more substantive version of physicalism (which involves for example repudiation of the intrinsically intensional) would indeed be a Quinean view, but it would be in part a consequence of his hostility to the notion of meaning rather than a foundation for it.

To see how such a reading of Quine might work in more detail I shall turn to examine the implications for meaning of an apparently entirely different view, namely traditional sense datum empiricism, when developed in a certain way. This may seem an exceedingly bizarre proceeding, since we are here very much in that territory of first philosophy, and foundations outside ordinary commonsense and science, which Quine so vigorously repudiates. Nevertheless there is interestingly, something, in common between such empiricism and Quine's position (as I suggest we understand it), namely the idea that theoretical meaning (in so far as we can speak of it at all) is founded solely on the relation of theoretical with observational statements. My conjecture is that it is exactly this similarity which Quine means to mark by saying that we have no choice but to be empiricists so far as our theory of linguistic meaning is concerned.[10]

What follows in the rest of this chapter is not, for the most part, directly about Quine, although I shall take the opportunity at certain points to indicate some resemblances between the theses and arguments under discussion and some well-known Quinean claims. I shall in the next chapter return to more explicit discussion of his views.

One point of interest in what follows will be the emergence of one sort of 'holism', which will play a pivotal role in determining what is to be said about meaning. This intriguing but vague notion will re-appear, importantly transformed, at later stages in the book.

3.2 SETTING UP A PREDICTIVE SENTENCE MACHINE

Imagine, then, that we hold two theses which are arguably definitive of a central strand of empiricism. We believe first that there are events in which we have unproblematic confrontation with reality: we exist and are conscious subjects, each one a percipient *tabula rasa*, and there are also real things in the world; the latter act upon or get presented to the former and the upshot is an experience in the subject in which he or she is aware, in an undistorted way, of what is actually there. Our second empiricist assumption is that the kind of item (object, fact) with which we are confronted in these experiences is the only kind of thing that we can intelligibly claim to exist; we can have no conception of, and *a fortiori* no belief about or knowledge of, any other kind of item; the concepts we have are and can only be of what we directly experience.

Let us suppose also that we have a language in which we can report upon the items we are confronted with – a 'fancifully fancyless medium of unvarnished news'. Let us call this the 'basic language' and abbreviate the sentences in it to 'S1', 'S2' etc. These will be type sentences of an indexical character describing the nature of our experiences. If we want some examples, we may imagine them to have contents such as 'hot now', 'half red and half green then' and so forth.

Suppose that, equipped with our basic language, we wish not only to be able to comment on what presents itself to us but also to predict what will happen. Perhaps we merely wish to predict for the satisfaction of seeing if we can get it right or so that we can prepare ourselves better to enjoy or withstand what occurs. But, more plausibly, on the assumption that we can ourselves intervene actively to determine the future, we wish to be able to predict in order to be able to control events. In either case we will need to establish inductively the existence of certain regularities.

Perhaps the observed sequences will be simple and we shall be able to express them neatly in our basic language with sentences like 'Whenever S1 and S2 then S3'. But perhaps what regularities there are turn out to be exceedingly complex and so cannot be handled in such a brief way. How then might we proceed?

It might become convenient to introduce a new form of notation. Let the items in the new notation be abbreviated as 'T1', 'T2' etc. Armed with these, our general shape of procedure in arriving at a prediction is to assemble as many observation statements of the basic language as seem relevant, to move thence to some more easily handled formulae in the new notation, to manipulate these according to prescribed rules so as to arrive at a different formula of the new notation and finally to move back from there to a sentence in the basic language which expresses our prediction.

It is important to stress at this point that the items in the new notation, together with the rules for introducing, manipulating and discarding them, are invented solely to facilitate the derivation of predictions. This is the instrumentalist stance which comes built into our form of empiricism. Let us call an assemblage of such items, together with suitable rules, a 'predictive sentence machine' or PSM. To have a PSM is just to have a device into which one can put some sentences of the basic language and which will, after certain crankings of the handle, deliver some other basic language sentences at the other end. We may, if we like, say that the items 'T1', 'T2' etc. are 'sentences'. But we must beware of assuming without further justification that they function like the sentences of the basic language – that they, for example, report or describe anything. Perhaps they do. But that will depend upon the exact workings of the PSM in which they occur. And it is to the varieties of different possible PSMs that we now turn.

What will an effective and useful PSM be like? There are various different cases here. In one it will be possible to devise a helpful PSM in which 'T1', 'T2' etc. are tied up one by one with (in most cases extremely long and cumbersome) truth functional packages of basic language sentences. So (to take an artificially simplified case) 'T1' might abbreviate 'S1 and (S2 or S3)', and 'T2' might stand in for 'S4 and S5 and S6'. Here the 'sentences' of the PSM can properly be said to describe the world. We have moved up in level of complexity but not in conceptual terms beyond the situation where we did not need a PSM at all.

It is part of what we imagine in imagining this that the rules of the PSM do not go beyond the rules we have for transforming and inferring in the basic language, i.e. do not go beyond the resources of classical propositional logic. If they do then we have a somewhat different situation. It is important to remember that the rules of transformation are as important a component of a PSM as its formulae. If we have PSM formulae introduced according to strict equivalences with basic language packages but manipulable in ways which have no intelligible analogue in the basic language – e.g. by permuting the letters, writing the sentences back to front, or otherwise applying a 'logic' which would be invalid for basic sentences – then it is not so clear that we can regard these PSM formulae as abbreviations for basic language sentences. We would have moved to a stance which cannot but be taken merely instrumentally, where we take it that we can do what we like with the formulae we devise, provided the result is all right in the end. And

we would thus not regard ourselves as answerable, in our manipu-
lations, to some descriptive meaning which the formulae possess.

Yet another sort of PSM would move us further again from the
idea that PSM sentences had descriptive meaning. To see how this
might be so let us consider a PSM which helps us – believers in
sense data who wish to predict future sense data – in something
like our actual world. Here the possibility of simple bundle correlation, for input to the PSM, is most unlikely to be realized.

To see this more clearly consider an example. Suppose that our
basic language is a visual one in which we describe two-
dimensional arrays of shapes and colours. Our predictive problem
is akin to that of trying to anticipate the shapes and colours which
appear on a screen in front of us – as in the cinema. If the patterns
resemble in complexity and structure those that we see in actual
cinemas then it is difficult to see how a PSM could make any useful
contributions unless it introduced something which – taking up for
a moment a non-empiricist, non-sense datum perspective – looked
like the concept of a third dimension. In such a PSM we would
move from a set of basic language statements describing a sequence
of two-dimensional arrays to a sentence like 'A small red cube is
circling a large blue sphere'. The internal manipulation rules of the
PSM might then allow us to derive 'The small red cube will soon be
behind the large blue sphere', from which we would in turn derive
some basic language statement about the disappearance of a red
square from our visual field.

Now it is clear that there is no way of simply pairing off sets of
basic language descriptions and 'sentences' of the PSM. Speaking
again from outside our empiricist assumptions, a given two-
dimensional array can be produced by projection from indefinitely
many different three-dimensional situations and, conversely, a
given three-dimensional situation can project, by variations of
angle and distance, to indefinitely many two-dimensional arrays.
Introduction of temporal sequences of two-dimensional arrays will
not help to eliminate this flexibility of linkage when we remember
that the three-dimensional vocabulary will contain such terms as
'growing' and 'shrinking'. A further feature which the PSM will
need to incorporate, if the world it copes with is to be anything like
ours, is something corresponding to the (perhaps undetected)

existence of mirrors, distorting lenses and the like. Building all these kinds of complications into the PSM makes it clear that reductive equations are not to be had. Hence when I spoke earlier of moving from basic language sentences to PSM sentences, that moving cannot be a matter of simple, mechanical replacement.

How then do we work the PSM? Given some set of basic observations we will have to make a choice of PSM sentence or sentences and similarly at the other end of the process when deriving our final prediction. The existence of this need for choice does not make the PSM useless. It only shows that operating it cannot be an entirely deterministic mechanical procedure and that we cannot expect it to deliver a unique set of predictions. Consider again the earlier example of the sequence of observations which leads me to introduce the PSM sentence 'A small red cube is circling a large blue sphere'. My prediction about the disappearance of a red square from my visual field may turn out wrong; perhaps the red square becomes superimposed on the blue circle but continues to diminish in size. It looks then as if I would have done better, in this particular case, to have made the move to 'shrinking' rather than 'circling' as my response to the sequence of observations of the changing size of the red square.

We can see additionally from this case that slack between basic observations and licensed PSM sentences may in practice be lessened by my adopting some policy with regard to what sort of PSM sentences to work with when I have a choice. Perhaps, for example, I have a policy of using if possible sentences which talk only of 'circling' rather than those which speak of 'shrinking' as well as 'moving'. We may represent this as my taking it that things remain the same size and move more often than they shrink and move. The policy thus corresponds to a further formula in the PSM language. This can be treated as another input, alongside the observation statements, which helps here to determine my ultimate prediction. But of course it is not an independent input; it is only one of the rules of the PSM and as such subject to modification in the same way as the others.

A PSM which is, in the way discussed, non-deterministic in operation is thus risky to use. But it may still be a good deal better than nothing, if the choices or probabilistically determined moves turn out right in a good number of cases. And I can always keep on the look out for ways to refine and improve the rules for PSM manipulation.

3.3   INDETERMINACY OF FUNCTION AND MEANING

Imagine now that we have a given body of data specified in the basic language and we are setting about devising a PSM. Is there any reason to suppose that our data will yield for us a unique, best PSM? Let us define the 'goodness' of a PSM purely in terms of its yielding accurate predictions. (If we allow such features as whether it is easy or fun to work with then the case for the existence of alternatives is strengthened further, since it seems likely that the various desirable features need not all be manifested together.) It is surely overwhelmingly plausible to suppose that the answer is 'no'. Even when we do not have to move beyond truth functions and the basic language to state the laws of the world there may well be notationally different but truth functionally equivalent ways of packaging the materials. And as soon as we move to PSMs whose sentences cannot be reduced then it is yet more compelling to suppose that alternative PSMs are possible, even if we in fact succeed in thinking up only one. The striking feature of such PSMs is that their notation moves beyond that available in the basic language, it breaks new ground. So the supposition that there is only one PSM turns into the implausible view that there is only one novel extension of the basic language which could be of use.

At this point a worry about the coherence of our empiricism in the face of the non-reducibility point may surface. We take ourselves to be empiricists, and so allowed only a limited repertoire of basic notions. But have we not breached these constraints in supposing that we have thought up these novel notations? The answer is that we have not. But to prevent the charge sticking we must hang on firmly to the formalist claim that to devise a PSM is merely to hit upon the idea of some pattern or shape which is manipulable by us according to certain rules. The shape and the rules are both specifiable in the vocabulary of the basic language and such merely syntactic items present no problems for the empiricist – at least no problems that we have not overcome already in imagining ourselves equipped with the basic language. The 'novelty' in question in a PSM is, on this view, merely the novelty one gets by assembling familiar syntactic types of item in new instances of familiar syntactic relations.

To get the flavour of the instrumentalist claim here we could consider as an analogy increasing the complexity of the mathematical symbolism we use to deal with spatial position by introducing elements standing for fourth, fifth, sixth etc. 'spatial dimensions'. It is at least not *obvious* that usefulness of the talk of 'the curvature of space' has to commit us to non-instrumentalist construal of such talk. To say, as the instrumentalist would, that we have here something which is merely *formally* analogous to the bits of notation which describe 'real position' is a move with some attractions. And part of its attractiveness is precisely that some of us do not think that we understand or can make any sense of more than three spatial dimensions.

Another feature of PSMs is worth remarking. As with any machine designed to perform a certain function, if one extracts one element of that machine and asks whether it is 'right', whether it is one whose presence we endorse, the enquiry will only make sense if we presuppose the existence and determinate working of the rest of the machine. The endorsability or otherwise of a component has to do with how it interacts with the other components in delivering the goods. There is no such thing as inspecting a piece in isolation and deciding that it is a good part for our machine. So we can assess a particular piece of notation which is a potential component of a PSM only if we know what other sentences the PSM contains and what the rules for manipulating them are.

The notion of a unified machine which is to be assessed by its performance of one function thus imports the first sort of 'holism' we have come across. It is holism about what is relevant to assessment of parts of a machine and it stems from the fact that it is only the machine as a whole which produces the output which interests us.

If we were to change our terminology and talk not of 'PSMs' but of 'theories' then these last two points are the familiar underdetermination of theory by data and Duhem's thesis that the various claims of a scientific theory cannot be tested in isolation. These are views about 'theories' which an instrumentalist will find obvious. And let us remember that Quine is a strong proponent of both claims.[11]

What, then, are the implications of all this for meaning? Can we speak of the meaning of a PSM or of its component elements? The empiricist/instrumentalist view of meaning is that an item has meaning if it is a (potentially true) description of what exists – namely sense data. Note that the meaningfulness of elements of the basic language – construed in the 'realistic' or 'mirroring' way I alluded to briefly at the start of this chapter – is not in question at all. This is taken entirely for granted. The question is whether a PSM or its parts have meaning – i.e. (on the given construal) whether they describe sense data.

A PSM as a whole may be said to have meaning, in the following way. To utter the whole set of sentences constituting the PSM, against the background of some known rule for entering, manipulating and leaving the system, can be taken as tantamount to saying 'The PSM constituted by these sentences and rules is a useful one'. That claim is, in effect, a description of sense data because it commits the claimant to a complex conjunction of conditionals of basic language statements – namely the one that is defined by conjoining all the conditionals we get by feeding basic language statements into the PSM, seeing what others come out at the end and linking input and output as antecedent and consequent. So here we can see why an instrumentalist might say such things as that a theory as a whole has empirical content. (Let us note in passing that this is another characteristic Quinean view.)[12]

But what of individual components of the PSM – sentences and words? It is clear at once that on the empiricist conception of meaning (and given non-reducibility) the individual components can have no meaning. To utter a sentence in a PSM is not to make some claim about what sense data have occurred or will occur; it is merely a necessary stage in the working of the machine.

It does not follow from this that the meaning of a PSM component is indeterminate, i.e. that there are various ways of assigning it meaning but one is as good as another.[13] What follows is that it is totally inappropriate to speak of meaning here at all, as inappropriate as it is for the non-morphemic syllables of a word. The syllables have a role in the language in enabling us to distinguish one word from another, but they do not mean anything in the way that a word does.

The mention of words raises another possibility. Words, after all, do not have meaning in the sense in which sentences do. They do not make true or false claims about reality. Rather they have their meaning in virtue of some systematic contribution which they make to the sentences in which they occur. So could we not say something analogous for PSM components?

Although the whole PSM is, in a sense, an enormous sentence, it will not do to press the word/sentence analogy; we cannot think of components of a PSM, components with the superficial appearance of sentences, as being words, with roles like referring or predicating. That philosophically standard way of talking about word meaning (and seeing sentence meaning as the resultant of it) goes together with commitments about existence – with a willingness to admit that there are objects which exhibit various characters and that words connect with these objects and characters. So, although word meaning is of a very different sort from sentence meaning, it still involves 'connection with the world'. And hence talk of 'meaning' as belonging both to sentences and to words involves little sense of strain.

But the syntactic structures which reflect this thing/property type of metaphysics are clearly lacking in the formal relations between a PSM and its components. So the most that we can derive from the proposed word/sentence analogy is the idea of systematic contribution to meaning, i.e. the idea of a characteristic sort of role that a PSM component could play in the overall functioning of the machine.

How can we specify the roles of individual constituents of a PSM? We could describe the workings of the whole machine, indicating at a certain point that we were talking about the constituent which was of particular interest. But this approach does not give us the idea of 'the' role of one component, something in which it may differ from other components, because every component gets the same specification – namely via a description of the whole machine. So, on this way of treating the matter all components are seen as having the same role, namely that of jointly constituting a machine which works thus and so.

In order to isolate one role and specify it in a way which does not bring in all the others we need some more economical vocabulary. With ordinary machines we do have such a vocabulary. We can talk of the *engine* of a car and of the *handle* of a mincing machine etc. The existence of such a standard vocabulary is made possible by the comparability of different mincing machines or cars. We can make sense of the question 'What item in that machine plays the role that this item does in this machine?' Can we do anything similar for PSMs?

It may sometimes be the case that a person wishes to enquire about the role in a PSM of some piece of notation which he has not come across before. If he is already familiar with some other PSM, which seems to be of closely comparable structure, then it may be informative to tell him that the unfamiliar sentence plays the same role as 'T1' with which he is already acquainted. The word 'means' might seem appropriate in such a report – e.g. 'T1' means the same as 'T2' – because we here link two 'sentences' and this will be something like the form of report we are already used to employing for explaining the (genuine) meaning of basic language sentences. In the basic language unfamiliar notation may need to be introduced and will be explained either ostensively or by production of another sentence with the same meaning.

Recent discussions in philosophy of language have made us familiar with the point that if the type of remark we have just mentioned – e.g. 'S1' means that S2 – is really to do its work of telling the enquirer how 'S1' relates to the world then 'S2' must occur in it unquoted. The semantic report is not a mere remark about synonymy.[14] (One could report on the existence of synonymy in the basic language – 'S1' means the same as 'S2' – but this is different thing from telling someone how the new notation 'S1' actually relates to the world.) 'T1' and 'T2', our PSM components, do not describe the world. So in their case it can make no difference whether we choose to put in the quotation marks or not. It is interesting to note that Quine (as opposed to Lewis or Davidson) seems to see no important difference between studying translation and doing semantics, and has made no move to alter or reformulate his position in the light of the distinction they draw.

So possession of meaning for PSM components (or the best we can do for an ersatz) amounts, on this line of thought, to the possibility of finding determinate ways of equating or pairing off elements in one PSM with those in another. If there is such a pairing then we can speak with confidence of 'the' meaning (i.e. roughly, function) of a PSM component and usefully specify such meanings by citing an appropriate sentence. Such 'specification of meaning' although it does not report a connection between sentences and the world will nevertheless report a real fact – by our empiricist lights – about the sentences in question. The elements of the PSM are really in the empiricist's world, as are also the facts that they have such and such perceptible features and occur in such and such patterns. The imagined determinate one-to-one pairing will be of this order, if it exists. If on the other hand there are reasons in principle for supposing that pairing sometimes or always cannot be determinately enforced then our ersatz 'meaning' for PSM components will lose its factual status for the empiricist.

Let us consider machines in general – floor cleaners, sausage-making machines, lawnmowers and the like. Is it guaranteed that if we take two that perform a similar function and deliver the same output we shall be able, on inspecting the innards, to pair elements in the one determinately with elements in the other? It may seem that the obvious answer is 'no' – there can be no certainty of such pairing. After all, even if the two machines deliver the same output they may be designed to cope with very different sorts of input. A machine for making sausages out of ordinary meat would work very differently from one designed to cope with an input of completely formed sausages encased in shells. The output 'clean floors' might be produced very differently if the input were dirty carpets rather than dirty tiles. So it would hardly be surprising if two PSMs designed to produce the same output (under the description 'accurate predictions') had very different structures, if different inputs, i.e. different bodies of experience to systematize, had been supplied.

My aim in pursuing this line of thought is to throw light on

Quine's indeterminacy of translation thesis. But we cannot suppose that the above unremarkable result has helped much. Quine's claim is that given two languages *however alike* there is no certainty of finding a unique best translation scheme from one to the other. On the contrary there will be various alternative schemes of translation which preserve all the community's dispositions to linguistic behaviour. This applies even when we are translating our own language into itself. The homophonic scheme may be the easiest option and the only one we can in practice think of. But there will be non-homophonic ones which pair off sentences having no intuitive claim to equivalence with each other at all.[15] If we regard preserving dispositions to linguistic behaviour in the face of the same experience as an instance of preserving input and output (of our PSM or whatever machine we are considering) then the Quinean claim generalized comes out as something like (but as we shall see not exactly like) this: That given two apparently identical machines which not only perform indistinguishably but also look alike when taken apart there is more than one way of pairing elements on the basis of identity of function. Now this *is* a prima facie startling claim, very different from the earlier truism. Can we throw any light on it by pursuing the instrumentalist line?

Quine links indeterminacy of translation with the underdetermination of theory by data. He claims that they are importantly different theses but that the latter underpins the former. Now in the instrumentalist reading of 'theory' the underdetermination of theory by data comes out as a particular version of the more general thesis that two machines which perform identically (processing identical input into identical output) may nevertheless have strikingly different internal organizations. This seems unexceptionable. But something important that it brings to our attention is that to grasp Quine's view properly we need to be willing to deploy, initially at least, the distinction between language and theory, or, in machine terms, the distinction between an array of equipment (nuts, bolts, cogs, belts, words, rules) and the machines that one might build from it. The *underdetermination thesis* more accurately expressed is that from some extensive, imaginable set of equipment two identically performing machines can be built, which are nevertheless significantly different in internal working. The *indeterminacy of translation*, extended to the case of machines in general, comes out like this: if we consider two equipment sets, not from the point of view mere shape (= pure syntax) but from the point of view of potential use in machines (= meaning), then there will be more than one way of pairing them. For example, even in two qualitatively indistinguishable equipment sets, it is not mandatory to pair off each cogwheel with its qualitatively indistinguishable counterpart in the other set; it could defensibly be paired with an axle, pulley or bolt, i.e. the cogwheel could be thought of as contributing the same function to potential machines as the axle, pulley or bolt. Can we make any sense of this idea?

Let us start by asking what underlies the underdetermination, what makes it possible that there should be two machines? The precondition is that the defining differences between input and output can be broken down into collections of subdifferences in a variety of ways. For example consider the contrast between chunks of meat and sausages. They differ in two important respects, texture and shape. So if one could first change the texture and then change the shape one could transform the one into the other. But equally if one could half transform both texture and shape and then complete both transformations one could produce the same result. Our sausage machines work on the first principle; we mince the meat and then stuff it into the skins. But we could imagine a machine which first produces sausage-weighted balls of partially re-textured meat and then puts these balls through a process which simultaneously modifies the texture and encloses the balls in properly shaped skins. Let us put this schematically. We have in the one case an X-er and a Y-er operating sequentially and in the other a W-er and a Z-er operating sequentially.

That these two machines are different is not in dispute – just as it is not disputed by Quine that two languages or theories may be different in the sense of being distinguishable collections of marks, contrasted in shape and manipulation rules. The question however is about pairing of elements on the basis of function performed. So let us ask 'What is involved in something being an X-er, e.g. a mincer?' This is not so clear cut as one might suppose. Transforming meat into sausages necessarily involves changing the texture of the meat. That is just a trivial consequence of the specification of the overall functioning of a sausage-making machine. But then there must be *something* which does this in any machine which actually delivers the goods. So that thing, what ever it is, can be called the mincer. As it turns out, the mincing function in our second machine is going on continuously throughout the course of sausage manufacture. But that could just lead us to say that the second machine consisted of an X-er and a Y-er (mincer and shaper) working in parallel, rather than in the familiar sequential way.

Suppose now that I have an equipment set sufficient to build either type of machine and that you do also. Suppose further that we have in fact constructed identical machines. It follows from what we have said above that even so it is *not* obligatory to pair off pieces of the equipment sets, functionally speaking, in the obvious 'homophonic' way. I may do that, of course, but I can also equate the pieces which it is most natural to regard as my W-er with those pieces of your equipment set from which you could have made an X-er had you chosen to construct the other type of machine. So for example my W-er involves a cogwheel; but I pair that cogwheel not with your cogwheel (which is actually doing exactly the same thing in your machine as it is in mine) but with the pulley from which you could have made the X-er. And conversely I pair my pulley with your cogwheel. How can I justify this? My grounds are that it is possible to regard an X-er as part of a W-er. It all depends on how I choose to segment the machines and whether the idea of, say, finding 'the mincer' seems to me important. The language and translation version of this is that I can translate you – who seemingly speak English and affirm just the same sentences as I do – as expressing by your utterances an entirely different view of the world, namely the view you would have had had you adopted the alternative PSM which I recognize to be possible.

There is something very odd about this in the case of physical machines and one may well want to resist these conclusions. There are, after all, physical constraints in ease of handling and repairing machines, which make certain kinds of segmentation overwhelmingly useful to us and rule out others as mere freewheeling fantasy. But these constraints will not help us to resist the Quinean-sounding conclusions in the case of the PSMs because in their realm technological limitations are at a minimum; the sentences and rules provide no resistance to any segmentation or manipulation.

We can see then how, following the instrumentalist line, the central Quinean thesis of indeterminacy of translation emerges with some plausibility. Moreover, this interpretation has the advantage of showing how the indeterminacy thesis links with the underdetermination one while still being a distinct claim.[16]

What then of the attack on the distinction between analytic and synthetic truths? On one way of looking at the matter, the non-existence of analytic truths (i.e. ones guaranteed by meaning) is a direct consequence of the non-existence of determinate assignment of function to PSM parts. Supposed discovery of analytic equivalences is just discovery that one bit within a language is a translation of another.

But there is another way of looking at the matter which is perhaps more illuminating. In 'Two Dogmas of Empiricism' Quine argues for the non-existence of a firm class of analytic truths (which I shall treat, as Quine does, as the same as the non-existence of necessary truths) on the grounds that, given bizarre enough data to systematize, any general statements or rules could in principle be discarded. He is sometimes criticized for confusing the question of whether one could be mistaken about necessity and come to recognize that mistake with the question of whether there are any necessary truths. He is said to move from a perhaps acceptable fallibilism to an unwarranted scepticism about necessity. But on the instrumentalist reading the criticism is unjustified. The best that the instrumentalist could do for the notion of 'necessary truth' in a PSM is to find elements, rules or functions, which have to be present in any PSM whatsoever. If we can find features which no usable PSM could lack then they could be said to be indispensable because of their function i.e. necessary on account of their meaning. But given that the test of a PSM is entirely in its working it would seem rash to take such a dogmatic stand that 'whatever is altered in my PSM *this* shall stand firm.' An easy-going and pragmatist attitude to PSM features should be the instrumentalist one. And this is just what we find in Quine.

3.4   INSTRUMENTALISM AND THE REVISABILITY OF LOGIC

It has frequently been remarked that Quine seems to be ambivalent about the status of classical logic. On the one hand he claims that it is revisable, up for holistic appraisal like any other element in our intellectual system (even if it is extremely unlikely that we will substantially revise it); on the other hand he insists that change of logic is change of subject.[17] I shall suggest that the instrumentalist ideas explored in the previous sections provide a framework for seeing how this clash might arise.

Let us make explicit the assumption that we have operated with so far, namely that the sentential operators 'not', 'and', 'if . . . then . . .' and so forth are part of the basic language and that when we speak the basic language we reason in classical style. This is no more than a reflection of the robust mirroring realist outlook we have at this level. But what of such operators and the principles governing their use in a PSM?

A problem immediately presents itself when we pursue this thought. Suppose we try to raise the question 'Is it conceivable that we should wish to modify the PSM so as not to include in it the law of non-contradiction or *modus tollens*?' We discover that we have not succeeded in asking anything coherent. Finding 'the law of non-contradiction' or the like in the PSM depends upon making sense of the idea that some of the PSM components are to be identified as meaning 'not', 'if . . . then . . .' and the like. Our difficulty is not just that we cannot identify any items as negation, conditional etc. unless they obey classical laws. It is the much more primitive difficulty that we have given no sense to the idea that PSM components could have this sort of meaning at all. Remember PSM components are merely shapes (or noises or whatever) which we manipulate. Their production by us is not assertion, they cannot be denied or inferred. So it looks as if the appearance of an 'and' or a 'not' in the PSM could be no more than a pun. And then the whole question of the status of logic in the PSM collapses.

But this is premature. We can, on reflection, see how logical operators might, in a not wholly punning way, be incorporated into a PSM and thus give rise to the question about the revisability of logic.

Let us note first that there is likely to be a tendency to abbreviate remarks about the PSM to utterances which, in a different context, would constitute actual operations of the PSM. If a large part of our lives consists in thinking and debating on how to improve our PSM we may fall into the shorthand of uttering merely 'T1' when we mean 'Let's put "T1" into the machine'. Or we say 'If T1 then T2' meaning 'If we put in "T1" we should put in "T2" as well'. And we say 'Not T2' to express disapproval of the inclusion of 'T2'.

This does not give us logical connectives as PSM elements but one further move puts the operators inside the machine. This move is taken if we develop the idea of a self-modifying machine, i.e. we recognize not only rules about how PSM elements should be manipulated but rules about how those rules should be modified.

It seems likely that in any case of modifying a machine, sensible modification will often come in groups. Suppose that I have a mangle which every now and then gets into an unfortunate configuration in which a part sticks out and trips me up. I partially dismantle the machine and discover that the obstructive item is linked to something else which occasionally moves in such a way as to push the offending part out further than usual. I can now relocate this further thing, alter the linkage, or pursue yet deeper into the works. But a very probable scenario is that I shall have to make a sequence of adjustments. For example merely undoing the linkage may produce some serious malfunction elsewhere, prevention of which requires further manoeuvres.

With a PSM one might analogously discover that every now and then it produces 'T2' and that use of that 'T2' leads to false predictions. 'T2' is produced, we discover, because the PSM contains 'T1' and in the operating instructions we have the rule 'Put in "T2" when "T1" is present'. Suppose I express this rule to myself in the abbreviated form mentioned above; I say 'If T1 then T2'. On discovering that operation of the machine is producing trouble in the way outlined and taking the view that the machine has got to be prevented from producing 'T2', I realize that I have certain options. Among these are, first, removal of 'T1' and, secondly, modification of the rule. But perhaps I am determined to hang on to the latter. My best policy then seems to be to remove 'T1'. Supposing this sort of modification to be needed fairly frequently I might devise for myself a higher level instruction which (using 'P', 'Q' to capture the generality I need) I find it natural to express as follows: 'If, if P then Q and not Q, then not P'. Or a related instruction might be 'If not Q then either not P or not (if P then Q)'.

I have, in doing these things, taken up a stance in which the PSM together with the rules for operating it (which all along I expressed using logical operators in imperatival sentences) becomes itself an assemblage subject to further rules of modification. I have rules about what rules I shall adopt for the manipulation of the basic elements. But it is important to remember that these higher level rules are not purported statements of truths. If we unpack the one given above in a particular case it comes out like this:

If you hang on the rule 'Put in "T2" if you have put in "T1"' and you do not want to put in 'T2' then do not put in 'T1'.

Or we might express it in a kind of intermediate notation thus:

If you include 'If T1 then T2' and also include 'not T2' then include 'not T1'.

What does 'including "not T2"' amount to? It is, in effect, writing myself a note to remind myself to take 'T2' out of the machine. But the writing of such notes has now become part of operating the machine. The notes themselves are, in a way, parts of the machine.

The upshot, then, of allowing the conception of the self-modifying machine is to make natural the use of items like 'not T2' which are, regarded from one perspective, parts of the machine but regarded from another are instructions on how to work the machine. 'Not' thus occurs in the machine and its occurrence is not a pun; its occurrence is an intelligible extension of its use in the basic language, namely in the description of and giving of instructions about the sense data and sentences.

Having in this way put logical operators into the machine we can ask a question about classical logic, namely 'Must we accept as an overriding principle of machine construction the need to keep logical operators distributed among the sentences of the PSM according to only classically acceptable patterns?'

Suppose for example that I have a PSM and, as a result of various operations, it comes to include 'T1', 'if T1 then T2' and also 'not T2'. I notice this configuration. Must I now say to myself 'There is something terribly wrong with this machine which I am obliged to attend to'? Do I become subject to necessities in my handling of my machine in virtue of having adopted this self-modifying policy and the notation which naturally goes with it?

The symbols 'not', 'if . . . then . . .' etc., could not appear in the PSM without being mere puns unless there was some presumption that I would at some stage of the operation of the machine take notice of the instructions that I give myself by including them. I am *ex hypothesi* in the business of modifying my PSM in a systematic manner and the general patterns of modification are what justify the use of these particular mnemonic marks. But this observation alone does not show that I shall find myself subject to necessities.

And there are two further considerations which show that it would be inappropriate to insist that classical logic be preserved within the PSM. The first is that PSM construction is only one among various projects which I may have. With the inconvenient mangle I may decide that I cannot be bothered to dismantle it. I will instead keep a good lookout for the obtruding piece and just shove it back in when it threatens to be a nuisance. Similarly with my PSM I may merely keep a good lookout for 'T2' when it turns up and remove it before it generates any misleading predictions, without bothering to readjust the innards so that it does not appear again. To do this is to adopt a PSM which says 'T2' and at the same time 'not T2'. But if life goes on all right why should I worry?

Well, it may be said, clearly you have not got an entirely trouble-free PSM; it is imaginable that you could devise a better one; you should stop lazing about enjoying your sense data and get on with improving your PSM. Perhaps I take this advice to heart. Or perhaps I like constructing PSMs. Or perhaps I think that I might get even better sense data if I got rid of this occasional awkwardness of the current PSM. So I have now as my goal the devising of the maximally smooth-working, economical, reliable etc. PSM. Does this restructuring of my objectives give us what we want, namely the idea that I should recognize myself as subject to a necessity of preserving classical patterns for the connectives? It does not.

The problem is that we do not have and cannot have a guarantee that there is a PSM which preserves the classical patterns and works better overall than the imagined non-classical one. Until I have found the alternative I am rationally justified in continuing to use the non-classical PSM and need have no qualms at all about doing so. The *ad hoc* policy adopted earlier on grounds of laziness may be the best policy even when laziness has been discarded. And, more elaborately, we can see how such things as quantum logic may turn out to be highly useful for incorporation into certain parts of the PSM.

My suggestion, then, is that this sort of approach might make some sense of a Quinean style of ambivalence about classical propositional logic. On the one hand we need it as an element in the basic language but on the other hand when it, or its extension, gets incorporated into a many layered PSM we want it to be malleable, as other PSM elements are.

4

Quine's Naturalized Empiricism

4.1 QUINE'S EPISTEMOLOGY

The contention of this chapter is that we can best understand Quine by supposing that he rejects sense data and the 'first philosophy' underpinnings of the instrumentalism explored in the last chapter, while carrying many structural features of the position into a naturalized version of empiricism. The retained features include the existence of a sharp distinction between observational and theoretical sentences and the constitutive thesis about theoretical meaning, namely that what makes theoretical sentences have whatever meaning they do have is their relations with observational sentences. The upshot is that the sceptical consequences for theoretical meaning implicit in instrumentalism also are retained.

To make this interpretation plausible I shall first examine the evidence for resemblances between Quine's later epistemology and instrumentalist empiricism. Then I shall, in later sections, consider the ramifications of the position sketched. The theme here will be that a non-instrumentalist interpretation lands Quine fairly directly into gross and obvious difficulties. The naturalized version of instrumentalist empiricism, on the other hand, does indeed require one to do some very delicate balancing acts, concerning notions such as 'real', 'true' and the like (balancing acts of a type which we find Quine attempting) but can be made to yield a whole picture which is less obviously incoherent, if exceedingly strange. In the final section I shall ask whether we need to accept this unfamiliar vision of ourselves.

In 1951 Quine wrote

As an empiricist I continue to think of the conceptual scheme of science as a tool, ultimately, for predicting future experience in the light of past experience . . . The myth of physical objects is epistemologically superior to most in that it has proved more efficacious than other myths as a device for making a manageable structure of the flux of experience.

In the famous paper from which that comes he also introduced his image of the web of belief: 'The totality of our so-called knowledge or beliefs, from the most casual matters of geography and history to the profoundest laws of atomic physics or even of pure mathematics and logic, is a man-made fabric which impinges on experience only along the edges.'[1] Thirty years later in 1981 his comment on his earlier formulation is this: 'It was an interim indication of an attitude and an attitude that I still hold.' But he adds 'My noncommittal term "experience" awaited a theory.'[2] His later theory of 'experience' is revealed in this:

> Our talk of external things, our very notion of things, is just a conceptual apparatus that helps us to foresee and control the triggering of our sensory receptors in the light of previous triggerings of our sensory receptors. The triggering, first and last, is all we have to go on.[3]

The striking feature of these quotations is the persistence in them of the ideas of something (sensory experience or triggerings of sensory receptors) which is to be predicted, foreseen, managed or controlled, and of something else (tool, man-made fabric or apparatus) which we devise to do the job. Let us look at the two elements in turn, starting with Quine's notion of experience, his rejection of sense data and his later idea of an observation sentence.

Quine speaks mockingly in *Word and Object* of 'a fancifully fancyless medium of unvarnished news', a 'protocol language', in which we could offer an 'account of the passing show' or of the 'unsullied stream of sense experience'.[4] It is clear that he thinks that we do not have such a language and that we cannot attain one by rational reconstruction. But if we look in more detail at his reasons for denying the 'fancyless medium' various interesting facts emerge.

He remarks that it is references to physical things which hold together the domain of immediate experience which would otherwise not cohere and that reference to physical objects gives us 'our main continuing access to past sense data themselves; for past sense data are mostly gone for good except as commemorated in physical posits'.[5] The thought here is that if I set out to think about what my sense experiences have been like in the past few minutes what I actually do is to consider the objects around me, how my eyes have been oriented and the like, and to reconstruct from this what I must have seen and felt. And surely this is right. The point seems to be that 'actual memories mostly are traces not of past sensations but of past conceptualization or verbalization'.[6] Later he says 'We cannot rest content with a running conceptualization of the unsullied stream of experience; what we need is a sullying of the stream. Association of sentences is wanted not just with non-verbal stimulation but with other sentences if we are to exploit finished conceptualizations and not just repeat them.'[7] The emphasis here is on the limitations of reports of the unsullied stream; by themselves they do not supply any predictive tools.

Consider also the following quotation.

> Even a strictly sensory idea is elusive unless it is reinforced by language. The point was made by Wittgenstein. Unaided by language we might treat a great lot of sensory events as recurrences of one and the same sensation, simply because of a similarity between each and the next, and yet there can have been a serious cumulative slippage of similarity between the latest of these events and the earliest of them.[8]

The view here seems to be that we can recognize similarity between one sensation and another but, as things are, not accurately enough to ensure that only ones exactly or really closely resembling the first get called by the same name; we lose grip on the standard of similarity set by the first, but only because of some confusing series of intermediate events.

One striking thing that emerges from these passages is that the rejection of sense data seems curiously half-hearted; the general impression given is that they occur but are elusive and tend to be remembered not at all or inaccurately. A sense datum instrumentalist with a bad memory would be happy with what Quine says. But perhaps this is just a rhetorical device on Quine's part; perhaps he is just trying to loosen the grip of a simple-minded sense datum view with an eye to more radical alterations later.

Much more important is the fact that none of Quine's objections are objections in principle to the very idea of an event with (many of) the essential characteristics of the supposed confrontations with sense data. In the latter part of *Word and Object*, and in subsequent writings, the idea of the sense datum report does indeed fade away – after its last ghostly appearance in the remarks above. But in its place we are offered the idea of an *observation sentence*, which, as we shall see, has a very good claim to be just another sort of 'fancyless medium', whose main difference from the sense datum report is its subject matter rather than its epistemological characteristics.

The notion of an observation sentence is introduced by Quine in *Word and Object* and the account is slightly modified and clarified in certain respects in other places.[9] What is interesting is that it is apparent that the guiding principle in constructing the account given is to arrive at a notion of a kind of a remark which is merely a response to what a person is currently confronted with. In the case of sense datum reports the judger can tell by introspection whether a remark has this character. But if we have rejected that way of approaching things and have adopted the third person perspective within which Quine works, we cannot find out just by looking at the linguistic behaviour of one subject whether his reports are of this kind. His responses will necessarily depend upon past experience as well as what he is currently confronted with, because he must have had some experiences in learning the language. And we cannot separate out, by looking at him alone, which of those experiences determine the meanings of sentences and which contribute to possession of collateral information which may influence the judgements made.

At this point in Quine's exposition one might think that the notion of a linguistic response which is merely a non-committal labelling of the current stimulus is doomed and that it is Quine's own rejection of the analytic/synthetic distinction (which is another aspect of the meaning/collateral information distinction) which has brought about this fate. But Quine is determined to restore the idea and does so by the ingenious move of bringing in other speakers. 'An observation sentence is one on which all speakers of the language give the same verdict when given the same concurrent stimulation. To put the point negatively, an observation sentence is one that is not sensitive to differences in past experience within the speech community.'[10] An interesting feature of this definition is that observationality is clearly a matter of degree. It will depend upon how wide a speech community we consider and how much agreement in verdict we demand. Quine explicitly acknowledges this; and the moral should be (I think) that the notion of a sharp observation/theory distinction is untenable and that other related theses (like thoroughgoing epistemological holism) follow. It is striking that this is not the path Quine takes; rather he chooses to ignore these concessions and to treat the notion of observation sentence as one with a sharp boundary and to suppose, in consequence, that an observation sentence can have a well-defined class of stimulations which elicit it and which it can be said to mean.

The observation sentence which emerges from this definition is notably unlike the sense datum report in not presupposing consciousness and in not being about something which is private to the subject. But in other respects it remarkably resembles it. The observation report is something which is a direct, non-inferential response to certain patterns of stimulations of nerve endings. It 'has its particular range of admissible stimulating occasions independently of wider context'.[11] And 'observation sentences peal nicely; their meanings, stimulus meanings, emerge absolute and free of residual verbal taint'.[12] Thus the observation sentence is free of the Duhemian web and can be verified or falsified in isolation. 'In my view observation sentences can indeed be cognized in isolation, independently of scientific theory as a whole, by the closeness of their association with stimulation.'[13] A corollary of this is that they are (pretty nearly?) infallible. And, as Quine himself remarks, 'speech thus confined would be strikingly like bare reporting of sense data.'[14]

There is an important qualification and clarification of this, concerning isolation and infallibility, which is worth noting. It is only when regarded holophrastically, with the meanings appropriate to sentences lacking significant internal or referential structure, that observation sentences can be regarded as being conceptually and epistemologically isolated. It is possible for us, however, to pay attention to the words that we discern in some observation sentence and think of the meaning of the sentence as something only to be characterized in terms of the notions that are brought in when analytical hypotheses about these words have been accepted. If we do this then we shall find that the observation statements look less like sense datum ones. Their meanings become enmeshed with those of theoretical statements and, because of this enmeshing of meaning, theoretical sentences come to have some bearing on the epistemological acceptability of these observation sentences. This may lead to the overturning of an observation statement by theoretical considerations. At this point it may look as though Quine has recognized the points mentioned earlier and is urging an observation/theory distinction which is merely a matter of degree.

But things are not so simple. He also says that what is then rejected is not the original observation report. Consider the following.

> These occasion sentences qualify holophrastically as observational, but their parts recur in terms in theoretical science. That is how observation sentences link up with scientific theory, bearing evidence. If a recorded observation wildly at odds with theory is ultimately repudiated, as may happen, still *what is repudiated is a dated statement of history, itself theoretical, and not the occasion sentence at its utterance.*[15]

Quine here says that what is repudiated from theoretical considerations is theoretical – a dated, and hence eternal, sentence concerning the existence of some theoretical item at the specified time. Thus it need not be taken to be the same as what was originally asserted, which was (so Quine seems to suggest) some indexical and holophrastically construed claim about the nature of current stimulation. This distinction (if I have interpreted the passage rightly) seems to be designed to preserve in full force the infallibility of the observational.

We have thus far looked at Quine's continuing commitment to the idea of observation reports which are risk-free labelling responses to stimulation. Let us now turn to the other element of the instrumentalist picture – namely the idea of the tool or apparatus which we devise to handle or predict our observations.

Quine writes, as we saw above, 'Our talk of external things, our very notion of things, is just a conceptual apparatus that helps us to foresee and control the triggerings of our sensory receptors.' He continues this passage as follows: 'The triggerings, first and last, are all we have to go on . . . What I am saying is not meant to be sceptical . . . But there remains the fact – a fact of science itself – that science is a conceptual bridge of our own making linking sensory stimulation to sensory stimulation.'[16] And at another place he says something related:

> Science itself tells us that our information about the world is limited to irritations of our surfaces and thus the epistemological question is in turn a question within science: the question of how we human animals can have managed to arrive at science from such limited information. Our scientific epistemologist pursues this inquiry and comes out with an account that has a good deal to do with the learning of language and with the neurology of perception. He talks of how men posit bodies and hypothetical particles, but he does not mean to suggest that the things thus posited do not exist. Evolution and natural selection will doubtless figure in this account.[17]

One thing to note here is that Quine explicitly distances himself from possible anti-realist implications of this instrumentalist sounding talk. And we shall need to return to the question of what Quine's realism amounts to. But for the moment we need to get clearer about what he means by the fact of science, namely that science is a bridge of our own making linking sensory stimulation to sensory stimulation. Which parts of our generally accepted picture of the world is he here calling on?

Most probably he has in mind the following kinds of consideration. The behaviour of our bodies, including our movements, production of noises etc., is determined by a combination of impinging physical stimuli (light rays, pressure, heat etc.) and the given internal state of the body. The current internal state is the result of previous impinging stimuli and previous internal states. Matters can be traced back ultimately to our genetic constitution and the environment in the womb. The theory of natural selection tells us that we have the kind of genetic constitution we do because its possession contributed to those who had it in the past behaving in ways which resulted in more of their offspring surviving than those of creatures with different genetic constitutions. Surviving and reproducing are, in large part, a matter of being so constituted as to produce, on a certain stimulus, behaviour which will result in certain future patterns of stimuli rather than others. The causal effects of the environment on the development of species and individual animals is all (given the non-existence of action at a distance) mediated via causal effects on the exterior surface of the animal. Natural selection mimics teleology. So one may say that our internal constitution (i.e. genetic structures, the development of the nervous system which it largely controls, and the consequent disposition of the nervous system to change under the impact of stimuli) is an apparatus, the biological function of which is to ensure that the organism anticipates and controls the triggering of sensory receptors in the light of previous triggerings. But different genetic constitutions might, for all we know, be equally effective in producing the same external behaviour, i.e. the same stimulus–behaviour–stimulus sequences. Equally, for the individual animal it is highly plausible that different neurophysiological structures could have developed in response to given stimuli and have produced indistinguishable patterns of future stimulus–behaviour correlations.

It is this set of facts, about physiology, evolution and so forth which, I conjecture, Quine sees as justifying his remarks about what science is and his related claim that we have no choice but to be empiricists as far as our theory of linguistic meaning is concerned. There are, as I shall suggest in the last section of this chapter, reasons for grave dissatisfaction with the reading Quine offers of the scientific facts. But these we shall set aside for the moment. The question we need to consider at the moment is whether the view of science, and in particular of the nature of the meaning of scientific sentences, is instrumentalist.

Here I would like to mention three considerations. One is the, already noted, constitutive flavour of the remarks about meaning which I quoted above, in section 3.1. The second is the distinctly instrumentalist tone of those Quinean remarks about science which we have just set out. ('Our talk of external things . . . is *just a conceptual apparatus*': 'Science is a *conceptual bridge* of our own making'.) The third is his treatment of the postulation of physically respectable inner items which might be thought to supply some facts for translation manuals to describe. This third topic deserves a little more discussion.

In a discussion of the idea of differentiating in point of correctness between two translation schemes which fit all observable behaviour, Quine remarks

> Since translators do not supplement their behavioural criteria with neurological criteria, much less with telepathy, what excuse could there be for supposing that the one manual conformed to any distribution of elementary physical states better than the other manual? What excuse, in short, for supposing there to be a fact of the matter?[18]

One thought Quine seems to be pursuing here is that it would be wrong to think that translators are using behavioural data to make guesses about neurological states. If they were then they would use more direct information about neurological states if they could get it. But they show no disposition to do this; the neurological data are of no interest to them. And so two translation manuals cannot be seen as differentiated in truth value by appeal to hypothetical differences in neurology. But the same holds, Quine also suggests, for items which might be the object of telepathy. Presumably he is here thinking of some supposed intrinsically intentional states of mind-stuff.

The supposed conclusion is that imagined inner items which are epistemologically underdetermined by observable behaviour – whether these items are neurological or mental – are not what translation is about. The argument of the passage quoted is not that we know that some sort of item – e.g. non-physical ones – would do the job, but unfortunately our physicalism rules out postulating them. As the mention of neurology shows, it is not the non-physical nature of the postulated items which is the sticking point, despite the rhetoric about 'distribution of elementary physical states'. Quine's point seems to be rather that the enterprise of translation, as we actually conduct it, just is not a theoretical enquiry after unobservables, whether meanings or neural states.

It is interesting to think of Kripke's interpretation of Wittgenstein at this point.[19] Both Quine and Kripke's Wittgenstein maintain that the kind of fact that we are tempted to put in, by way of fleshing out what makes meaning statements true, turns out not to be what we were after. But, on the interpretation I wish to recommend, the parallel breaks down beyond this point. Kripke's Wittgenstein (whom we shall discuss further in section 7.3) thinks that we cannot find such facts about meaning because of a link between the notions of meaning and the normative. Also he thinks that the point is quite general and suffices to undermine the idea of a fact about meaning for all kinds of sentences. Quine, on the other hand, thinks that observation statements have clear stimulus meanings. And his reasons for denying facts about theoretical meaning do not have to do with norms. Moreover Kripke's Wittgenstein thinks that we cannot, on reflection, make sense of the idea of there being a fact about meaning; we cannot get our minds round any coherent conception of what such a fact could be like. Quine does not seem to be hesitant on these grounds: if translation procedures could be shown to deliver a unique manual, Quine implies, then we need have no qualms in talking of facts about meaning: such facts would simply be what was stated by the relevant parts of the uniquely correct manual.

But if it is not the non-physical nature of meanings which is the trouble, nor yet the fundamental unintelligibility of facts about such things at all, what is Quine's root thought here? An instrumentalist assumption about the nature of theories provides at least one answer to this question.

It may be thought however that the three points I have just mentioned are but flimsy evidence on which to base an instrumentalist reading of Quine, in the face of his denials of sceptical intent and repeated professions of realism. So I shall turn in the next sections to a fourth and stronger kind of consideration, namely that of internal consistency. I shall argue that, contrary to what one might at first suppose, Quine will have much more trouble maintaining coherence if we read him non-instrumentally than if we read him instrumentally.

4.2 ONTOLOGICAL RELATIVITY AND DISQUOTATION

That Quine's views about meaning rest upon the constitutive thesis about the relation of observational and theoretical meanings, which is in turn bound up with something of significantly instrumentalist style about the nature of theory, has seemed to many implausible because, as we have seen, Quine again and again denies that his stance is sceptical and claims to be a realist about the subject matter of theories.

So the crucial question, for the spelling out of Quine's doctrine which I wish to defend, is whether we can make sense of Quine's realism in a way which preserves at the same time both a significant element of instrumentalism and also something which Quine would call 'realism'. I believe that we can, but what emerges under the name of 'realism' is something which does not come under any of the three types discussed in chapter 1 and which many might have difficulty in recognizing as a form of realism at all.

The alternative and more usual way of spelling out Quine's thought has the attraction of starting with something much more robust and obviously 'realistic' – namely by taking Quine to be something like a mirroring realist. But I shall suggest that this (together with its related reading of the argument for indeterminacy of translation) is untenable. If we pursue it we shall find ourselves attributing to Quine some fairly obvious muddles and incoherencies. Moreover it is inconsistent with much that he himself explicitly says about the notions 'truth', 'reality', 'empirically equivalent' and the like.

I shall first try to make this claim plausible by examining the matter of 'ontological relativity'. This will provide an example of the kind of difficulties we get Quine into if we take his realism too naively. It will also introduce the important matter of his treatment of truth. In the next section we shall move on to further consideration of his realism and its relation to indeterminacy of translation, and his naturalism.

Mirroring realism has as a natural corollary a correspondence theory of truth and a belief in the obtaining of referential relations between names and objects and between predicates and the classes of things of which they are true. Quine's professions of realism, together with his well-known approval of the extensional semantic idioms, may combine to suggest that he is sympathetic to these views.[20]

Suppose that this were so, what sense could we then make of his doctrine of 'ontological relativity', which he states as follows: 'It makes no sense to say what the objects of a theory are, beyond saying how to interpret or reinterpret that theory in another.'[21]

The claim of ontological relativity, or 'inscrutability of reference' as Quine sometimes calls it, is a close relative of the indeterminacy of translation. In *Word and Object* it is not sharply distinguished from it and is presented as the main line of support for indeterminacy of translation. It is only with 'On the Reasons for Indeterminacy of Translation' that we find the shift to emphasis on the central part played by underdetermination of theory by data. It is this later line of thought which we have discussed up to now. But in 'On the Reasons for Indeterminacy of Translation' Quine still assigns an important role to the inscrutability of reference. It can provide support for indeterminacy via 'pressure from below' – as opposed to the 'argument from above' of underdetermination.

The idea of inscrutability of reference is this: if I am translating a foreign language I will start by finding sentences which, as wholes, are asserted or denied in conditions the same as those in which certain sentences of my own are asserted or denied. But I cannot make substantial progress, especially in translating highly theoretical sentences, unless I move beyond this to detect sub-sentential units in the foreign sentence which I can pair with my own words. I must, in Quine's terms, adopt some 'analytical hypotheses'. Quine's claim is that this can be done in a variety of competing ways. To take the familiar example, I could equate their term 'gavagai' with my term 'rabbit' and some other term of theirs with our 'is identical with'. This might give me the right assent and dissent conditions for some utterance containing both terms of theirs. But, says Quine, if I paired 'gavagai' with 'undetached rabbit part' I could adjust the translation of the other term – taking it as equivalent to 'is part of the same animal as' – thus preserving the overall assent and dissent conditions of the sentence.[22]

This is not itself a very exciting form of alternative translation. Some one who says 'This rabbit is identical to that' and someone who says 'This rabbit part belongs to the same animal as that' have, in some sense, 'said the same thing'. And if indeterminacy went no further than this we would hardly be worried. Quine's claim however is that in other cases of less observational sentences the two elements of the original analytical hypotheses will cease to cancel each other out and we shall be led to offer two competing translations for the one native sentence which in no plausible sense 'say the same thing'. In these cases moreover, because the sentences are highly theoretical, we shall find that we have no evidence to support one translation rather than another. This is how inscrutability of reference is supposed to support indeterminacy of translation.

We need not concern ourselves with Quine's arguments for the existence of different analytical hypotheses or why they should be supposed to cease to cancel each other out. Let us look simply at how Quine puts what he claims. He says that it makes no sense to press the question 'What does "gavagai" refer to, rabbits or undetached rabbit parts?' There is no fact of the matter about what it refers to. On the other hand it does make sense to enquire what it refers to relative to some theory, i.e. relative to some translation manual for linking terms in different languages. He explicitly likens this to Leibniz' replacement of the idea of absolute space with that of relative space.[23]

Hartry Field launches an interesting attack on this position.[24] He claims that the notion of 'reference relativized to a translation manual' makes no sense. Consider '"Gavagai" refers to rabbits relative to manual M1 and to undetached rabbit parts relative to manual M2.' The remarks seems to set up some genuine link between the word 'gavagai' and rabbits – but only relative to a manual. But what will the manual do? It will only tell of a relation between the *word* 'gavagai' and the *word* 'rabbit'. A relation between 'gavagai' and actual rabbits is only thereby set up if we assume the existence of an unrelativized relation between our word 'rabbit' and rabbits.

Can it really be that Quine has fallen into this muddle of trying to set up a genuine, if relativized, reference relation, oblivious of his claim that the same inscrutability infects our own utterances and hence oblivious of the fact (according to him) that my lingking 'gavagai' and 'rabbit' in a manual cannot secure any connection between 'gavagai' and rabbits that it does not equally secure between 'gavagai' and undetached rabbit parts? Field's view is that he has and that he needs to be rescued from it by an ingenious doctrine of partial denotation, which Field explores in the rest of his article.

But we can get a lead to another reading which has Quine looking less muddled (if more bizarre) by considering something Field himself says in a footnote.

What we do in translation manuals is set up relations of co-extensiveness or co-denotationality. But Quine thinks that we are not simply limited to locutions like '"Gavagai" is co-extensive with "rabbit"', because we can say also that 'rabbit' occurs in a 'background language' which we acquiesce in 'taking at face value'.[25] But what is this 'taking at face value'? It may look simply like sweeping Field's problem under the carpet. But Quine might have more to say in defence of the idea, by spelling out the analogy with Leibniz' view of spatial location talk. On that view we cannot sensibly ask for the absolute position of some object x, but we can say what spatial relation x has to some other object y; and we can avoid an infinite regress in fixing position by *pointing* to y. This is a move which, according to Quine, removes need for further discussion, just as 'acquiescing in our mother tongue' is the move which ends discussion of reference. But, says Field, 'there is a crucial disanalogy here: on Leibniz' theory we can understand relativized claims about the relation of physical objects to places *only because places are understood as constituted by the relations of physical objects*; whereas no one holds that physical objects are constituted by the relations of words.'[26]

But is it so clear that Quine rejects the idea that 'physical objects are constituted by the relations of words'? Of course in the natural first reading of 'constituted' it is absurd. Physical objects are constituted by atoms, fields of force or what have you, as specified in physical theory. Suppose however that one were an instrumentalist?

On the relational theory of space one denies the existence of absolute space but admits the reality of objects and relations between them; talk of 'place' is just a convenient abstraction from, or shorthand for, talk of objects and the relations between them. On an instrumentalist construal of theoretical sentences, one denies the existence of extra-sentential entities but admits the reality of the sentences and the relations (of shape, role etc.) discernible between them. Talk of 'objects' is thus for the instrumentalist merely a convenient way of remarking on certain high level features (of organization, structure etc.) of those patterns of useful sentences. Thus the doctrine that Field thinks no one, even Quine, could be so crazy as to hold, is just what an instrumentalist actually thinks.[27]

It was the introduction of the idea of a real relation of reference which precipitated Field's Quine into the muddle. But it is clear, if we look further, that Quine's approval of the extensional semantic idioms is not to be understood in this way. For him 'true', 'refers' etc. are mere devices for disquotation, useful tools for 'semantic ascent'.[28] Let us put this view at its simplest. When I utter 'The moon is round' in the normal run of things, I use that sentence to do whatever is its proper job in language. I may also form a name of the sentence and hence a device for talking about it by putting quotation marks around it. So insulated it does not perform its normal task. But if I now add 'is true' I have used a linguistic device the central purpose of which is to undo the effect of the quotation marks – i.e. to produce a more complicated looking syntactic sequence which has the same potential role in discourse as the original, quotation free, sentence. Similarly the phrases 'the referent of "..."' and 'is in the extension of "..."' are devices for undoing the effects of quotation marks on singular terms and predicates.

On this approach, what should we say of contexts (as for example in translation manuals) where we say such things as '"Snow is white" is true iff snow is white'? Here we do not simply disquote but seem to use the devices to speak of a link between a quoted item and some thing or condition in the world. The disquotationalist has an account of this too. He says that we give a hearer some grasp of how to use a foreign, quoted, linguistic item by exhibiting to him a sentence of our own which he already knows how to use and which has the same use for us as the foreign sentence for the foreigner.

(Remember Quine's comparison of acquiescing in our mother tongue and pointing.) On this approach it is not of any particular significance that the clause on the right-hand side of the 'iff' should occur unquoted. Its unquotedness signals merely that the speaker thinks that he is now using a clause already understood by both himself and the hearer he is trying to help – i.e. that he has reached a background language.

A proponent of this view would reject the idea that unquotedness is important on the right-hand side because in such remarks we are 'doing semantics' as opposed to merely reporting synonymy relations. Recall again what we remarked in chapter 3, that Quine seems quite unmoved by those who have attacked his translational approach to the study of meaning on the grounds that it confuses these things.

4.3 QUINE'S VERSION OF REALISM

Let us return to the question of what we are to make of Quine's insistence that he is not a sceptic.[29] I shall start by raising another difficulty, similar to the one Field discusses, which appears in Quine's position if we suppose that Quine's realism is of any substantial, i.e. non-instrumentalist, variety (whether it is mirroring, quietist or whatever). On this view we take it that Quine's 'conceptual apparatus' talk about science is not instrumentalist but is rather just an expression of the familiar idea that in science we make hypotheses about items we cannot perceive and that one test we apply to such hypotheses is whether they enable us to make accurate predictions about what we can observe.

How, in this framework, is the argument from underdetermination of theory by data to indeterminacy of translation supposed to work? The instrumentalist/constitutive considerations I have been exploring are out. Instead it seems probable that we will have to invoke a line of thought relying on a substantive version of physicalism, as we sketched in section 3.1. Let us recapitulate that argument.

We have two theories, T1 and T2, which are incompatible but each consistent with all the observation sentences. We accept T1.

We imagine all the physical facts to be fixed, i.e. all the facts about positions of fundamental particles, movements of bodies, utterances of noises, etc. We will doubtless use the terms supplied us in T1 to charactarize these facts and the characterizations will not include any mention of meanings. Next we recognize that it is consistent with the statement of all these facts to say of some alien scientist both that his theoretical utterances are to be translated as expressing T1 and also that they are to be translated as expressing T2. So given the data available to us (which is all physically specifiable) about his utterances and what stimulate them (and given all other physical facts as well for good measure) we still find that hypotheses about theoretical meanings are underdetermined. But our physicalism insists that there are no further facts which could make one of the translation hypotheses true and other false, for there can be no factual difference without a physical difference. Therefore there is no fact of the matter about which theory the foreigner accepts and no fact about what his theoretical utterances mean.

The tension in this story emerges as follows. On the one hand we refuse to identify the 'truth' of a theory with its coping adequately with all the data. This is the identification which our non-instrumentalist realism rules out. We say that two theories may cope equally well with all the data but that, if they clash, one of them will in addition have some further virtue which the other lacks, namely that of describing how things really are. In saying this we clearly allow for the possibility that there should be two syntactically distinguishable systems each of which has the syntactic property of generating all the true observation sentences, but one of which has, whilst the other lacks, an important semantic property – namely that of saying something true. On the other hand when we consider the foreign scientist's utterances, we must, on Quine's view, deny that there can be any fact of the matter about whether his set of sentences has or does not have this semantic property. It can be translated equally correctly by that set of our sentences which has it and by the set which lacks it.

But what could justify the discrimination implicit in this between what we are prepared to say of our sets of sentences and what we say of his? It seems unmotivated and Quine is indeed anxious to emphasize that the indeterminacy of translation can be applied in our own case. Thus we may ourselves accept T1 and reject T2, in the sense of choosing one set of theoretical sentences to utter rather than the other. But we must say of ourselves that in uttering the sentences of T1 we can be translated either homophonically as holding T1 or non-homophonically as holding T2.

And now what are we to make of the 'realism' we earlier professed? That realism offered us a view on which an important difference existed between T1 and T2, while the current view makes a nonsense of that claim. If my uttering the sentences of T1 is acceptable, whilst it is also the case that in uttering them I can defensibly be taken to have 'meant' T2, then I might as well have uttered T2 instead; and if I had it is hard to see how it would not have been other than equally defensible.

This seems such an unpalatable and muddled position that we should, if at all possible, avoid attributing it to Quine. And there is ample textual evidence that it is not his view. The first point to note is his theory of truth, which we have already discussed. Acceptance of a disquotational theory is not a position with clear metaphysical commitments of its own. It is compatible with mirroring realism, with 'quietist' realism (of the sort mentioned in chapter 1) and also with instrumentalism. But as deployed by Quine it is clearly designed to offer us a view of 'true' which frees us from the temptation to suppose that we must hypothesize some correspondence relation, of the type implicit in mirroring realism. And Quine is hostile to the idea of such a relation. He speaks of the correspondence theory as 'a hollow mockery'[30] and points out with relish the consequences of his views about meaning for the notion of 'state of affairs' which would be required at the world end of such a relation.[31] It is, on this evidence, surely possible to suppose that he means to deploy the disquotational view in such a way as to make instrumentalism seem more palatable than it otherwise would; instrumentalism does not debar us from talking earnestly of truth.

The second relevant point from Quine's writings which bears on this matter is his handling of the hypothetical situations where we are confronted with two empirically adequate theories. His moves here are subtle. In the version of 'Empirical Content', originally published in 1981 in *Theories and Things*, Quine wrote 'Still, let us suppose that the two formulations are in fact empirically equivalent though not known to be; and let us suppose further that all of the implied observation categoricals are in fact true, although again not known to be. Nothing more, surely, can be required for the truth of either theory formulation. Are they both true? I say yes.'[32] But Roger F. Gibson pointed out a disagreement between this and a passage in *Theories and Things* where Quine also talks of alternative empirically equivalent theories.[33] (He is here considering theories that may be derived by the use of proxy functions and of considerations having to do with ontological relativity. But the issues which concern us are the same.) Here Quine says 'But it is a confusion to suppose that we can stand aloof and recognize all the alternative ontologies as true in their several ways, all the envisaged worlds as real. It is a confusion of truth with evidential support. Truth is immanent and there is no higher. We must speak from within a theory, albeit any of various.'[34]

Quine's response to Gibson's remarks was to modify the earlier cited passage (which as it stands is clearly congenial to the instrumentalist interpretation I wish to defend) to bring it more in line with the other. But let us remark that there surely must be some quasi-instrumentalist strand which led Quine to the first formulation; someone who was a straightforward mirroring realist would never have dreamt of writing it. Also Quine's inclination when faced with the idea of incompatible theories is to try to minimize the need for choice. He points to the possibility of reinterpreting terms in one theory so as to present it as a notational variant of the other or to the possibility of simply conjoining them. (If he were able to say that different but empirically adequate theories are impossible he could avoid the muddle we examined at the beginning of the section – but equally he would have lost his argument for the indeterminacy of translation.) And in fact Quine does recognize that there may, hypothetically, be occasions where choice cannot be avoided. On this, his final and subtle position hardly amounts to a robust version of realism. Rather he insists truth is *immanent*, we must speak *from within a theory*.[35] And it is this thought which provide the crucial clue to the nature of his realism. If we follow this through we can credit him with a coherent, if strange, vision.

To see how this may be so, let us return to some remarks in *Word and Object*.

> Have we now so far lowered our sights as to settle for a relativis-
> tic doctrine of truth – rating the statements of each theory as
> true for that theory, and brooking no higher criticism? Not so.
> The saving consideration is that we continue to take seriously
> our own particular aggregate science, our own particular world
> theory or loose fabric of quasi-theories, whatever it may be.
> Unlike Descartes, we own and use our beliefs of the moment
> even in the midst of philosophising, until by what is vaguely
> called scientific method we change them here and there for the
> better. Within our own total evolving doctrine, we can judge
> truth as earnestly and absolutely as can be; subject to correction,
> but that goes without saying.[36]

The emphasis here comes back to one aspect of Quine's naturalism, namely the idea that we cannot do without actually accepting
some theory of the world. (It is worth remarking on the slightly
unusual phraseology: we are said to 'use' our beliefs). There is no
entirely non-committal standpoint, no possibility of Cartesian jetti-
soning of all substantive and risky commitments, no finding of
some certain starting points for a first philosophy.

One might enquire at this point why talk about meaning was not
finally vindicated – as far as the possibility of realistic construal is
concerned – by parallel moves. Do I not always and unavoidably
'take seriously' some view about what utterances, my own or
others', mean? Quine's answer, at least for the case of other people,
is 'no'. He says 'The parameters of truth stay conveniently fixed
most of the time.' (We may take him here to be talking of truth in
connection with sentences of physical theory and 'the parameters
staying fixed' is our continuing to take seriously some background
picture.) But he continues 'Not so the analytical hypotheses that
constitute the parameter of translation. We are always ready to
wonder about the meaning of a foreigner's remark without reference to any one set of analytical hypotheses, indeed even in the
absence of any.'[37] Quine's view then is that I can carry on theorizing and talking about physics without accepting any one theory
about what other people mean.

But again what holds in my relations with the foreigner holds in my relations with myself. So the upshot is that I can operate without 'taking seriously' (in the relevant sense)any assumptions about what I mean by my own remarks. And now the shape of the whole Quinean construction can be seen more clearly. The claim is that a bit of my world picture that I do and cannot but take seriously – namely the bit that starts with talk of material objects and proceeds to theories about them – will, when reflectively examined, lead me to see that the other bit of the picture – namely the bit about meanings – is one that I do not and should not take seriously.

But now we want to know what it is to 'take an utterance seriously'. And the price to be paid for avoiding the obvious muddles, the ones that we saw in the discussion of Field earlier in this section, becomes apparent at this point. The price is a radical impoverishment of the picture we have of ourselves, or rather an inability to endorse fully certain apparently central elements of that picture. This occurs because Quine cannot allow anything but the thinnest account of what 'taking seriously' amounts to.

The natural account of what it is to take something seriously calls upon those notions which Quine wishes to see as secondary. For example we might well say that to take an utterance seriously is to believe *what it says*, or at least to suppose that there might be *good reason* to believe that it says something which might be *true*. But all the italicized phrases (except 'true') are ones which Quine tells us do not occur in descriptions of what really goes on. ('Reason', although we have not discussed it explicitly, clearly goes along with meaning, because it is in virtue of their meanings that sentences or beliefs enter into relations of epistemological relevance to each other.) And the account he gives of 'true' merely points us back to the idea of 'taking seriously', since to say something is true is, on his view, merely a disquotational manifestation of my taking it seriously.

We can return here to a reflection on Quine's realism and what differentiates it from instrumentalism. Earlier I offered a formulation of the anti-instrumentalist thought in these terms: empirically equivalent theories may differ in that one has a virtue that the other lacks. Quine's remarks suggest that he wants to respect this thought. But it turns out that the only fundamental difference he allows for, the difference which takes the whole burden of distinguishing the 'true' from the 'false' theory, is the fact that I actually use ('take seriously') one and not the other. Quine's non-instrumentalism, on my reading, consists only in this: he thinks that we are always actually employing one of our instruments and so, in some respects, cannot stand back from it; but we can stand back from it enough (he supposes) to see its instrumental nature and hence to derive sceptical conclusions about meaning.

We may indeed admit that being used or not used is a difference between the theories; and it is difference which, given disquotation and so forth, allows me to make realist-sounding remarks. But it can hardly be said that I have revealed a *virtue* which one theory has and the other lacks or that I have *made sense* of my adopting one rather than the other in terms of my taking it to have that virtue. I am returned simply to the blank fact that this is the theory that I *do* work with.

We are, of course, allowed by Quine to say those intensional things about ourselves – about reasons, beliefs, meaning and truth – in which we express our convictions that our utterances have virtues. He is not in favour of outlawing such idioms. But in saying these things we do not, according to him, capture anything that is really going on. What is really occurring, he claims, what I can say 'seriously', is that we are caused to make certain noises in ways which then cause us to make other noises and so forth.

But even this remark ('What is really occurring is . . .') comes to have an empty ring when we realize that it is itself just a noise we are caused to make. Even for it, I am not allowed to explain what my taking it seriously amounts to in any way which goes beyond the fact that I recognize that I am disposed to utter it. We thus end up, it seems, not only not taking seriously our remarks about meaning but, in some sense, unable to take seriously anything we do.

This is only a brief outline of the reflections that gazing at the Quinean picture leads us into. We shall return to the topic at the start of chapter 6 and explore the matter further. It is, however, already apparent that Quine's vision is exceedingly strange and uncongenial. Should we, nevertheless, endorse it?

4.4 SHOULD EMPIRICISM BE NATURALIZED?

There are two questions I would like to address in this section. First, assuming that the sketch I have given of Quine's position is correct, should we adopt that position? And second, can I substantiate my claim that the lure of mirroring realism (in its empiricist form) has a great deal to do with Quine's view? The second question may seem especially pressing, since the Quine who has emerged could hardly be said to be a central case of a mirroring realist. So we will start with it.

Mirroring realism is, I contend, at the heart of the matter in this sense: that it is a commitment to the idea that *if* meaning is to be respectable at all *then* it will fit the mirroring realist model, which drives the whole construction. How does this come about?

I would like to remark first, and rather baldly, that it is *not*, straightforwardly, 'a fact of science itself that science is a conceptual bridge of our own making linking sensory stimulation to sensory stimulation'. Such a view of science is not a mere commonplace of scientifically educated commonsense. The sciences Quine cites, physiology, theory of natural selection and so forth, tell us nothing directly about meaning, the nature of science or any such things. They do indeed tell us a great many fascinating things about light waves, retinas, nerves, neurones, genes, phenotypes, reproduction, survival etc. But we cannot superimpose upon the picture built up in these terms some story about meaning, beliefs, reasons, theories and so forth without making further assumptions about *those* notions, assumptions which are not supplied by physiology or natural selection theory. Quine may sincerely deny commitment to a first philosophy – but it would be impossible to get insight into meaning on the basis of physiology etc. without some ideas about meaning got from elsewhere, because physiology etc., in their central and uncontroversial parts, just do not deal with such matters.

And it is indeed evident that Quine does make some assumptions about meaning, about what a clear case of one item meaning something would be like. His paradigm is that of a situation in which items meant (stimuli) produce without significant mediation other things (responses), in such a way that a systematic and absolutely reliable correlation between their natures exists. And where has he got the paradigm from? He has got it from mirroring realism in its empiricist form.

I offer this as a historical claim and a brief look at Quine's intellectual development, and at what he himself says about it, will substantiate it. The influence of Carnap upon Quine is very great and openly acknowledged. The major intellectual enthusiasms and insights of the young Quine, in the areas of epistemology, metaphysics and theory of meaning, sprang from his contact with the Vienna Circle, and particularly with Carnap.[38] Consideration of Carnap's system at this time reveals it as providing an interesting precursor to Quine's.[39] Carnap held that we have a body of immediate experiences, described in 'protocol sentences', which we need to systematize. In order to do so we choose pragmatically among various different linguistic frameworks. Each framework involves its own particular set of terms, the meaning of which is fixed by analytic principles, linking sentences using the terms to protocol sentences and to sentences containing other terms. So, once a framework is chosen – the so-called 'external question' has been decided – then questions posed in the chosen vocabulary – the 'internal questions' – will have definite answers dictated by the course of experience. Quine's response to this, which we can see developed in a number of his early papers (most notably 'Two Dogmas of Empiricism')[40] is to deny the tenability of a sharp distinction between internal and external questions and consequently the tenability of the analytic/synthetic distinction. To deny this distinction is to pass what Quine calls the fourth milestone of empiricism (the earlier ones being the shift of attention, when considering vehicles of meaning, from ideas to words, the shift from words to sentences and the holistic shift from sentences to theories).[41] At this point, having passed the fourth milestone, and if we still accept the idea of protocol sentences reporting on immediate experience, we have reached the instrumentalist position as elaborated in chapter 3.

The next development, required according to Quine to move on past the fifth milestone, is to repudiate first philosophy and espouse naturalism. And now we can turn back to the first question posed in this section and ask whether we should adopt the final Quinean position. Two sorts of consideration are relevant. One concerns the acceptability of the mirroring realist paradigm and the other concerns Quine's correctness in supposing that the scientific facts, even if they do not supply those ideas about meaning, do indeed dovetail with them and give them support.

We cannot deal with the first sort of consideration properly until we come to discuss Wittgenstein's worries about mirroring realism and his rejection of the passive, imprinting, conception of meaning. Here I shall only put down a marker to the effect that there is something seriously wrong with the paradigm and hence that we should not desire to find naturalized structures into which we can read it.

But considerations of the second kind alone suggest serious worries about the internal cohesion of the Quinean system. Quine's claim is that we find reproduced within physiology etc. the structures that a sophisticated sort of sense datum empiricism claimed to find embodied in instrospectible experience and our deliberated response to it. But to read the scientific facts this way involves a good many procrustean manoeuvres. Someone who was not already thoroughly committed to the empiricist picture might well be more struck by the difficulties in the programme than Quine seems to be.

We have already seen that he has to skate over the difficulties of the fact that observationality is a matter of degree. Further recent work makes it look a murky and complex matter whether many or indeed any utterances are related to patterns of stimulation in the way Quine imagines.[42] And it is even less clear that utterances which fulfil this condition (if there are any) form a sharply distinguishable observational base for scientific theorizing. Related worries arise from the way Quine mingles the personal, intentional level of description with the subpersonal and causal. Scientific theories, he says, are of our own devising. This is unexceptionable. And equally it is unexceptionable that neural changes are caused in us by the triggering of sensory receptors. But the attempt to superimpose the one scheme of description upon the other produces various obvious tensions. One has to do with the content which, at the personal level, we would naturally take our evidential statements to have. We suppose them to be about tables, trees and so forth and are not aware of any 'holophrastic' level at which another sort of claim is made. But Quine tells us that it is these holophrastic claims upon which we base our theorizing. Another difficulty concerns the idea of whether judgement and choice are involved and, if so, how. At the personal level we suppose that it may sometimes be up to me which hypothesis I adopt, since the evidence does not point unambiguously one way rather than another. Indeed it is part of Quine's underdetermination thesis that this should be so. But at the subpersonal level there will be no underdetermination; the fact that different neural structures could underlie similar external behaviour does nothing to show that there is some causal indeterminacy about which structure I actually come to contain.

The point of the above sketchy remarks is not to show that Quine's superimposition is obviously untenable. It is only to make clear that it *is* a superimposition and that it is fraught with difficulties which Quine does not resolve. The conclusion is that his view is far from commonsensical or mandatory and hence that we may justifiably regard the extreme bizarreness of the position it leads us to as grounds for suspicion of the premises.

5

The Mona Lisa Mosaic

5.1 SEMANTIC HOLISM

In this chapter I shall set out another argument concluding that
there are no facts about meaning and that ascriptions of meaning
are subject to indeterminacy. It may be that I have been obtuse
and unjust in my earlier interpretation of Quine and that the (it
seems to me considerably better and more interesting) argument
which I am now about to sketch is the one he is really putting
forward. Another possibility is that the argument of this chapter
represents one strand in Quine which he never gets properly
disentangled but which has been extracted and presented in purer
form by a sympathetic developer of Quine's ideas, namely
Davidson.[1]

The new line of thought depends crucially upon 'holistic' consideration – but it invokes holism interpreted in a significantly
different sense from that presented in chapter 3. There we started
from the idea that the property we were interested in – meaning –
has a clear primary sense in which it belongs only to certain wholes,
namely observation sentences and entire theories. These things,
said our earlier theory, perform some function, namely that of
labelling an individual stimulus or encapsulating a whole course of
experience; and we can see that they do so from contemplating the
connection which they as wholes have with the things meant, quite
apart from any consideration of their internal structure or of the
meaning of other items; smaller units, words or individual theoretical sentences, may be said to 'have so and so meaning', but only in
a derivative sense (as the parts of a sausage machine may be said to

'make sausages'); and this sense must be explained in terms of an identifiable contribution made to the functioning of the whole.

The kind of holism we shall now consider, however, starts from a different idea, namely that possession of meanings is quite properly, and in no secondary sense, ascribed to small units such as words or sentences of a theory. But, it adds, possession of this meaning demands the presence of other similar meaning-bearing items of a suitable sort, which together with the individual item considered, form some assemblage; and, it says further, the meaningfulness also requires the absence from that assemblage of certain items of an unsuitable sort. If these conditions are fulfilled then there will, it seems likely, be a sense in which the assemblage as a whole has meaning. And, given what we have just said, its existence and meaningfulness are required for the meaning of the elements. But the dependence is, on this view, mutual. The meaningfulness of the whole is not prior to that of the parts, in any significant way, conceptually, causally or metaphysically. We cannot make sense of the idea that the whole should have the meaning it does without the individual parts bearing their appropriate meanings. So the slogan 'the fundamental unit of meaning is the whole' would be highly misleading as a summary of this sort of holism, although accurate enough for the earlier variety. The central idea now is rather that meaning necessarily involves complexity.

There are, plausibly, at least three levels to this complexity – that of word, sentence and (for want of a better word) discourse. But I shall not, in what follows, say much about words, concentrating rather on some features of the required connections between sentences and other sentences in discourse. (It may be that the existence of words is a corollary of the existence of further features of the sentential patterns needed for meaningfulness, but I shall not pursue this thought).

To help get a grip on the kind of meaning holism now under consideration it may help to look at a case where a very similar sort of reciprocal dependence is found, namely pictures and their elements. I have in mind here that kind of pictorial representation which may be found both in artefacts and in such natural objects as clouds or stains on the wall.[2] We shall be concerned, initially, only with the sort of manifest content which can be seen in a picture in virtue of its visual qualities, without special knowledge of its maker's intentions or the identity of any model it may have had.

In a picture of a face, it may be clear that a certain circle represents the right eye, a line represents the nose and so forth. But the circle standing entirely by itself could not represent the eye. It requires the presence of (at least some) other suitable items which can be seen as representing (at least some of) nose, mouth, other eye, etc. The assemblage as a whole is a picture of a face and the circle represents an eye only in the context of the other items which together make up that picture. So one could be tempted to say that the whole picture was the primary vehicle of representation. But this would be to ignore the fact that this whole only represents a face because the individual parts have their representational roles.

I do not wish to say that anything representing a face must have such internal complexity. A simple item, such a white blob, may indeed do so and also lack significant relevant structure within itself (as the simple circle may represent an eye without having internal complexity connected with pupil, eyelid etc.). But for the blob to represent a face in itself requires placement in a suitable setting, say a picture of an immense crowd.

So the general conclusion is that one cannot come to grasp the picturing role of some item, whether simple of complex, without attending to the picturing role of other items, whether simples juxtaposed to the first, if it is itself simple, or elements of it, if it is complex. Where there is pictorial representation there will always be complexity and hence possibility of talking both of what the whole picture represents and also of what the elements represent.

I have talked so far of the required presence of other items needed to make something simple, like a circle, represent an eye. But equally we can see that the absence of certain disruptive influences is required. The very same lines and circles that represent a face might, occurring in the context of some further lines and circles, clearly not be a picture of a face or not suggest a face at all, but be instead a straightforward picture of a salad on a plate, the wheels of a machine, or almost anything else one's ingenuity might devise.

When I speak of semantic holism in what follows it is a thesis suggested by this example that I shall mean. More specifically it is the claim that an individual sentence is both correctly said to be the unit of meaning (in some sense) and is also such that it can have the meaning it has for a person only if it occurs in a certain setting, which both contains other sentences used by that person to which suitable related meanings can be assigned and also lacks sentences inappropriate to that meaning.

We may leave the notions of what is 'suitable', 'inappropriate', etc. in a vague state for the purposes of the overall argumentative strategy, although I shall have a little more to say about them in section 5.3. But it is worth noting that an epistemological flavour is discernible in our semantic remarks at this point. What is suitable and what inappropriate has to do with what is involved in a person's being in a psychological state with a given content, for example, with how fragmented, partial, contradictory and so forth thoughts can be while still being thoughts. The questions will be ones like 'Could someone think this while also thinking that, or while failing to think such and such?'

Epistemology, narrowly construed, tells us about what people *ought* to judge or not to judge in certain circumstances, about how confident they should be and about whether their thoughts constitute knowledge. It is thus normative and might not seem to have much to do with what people actually do think or might possibly think. But the kind of outlook being discussed in this chapter makes the assumption that 'thinks' is, in Rylean terms, a success or achievement word.[3] One does not think at all unless one, to some extent, succeeds in doing what, *qua* thinker, one ought to do – namely, satisfying the norms which epistemology (among other enquiries) aims to lay out and clarify. The claim here is extremely weak. It is only that *completely* unsuccessful and chaotic thought, thought in which no shred of truth or rational connectedness is discernible, is an incoherent notion. It does not deny the possibility of extremely bizarre beliefs, great degrees of muddle, contradiction and so forth.

What of the notion of a 'setting' which has been invoked? In the case of a pictorial representation there will (usually) be some clear boundary to the area within which relevant items could occur, a boundary such as the edge of a sheet of paper or a frame. But in the case of a person it is difficult to see how one could find any such boundary at a place short of the limits of the whole assemblage of what the person says. (In as much as this includes responses to things said by others, relevant items may well be found even further afield; but we shall not pursue this complication.)

The earlier claims made, that meaning requires suitable presences and absences, and relatedly that thinking is a success notion, have considerable plausibility. But this last move may seem more startling. On reflection however it will become less outrageous. The first impulse to deny it may come from the (correct) perception that the requirement for the presence of relevant items may well be satisfied in a small and temporally limited set of utterances. Yet it is not the presence condition but the absence condition which requires us to look wider. And what principled reason could one give for ruling out any stretch of what a person says from consideration? All stretches *ex hypothesi* include things said and done by the very same person and hence subject to the constraints (however minimal) which are required for them to belong to the unified psychological life of the one subject. In as much as we weaken any such rationality and coherence conditions – for example, allowing the thoughts to divide into two groups the union of which violates the constraints – we have started to think in terms of sequential or parallel occupation of the one body by two persons. (It may well, for example, become necessary to know, when interacting with the person, which group of thoughts is operative.)

It is worth explicitly distinguishing semantic holism in the sense sketched above from the thesis which Fodor discusses under that name and which he summarizes as follows: it is 'the idea that the identity – specifically the intentional content – of a propositional attitude is determined by the *totality* of its epistemic liaisons'.[4] If one embraces semantic holism in Fodor's sense then one is forced to the conclusion that two people who differ at all in their views about evidential relevance cannot share any propositional attitude and hence cannot mean the same by any utterances they produce. Fodor, understandably recoiling from this outcome, suggests that the best hope for setting up a non-holistic account of meaning is to put denotation – determined on a one-by-one causal basis for meaningful items – in the central place.

But the result of doing this, at least in the way Fodor proposes to, is that, as he allows, we have to contemplate the possibilities that 'people can believe things that are *arbitrarily* mad' and that 'entertaining the thought that three is a prime number could constitute an entire mental life.'[5] Fodor professes himself happy with these views but they are arguably at least as intuitively unacceptable as the untoward consequence of Fodor's version of holism remarked on above, namely that people with different views cannot mean the same.

So, were Fodor's kind of semantic holism and his causal–denotational theory the only two options, we would be in a bad position. Fortunately there is at least one more possibility, namely the more moderate holism to be examined here. The crucial difference is that our holism claims only that for a certain meaning to be expressed, the whole constituted by the person's utterances must be suitable, in terms of presences and absences. But we have not said that there will be only one suitable setting in which a given meaning can occur, so we are not committed to the view that any difference between two wholes must make every meaning expressed in the one differ from every meaning expressed in the other. And to say (as we will later) that every statement in a whole collection is relevant to (has a potential bearing on) the meaning of any other given statement is not to say that a change in the former must necessarily correlate with change in the meaning assigned to the latter.

Nevertheless there is, perhaps, a highly paradoxical implication of the view lurking in the wings, namely a revival of the indeterminacy claims about meaning. And it is to consideration of this that we now turn.

We have so far been talking metaphysically or constitutively about what is required for an utterance to have a certain meaning. However, there are, it seems, implications in this for the methodology of the enterprise of ascribing meaning to the sentences of someone else's language. The methodology will be subject to holistic constraints – in a sense which I shall try to lay out more fully in the next section. But, it will then be argued, when application of a concept is governed (only) by this sort of methodological constraint then it is implicit in the rules for its use that each of two incompatible meaning ascriptions may be equally and fully in order. Hence the concept does not obey the law of non-contradiction and, in accordance with the connection outlined in chapter 1, cannot be regarded as describing the real.

The interest of the argument to be explored is that it invokes only the comparatively innocuous seeming premises we have discussed and is not cumbered with baggage of a controversial empiricist character. We start off the argument allowing ourselves to be realists about both the observable and the unobservable and unburdened by any views on how to spell out that contrast or whether it is important. We also carry no commitments about how concepts may be acquired or of what they can be concepts. All we have in the way of substantive premises are the outlined views about meaning, which might well be thought plausible and to reveal something interesting and distinctive about the notions of semantics and psychology as opposed to those of physics.

5.2   HOLISM AND INDETERMINACY: THE MOSAIC ANALOGY

In this section I shall try to make the argument from holism to indeterminacy vivid and plausible by examining a particular case of the picture analogy already mentioned. The advantage is that in the example to be discussed the essential logical features are clearly exhibited and, moreover, the conclusion is not seriously paradoxical. The case is that of constructing a mosaic. In the next section I shall move back to the case of language and meaning, showing how it can plausibly be construed as an instance of the same conceptual pattern.

Imagine that I am set down before a certain scene – a woman, Lisa, sitting in front of a landscape. I am supplied with a large flat tray and a box of little chunks of glass, ceramic, stone etc. of various sizes and colours. The task I set myself is to produce in mosaic a recognizable picture of the scene. One constraint on the enterprise is that I must use, if at all possible, all of the pieces I am supplied with; I must not throw out a large proportion in order to leave myself with a handy set. Another constraint is that I must not myself manufacture pieces to fill in inconvenient gaps. I am given no guarantee that the pieces are peculiarly suitable for the job – my task is not like that of doing a jigsaw. I do not lay down in advance what size the final picture is to be, nor do I demand that I should depict the scene from the viewpoint I currently occupy or that I should use any particular style of representation. Moreover the business is open-ended, since from time to time I may be supplied with new batches of pieces which must also be used.

How would I set about the task? Perhaps this way: by sorting the pieces for colour and size, noting proportions of various colours in the actual scene and matching as well as I can the elements of the real scene to the materials supplied. I may plunge in by matching some pieces to her hair, some to her hands and some to the distant hills. Having put these in place I am limited in my later choices. I may be lucky and discover that it all works out; but if I have not been careful enough I may find myself without enough left to model her face satisfactorily, so I must start again.

Many kinds of developments and outcomes are possible. Perhaps I complete one acceptable picture and, bored with nothing to do, I tip the pieces out and start again, producing another equally good picture from a different viewpoint and in a different idiom. Perhaps a promising picture has to be scrapped because a new batch of pieces arrives and cannot be fitted in. But perhaps again the new lot can be fitted in just by expanding the old arrangement. And so on.

In the context of this task and the various possible outcomes, consider the questions 'Where does this piece go? Is it a left eyebrow piece?'

There are various ways in which these questions can be construed, but on only one interpretation do they have a clear-cut answer, namely when they are taken as asking after a decision already made. On other interpretations there is no guarantee that there will be only one answer to where the piece goes and hence no guarantee that one could not answer 'Is it a left eyebrow piece?' with both 'Yes' and 'No'.

On one interpretation the questions may be taken timelessly – suggesting that there is some one role that any piece should play in all defensible arrangements or suggesting that there is one final best arrangement in which it can play only one role. But the assumption that all defensible arrangements must assign the same role to a given piece is wrong. New pieces may always arrive and disrupt a given satisfactory arrangement, necessitating drastic displacements. And, much more importantly, with a given set of pieces – even the final complete set supposing we know when that has arrived – there may be alternative ways of constructing an acceptable picture.

It may be that with the final set of pieces one arrangement stands out as vastly preferable to all others – e.g. the pieces may form a jigsaw. But our impression that there is only one arrangement may be due to lack of imagination. The terms of the task show that we cannot insist a priori that there shall be one and only one best arrangement of any given set of pieces.

If I cannot insist that there is no one best role of a particular piece, can I at least rule out certain roles for it? Again the answer seems to be that a priori I cannot, although (as with the assignment of a given role and for the same sort of reason) a particular given collection, e.g. a set of jigsaw pieces, may in practice rule out a particular move. It is even clearer that if I take a piece or small collection of pieces in isolation then I cannot, by inspection of them alone, dismiss certain roles as ones impossible for them to play. For example one might suppose that a particular bright red piece could at least be ruled out as an eyebrow piece. But if the pieces supplied turned out, on inspection, all to be in various shades of red, then the eyebrow is just where it might end up.

Another interpretation of the questions 'Is this a right eyebrow piece?' and 'Where does this go?' sees them as asked of me when I am half-way through completing the task with a given set of pieces. So it enquires, in effect, 'Given that you have already placed a good number of pieces and determined a certain style, colour scheme and degree of detail for your picture, where will this piece go?' Here there is more likely to be determinacy in the answer; the greater the number of pieces already fitted and the clearer the style, the less choice I have on where the remaining pieces shall go. But even so determinacy cannot be guaranteed.

These indeterminacies do not mean that we would have no use for the predicate 'left eyebrow piece'. Context will often serve well enough to distinguish the various questions being asked, or claims being made, by its use; and by employing it conversational moves can be made in a less cumbersome way than would otherwise be required. But the indeterminacies do show that anyone who thought that this predicate operated like more straightforward descriptive ones, such as 'red' or 'square', would be mistaken. In particular he would be mistaken in supposing that there was some 'fact of the matter' in virtue of which he could insist on getting a clear cut answer to the timelessly intended questions.

What are the general structural features of the situation that explain the indeterminacy and by discovery of which we might hope to throw light on the case of meaning?

We have a group of objects, the mosaic pieces, to which two sets of predicates are applicable. One set is relatively unproblematic – 'red', 'square', 'member of a large group of like-coloured pieces' etc. Let us call them the U-predicates or (relatively) unproblematic predicates. These predicates are the ones about which we are realistic. We take it that there are facts about whether the pieces are correctly described by them and that investigation can put us in a good position to make largely reliable, if not infallible, judgements about what properties of this kind the pieces have. The other sort of predicate – let us call them P-predicates to remind ourselves of their problematic status – are applied on the basis of the U-predicates. There are such things as 'being a left eyebrow piece' and so forth.

The P-predicates come as a set. As was stressed in section 5.1 above, for one to be applicable at least some others from the set must be applicable. Nothing can be an eyebrow piece unless there are at least some pieces which can be taken to represent nose, forehead, eye, etc. The items to which P-predicates apply must have certain relations. But these relations are defined at a high level of abstraction; they concern such things as contrasts between U-properties and contrasts between contrasts between properties. That some things stand in such relations does not presuppose much about the actual nature of the items related. Let us say that P-predicates generate an *abstract pattern of demands*. For example, an eyebrow piece and a forehead piece must exhibit some visual contrast, a contrast which would be possible to use to represent the difference between hair and skin. Being certain shades of brown and pink respectively would do the job, but so would many other differences such as being spotted and plain, black and white, small and large, etc. A hair piece and a cheek piece must also exhibit such a contrast. Moreover within one picture the two contrasts should be similar. How similar will depend on features of the general style of the picture. But I might well find myself in trouble if I failed to co-ordinate the two contrasts I intend to employ.

The crucial points in generating the indeterminacy are now thrown into relief. The only constraint on a defensible application of P-predicates is that the properties described by the U-predicates of the items to which they are applied provide a realization of the abstract pattern. So to apply P-predicates we try to match the abstract pattern of demands with some actual set of contrasts, relations etc., constructed from the U-predicates of our given set of objects. But the U-predicates of the objects contrast and relate in many different ways. Also the set of P-predicates, together with the abstract set of demands it generates, is open to extension or revision as we perceive more of the scene or decide to represent it in greater detail, and the demands so generated are not clearly ordered. An abstract pattern, in other words, is not a fixed matter dictated once and for all by the scene we are to depict. All that is required of it is that it be rich enough to enable us to recognize a picture embodying it as of the desired scene.

In constructing a picture we have then two points at which we may be required to make a choice. One point is that at which we fix on how much of the scene is to be represented, in what style, level of detail and so forth. The other is that at which we fix on how the U-properties of the pieces shall be deployed to fulfil the pattern of demands generated by the earlier decision. At neither point is there any guarantee that there will be one unique best decision; hence the indeterminacy. It is worth stressing, however, that the second factor mentioned is, by itself, quite sufficient to generate indeterminacy. Even if we had something fairly firm in the way of instructions about what features of the scene are to be represented in the picture we would still have no guarantee that we could not deploy our pieces in two different ways to carry out the task.

Why should it seem apt to describe application of the P-predicates as 'subject to holistic constraints'? The point is this. Given an item or group of items I cannot, just by examining them in isolation, decide what P-predicates are applicable to them. However well they fit together to make an eye, I must not say straight off that an eye is what they represent. I must first look to the whole set of elements to make sure that the other P-predicates have suitable resting places and hence to make sure that I am working with the most convenient sub-set of P-predicates and abstract demands. Whether I am operating a convenient set, and have made workable initial moves in applying it, depend upon the structure of the total set of elements. Thus every element is relevant to the placement of every other element. It is the need to keep an eye on the whole which thus operates as a distinctive constraint on this kind of enterprise. And it is the fact that the P-predicates come as a set which in turn underlies that methodological constraint.

This sort of holism is to be sharply contrasted with some general policy, applicable to any judgement, of keeping an eye on all the evidence. Our current holism is rooted in something peculiar to the predicates involved and consists in a necessity to perform certain specific kinds of cross-check on a certain particular group of items. The general policy of watching the whole of the evidence on the other hand is rooted in views about the unreliable nature of our capacity to acquire knowledge and views about the ramifying and interconnected nature of the world. In the routine application of many predicates this general policy does not give rise to the need to check against the rest of our beliefs; and when larger scale re-appraisal does seem in order the policy does not enjoin that any specific sort of check be undertaken. So, as I have stressed, the indeterminacy generated by the holism in the mosaic case is of a different character from the admission that future evidence may shake some of our current firm beliefs. As we shall see in section 5.4, the epistemological matter of needing to keep an eye on the whole of our current view, and the consequent coherence element in justification, does play an important role in the indeterminacy argument. But we must nevertheless keep epistemological holism sharply distinguished from the indeterminacy being discussed.

What the mosaic case illustrates is that a predicate like 'left eyebrow piece' (as I have imagined it used) is a different sort of linguistic item from a predicate like 'red' or 'square'. The point of having this P-predicate is, we might say, different from the point of having these U-predicates. The point of a P-predicate is, roughly, to be able to report on or ask after certain projects or decisions; the point is not to ask about items independent of our choices. And the defensibility of those decisions involves a different sort of consideration (namely about the picture as a whole) from the considerations involved in the defence of particular judgements involving U-predicates. The upshot of all this is that it is not difficult to persuade oneself that there is 'no fact of the matter' to be got at here.

5.3   HOLISM, INDETERMINACY AND LANGUAGE

How might all this apply to the case of meaning, i.e. to the problem of understanding the utterances and identifying the thoughts of another person? This is what I shall now try to spell out.

In a radical translation project as usually conceived we have two problems, that of translating the language of our subject and that of finding out what he believes. The tasks are different because a speaker may not say everything he believes and he may not believe everything he says. I want to avoid all the puzzles generated by these facts and will adopt instead the fantasy of a simplified situation – that in which we are confronted by someone I shall call 'the candid babbler'. The candid babbler is a person who conducts all his mental life, his noticings, musings, reasonings, concludings etc. overtly and in words and who never knowingly speaks falsely. With the candid babbler the problem of translation and that of ascribing thoughts are collapsed into the one problem of understanding his utterances.

The fantasy of the candid babbler is useful not only as a conceptual device for isolating the interpretation/translation problem from the conceptual soup we want to clarify, but also for other reasons. Thinking of our problem as that of understanding a candid babbler brings out a plausible presupposition, common to the approaches of both Quine and Davidson, namely that in understanding another person what we must go on is his or her utterances and behaviour in response to confrontations with the environment. There is some level of description which is available prior to (detailed) identification of meaning and which is the only thing on which we can call to supply material, conceptually or epistemologically, to ground specific ascriptions of content.[6] If the facts here are not enough to yield determinate interpretations, says this methodology, there is nowhere else to go; in particular we must not appeal to further inner events which are intrinsically intentional, i.e. to Cartesian 'thoughts'.

Our starting point for interpretation will be the utterances themselves. These play a role parallel to that of the mosaic pieces. The features corresponding to the size, colour etc. of the pieces are the phonetic character of the utterances and what we might vaguely call the circumstances – such things as the environment of the speaker, the movements he and his hearer's go through before or after the utterance, what other utterances precede or follow etc. These are described by our U-predicates. The P-predicates are ones by which we assign meaning – 'said that it was raining', 'concluded that the train was late', 'reminded her that she must take her umbrella', and the like.

To interpret is to make intelligible, and this in two senses. First there is the minimal sense where it simply means 'such as to have a meaning assigned'. But secondly there is a richer one, where 'intelligibility' also involves our seeing how the person could have come to have those thoughts; this intelligibility requires us to see some point, sense or defensibility in the other's thoughts. The first sort of intelligibility does not directly involve the second. Thus one may, on authority from others, come to use some translation scheme which enables one to provide a reading for various marks, noises or gestures, while it still seems to one that in another sense the interpreted marks, noises etc. 'make no sense'. But the two ways of using 'intelligible' do hang together in the long run, because use of interpretation in the first sense must ultimately be rooted in the second. It is understanding creatures in the sense of seeing them as beings with a point of view of their own, a point of view of which one can get some inkling, that justifies postulating translation schemes. If this idea fails us in some particular case, then we lose the idea that there is a person, a point of view, at the origin of some putatively meaningful items. But if it becomes clear, so to speak, that there is no one there, then the meaningfulness drains away.

The condition of 'intelligibility' that we here impose on interpretation is an obscure matter. It is not clear how much sympathy with or insight into another point of view (set of opinions, project, way of thinking) I have to have in order to find it intelligible. It is not clear that it is an all-or-nothing matter.

But we may suggest at least two constraints which the condition places upon interpretation. First our babbler, or candidate for interpretation, will only be intelligible if we can see him to be thinking, in part at least, about the world we share with him. This is a fairly elastic constraint. It does not rule out our making sense of someone who turns out to be unaware of his immediate surroundings and tuned in to broadcasts from the Andromeda Galaxy; nor does it rule out our making sense of someone who claims to be aware, some of the time, of things we cannot detect. The point is only that if his thoughts were solely about things which were entirely inaccessible to us then we would never make any sense of him.

The second constraint is that our candid babbler cannot be seen as thinking about anything at all unless he can be made out to be at least minimally rational, i.e. to exhibit some sensible pattern in his thoughts. It is important to be clear about the logical shape of this claim. The point is not that there is some particular pattern (*modus ponens*, universal instantiation, avoidance of the gambler's fallacy or whatever) which I can now specify and which he must exhibit. The constraint is only that he must exhibit some pattern or other which allows us to see him as reasoning, however misguidedly.

The upshot of these two requirements is that the P-predicates we wish to apply to him come as a set. Both the nature of rationality (as we conceive it) and the nature of the world (again as we conceive it) help to suggest what the members of the set will be. And, as in the mosaic case, the predicates generate a structure of abstract demands, for example, that utterances assigned different meanings should, in general exhibit phonetic differences and that utterances assigned related meanings (where one would evidentially support or be supported by the other) should occur sometimes in certain sorts of temporal sequence.

From this it follows that holistic constraints operate in the application of these P-predicates. We must not use one of them unless we are sure that the others have resting places and that radically disruptive elements are not present. The defensibility of an assignment of meaning to an item depends on how things work out across the whole set of utterances. Indeed the task of interpretation is now surprisingly close to that of mosaic construction. It is to take some gabble of noises and to tie them up to facts in the world in such a way that their utterer is shown to be someone who succeeds in representing that world in a recognizable manner. Another person is a living picture of the world. But (if the analogy holds up) it is *our* business as interpreters to arrange the assemblage as a whole into an actual picture. A person may also do it for himself, but he has no special authority such as might be given by access to Cartesian items.

The method will be to plunge in with some likely looking initial hypotheses and then to hope that the rest of the assignments can be fitted in. Deciding to adopt a certain translation scheme is like adopting a certain scale and style in the construction of the picture. It commits us to the existence of certain other U-characterizable items to fulfil the rest of the abstract pattern. And if these are not to be found, or if in addition some further radically different and unforeseen items appear, we shall be in trouble.

But as with the mosaic there is no guarantee that two or more ways of fulfilling the abstract demands cannot be constructed. Part of the flexibility comes from the fact that we have some discretion in fixing the set of P-predicates we work with, i.e. we can attribute bizarre beliefs to our subject (if we can find enough of a setting to make them intelligible) and we can make him more or less observant. But even if we imagine this degree of freedom to be not very extensive, even if we take it that there are a good many opinions, rules of inference etc. that must be found in any recognizable thought about the world, the possibility still remains that we might be able to find more than one way of tying up those obligatory opinions with the utterances we take to be their vehicles.

So, in summary, the methodology of interpretation is holistic. It can only consist in matching some chosen set of abstract demands generated by the P-predicates with the actual patterns detectable in the U-predicates. But given that we have a choice of subset of

P-predicates and, more importantly, that there may be different ways of arranging U-predicates to satisfy the demands, there can be no guarantee that there is some unique best interpretation of a particular utterance. Two entirely defensible translations schemes might assign it radically different roles.

Hence the conclusion is that investigation of the nature of meaning ascriptions themselves – the distinctive methodology of applying them – shows that insistence on a 'fact of the matter' is out of place, because even minimal realism is not defensible here.

5.4 CAN WE RESTORE DETERMINACY?

We move next to consider a counter-argument and some responses to it. Someone might point out that the existence of holistic constraints on placement of mosaic pieces is not by itself sufficient to ensure that there is no fact of the matter about whether a given bit is an eyebrow piece. We have implicitly used another important assumption, the alteration of which allows us to construct a case in which the application of such P-predicates is both subject to holistic constraints and also determinate.

The extra assumption is this: that the pieces from which we are to construct the picture have no natural suitability for the task. They have not been produced with a view to constructing a picture, so their number and colour are in no way controlled by the elements in the scene which they are used to depict. Rather the construction of the picture is entirely my project and the constraints on methodology result from my decision on what shall count as a successful completion of the project. Knowledge of the causal origin of a piece (e.g. as part of the rejects from a crockery factory) is thus of no relevance to my decision on where to place it.

But let us alter this assumption. Imagine that my task is as before *except that* I see my raw materials actually being produced by some device and I operate on the hypothesis that it is a device which has been built precisely in order to produce materials to construct a mosaic of the scene with which it is confronted. The device operates, I surmise, by directing some light sensitive mechanism at an area of the scene and stamping out a mosaic piece in accordance with the intensity and nature of the light arriving. But (let us imagine) I do not know as yet what optical resolution the device incorporates, what sort of scanning pattern it has, whether it introduces some systematic distortion of perspective or colour in its stamping process, whether it spits the pieces out as soon as it produces them or randomizes them inside first. Given this ignorance, my methodology in constructing the mosaic must, in practice, be the same as before, namely, entirely holistic. Consequently something like indeterminacy may arise. I cannot conclude from the fact that some group of pieces arrives together and work excellently to represent an eye that they must remain in that position in my finished picture; I may well be able to make two equally good pictures from the same set of pieces, and so on. Nevertheless the indeterminacy now looks more like the underdetermination of theory by data, because the predicate 'right eyebrow piece' will now have a new meaning, one upon which there is a determinate answer to the question 'Is this a right eyebrow piece?' – namely it will mean 'piece produced by the machine when scanning her right eyebrow'.

One might object to the claim that the methodology still incorporates a central holistic element on the grounds that, in theory at least and were my ignorance less, there should be more direct ways, which would supersede the holistic ones, of deciding what P-predicate to apply to a piece. Might I not actually see a piece being produced as a result of scanning her right eyebrow? Might I not have enough insight into the workings of the machine to assign a causal origin and hence a pictorial role to a piece, without the consideration of any other factors?

The answer is that I cannot do this unless I have reason to suppose that the holistic constraints are also obeyed – that the other P-predicates will find suitable resting places and that some set of abstract demands are fulfilled. I may have this assurance on inductive grounds – previous success with this machine on other scenes – or because I know in detail how the machine works. So I may, given these sorts of evidence, be prepared to override holistic considerations in the short term. But I can only properly do this because I take it that in the long run the constraints will be observed. It is exactly this that induction or the design evidence makes me think. If it begins to look as if I am wrong in anticipating this, i.e. my reliance on the non-holistic indicators for placement of pieces continues over a long period of time to produce a non-picture, then *ipso facto* I lose my confidence in the device, think I have misdescribed it or that it has broken down. And at this point 'left eyebrow piece' will cease to have determinate application on the basis of causal factors and will revert to the role or collection of roles we originally assigned to it.

My well-supported conjecture about the nature of the device thus does not enable me to ignore holistic constraints in applying P-predicates. Belief that the constraints are satisfied is part of what I endorse in describing the device as I do. But, and this is the important point in rendering the predicates determinate, if my conjecture about the device is correct it provides a standard by which I can sensibly choose between alternative picture constructions both of which satisfy the holistic constraints – a standard by which I can say 'This is the picture the machine was designed to produce' or 'This is the machine's picture'. Thus we come to an outlook in which a concept, 'right eyebrow piece', is subject both to holistic constraints and also to causal conditions. And if we get an insight into the workings of the machine we can employ the causal information to fix on placements for pieces. It is when holistic constraints are the only ones operative that indeterminacy ensues. The more complex concept now available is free of that feature and hence fit to describe an aspect of reality.

How could we apply a move of this sort to the case of meaning? The obvious suggestion will be that some non-holistic, e.g. causal, constraint be incorporated, as an extra element, into the meaning of talk about meaning. Utterances will be linked with particular states of the world which causally explain their occurrence. Thus alternative schemes of translation which satisfy the holistic constraints can be evaluated differently and meaning rendered determinate.

Something of this sort seems prima facie very plausible since no collection of bits of behaviour can be utterances or expressions of belief unless they are under the control of, formed in response to, the events and states they are about. So, one might say, if a person has a belief as a result of causal interaction with a certain state of affairs in the world (with many other provisos of course), then it is a belief that that state of affairs obtains.

But although this general programme is easy to sketch in outline, it is difficult to carry through in detail. It encounters many difficulties, some of which may be deep ones of principle. For a start it is clear that in applying it to determine content in the case of some particular utterances we shall need a way of sieving out utterances which are not assertive at all and also sieving out ones which are assertive judgements produced by 'improper' causes, such as Humean associative mechanisms or self-deception. If we attended to causes to fix content in these cases, we would go badly wrong.

It cannot but improve the chances of the strategy we are considering to imagine all these problems done away with. So let us modify our specification of the candid babbler to demand that he be an extremely literal minded fellow, all of whose utterances are concerned to express truths about the world and all of whose judgements are arrived at by epistemologically respectable routes. This latter cannot be taken to mean that the babbler never makes mistakes in reasoning, otherwise he becomes too unlike us to be interesting. So we will allow that he may be in error in reasoning, in the sense of being committed to far-reaching and principled mistakes. But he does not make trivial slips and is consistently rational by his own lights.

In the case of such a subject can the causal antecedents of belief fix meaning? It is here that some difficulties of principle appear and that Quinean considerations about epistemological holism become relevant. In the case of the mosaic-making machine we were able to home in on those particular causal antecedents which were of importance because we were able to distinguish sharply between the standing causal conditions for the production of pieces (namely the permanent design structure of the machine) and the varying conditions of input which explain, in particular cases, the varying output. But we are not like the machine. Certainly we are like it in that facts in the world impinge on us and causally contribute to our acquiring beliefs about them; moreover causal connections of these kinds may well be necessary for some sorts of meaning. It would be absurd to deny this. But when facts impinge upon a person, they for the most part encounter a subject already possessing a complex world view, itself the outcome of innumerable previous encounters. The 'output' of judgement on a given occasion thus depends not only upon current 'input' (if it depends on it at all, which, in cases of highly theoretical reflection seems problematic) but also upon previous inputs. How then do we choose among the causal antecedents of a judgement those which we take to be relevant to its content? The strategy under consideration requires that we be able to do so determinately, e.g. in the light of some other determinate (causal?) facts. But what if this cannot be done and the choice has rather to be made on holistic grounds?

We may approach the problem from another angle by introducing in more detail the theme of epistemological holism. The central claim here is that the correct epistemological status of a judgement cannot be determined by looking at the judgement in isolation. A judgement cannot be certified as something one ought to have a great deal of confidence in, or something one ought to throw out, except by considering how it relates to the whole body of beliefs.

Acceptance of this sort of holism does not mean that we have bought the idea that whenever we consider some question we ought to survey the whole body of our beliefs before answering. This would be absurd. Clearly a great deal is taken for granted and does its supportive epistemological work unnoticed in the background. The need to acknowledge this should not disconcert the holist. But all the same, his picture seems much more plausible for some kinds of beliefs and their relations than for others.

Let us consider some examples. Suppose that the question has arisen 'Is this flower a fritillery?' The other beliefs which I am likely to bring consciously into play concern the colour, habitat etc. of this flower and the colour, habitat, etc. of fritilleries. Beliefs such as that I can read, that a certain word is 'purple' or that the sun is shining are not going to figure explicitly in my deliberations. Yet it is surely plausible to say that my assumptions on these matters play an important background role in the matter, in that were I to change my views on them I might well change my verdict on this flower. But are *all* my other beliefs playing a similar behind-the-scenes supportive role? What about the belief that men have flown to the moon or that William II had red hair? It is certainly not clear that change in these would alter my judgement about the flower.

The holist however will reply to this that these other beliefs *might* support or disrupt my views about the flower because one cannot rule out as impossible circumstances in which they would be relevant. It could be the case that my confidence that I can correctly interpret what it says in this foreign flower book rests in part upon the fact that I can interpret some other sentence in that language as saying that William II had red hair. Or it might be the case that the fact that men have flown to the moon is part of the support for a view of gravity which connects with a view about geology which dovetails with a view about habitats which . . . and so on. We are not in a position to rule these out as intelligible accounts of what someone might, given certain other evidence, come to believe. And if someone did believe such things then the beliefs about the moon or William would have supportive and also potentially disruptive roles in connection with the judgement about the flower. The upshot is that my belief that William II had red hair is doing something important *vis-à-vis* my judgement about the flower merely by not exercising the disruptive potential it would have if the right mediating body of beliefs came to be accepted. In other words, the fact that my belief about the flower is consistent with my belief about William is not as trivial as it looks. And it is only given the structure of my whole set of beliefs – given the lack of intermediating items of certain kinds – that they are consistent.[7]

What are the relations of this kind of epistemological holism to semantic holism? The former may serve as a premise from which the latter may be deduced, provided that suitable extra premises of a verificationist character are to hand. But if we reject such extra premises then it seems much less likely that there should be a link.[8] This line of thought would take us back in the direction of the themes of chapters 3 and 4 and it is not how semantic holism has been defended in this chapter.

What about a converse connection? If one accepts semantic holism (as introduced in section 5.1 rather than in Fodor's sense) does epistemological holism follow? It does not. To consider the failure of epistemological holism one must imagine a schematic situation where, for some p and q, in establishing whether or not p it just could not, ever or for anyone, be relevant whether or not q.

This is prima facie plausible for various judgements, for example whether this is a fritillery and whether nine times nine makes eighty-one. Let us, for the sake of argument, take it that the plausible supposition is correct. Does the denial of semantic holism follow? To say that it did would mean that I was now in a position to establish that a certain remark of another person expresses the judgement about the square of nine without considering everything else that person says. But why should this follow from the epistemological irrelevance of the fritillery judgement? The point of the inspection of everything else the person says is to establish the absence condition required by whatever demands we have for minimal coherence and rationality. The epistemological irrelevance of the fritillery judgement helps us to establish this; the fritillery judgement is not going to do any disruptive work in. making our subject turn out to be incoherent. But that does nothing to undermine the idea that meaning requires a discourse-wide absence condition, and hence does nothing to undermine semantic holism.

The upshot then seems to be that semantic and epistemological holism are independent theses. What then underlies the latter? The claim in the earlier discussion was that intelligible links between any two judgements could be set up; one could always imagine a case in which the one bore upon the other. (On closer inspection we shall see this to be so, contrary to our earlier concession, for arithmetic and botany. For example, botanical views about fritilleries might bear upon the question of whether I was or was not drugged and so upon the question of whether I should accept the conclusion of this seemingly valid proof about the square of nine.) But why is this so?

The answer seems to have to do with the fact that we are not in a position to insist that the world exists in isolated watertight compartments. To establish epistemological non-holism we would have to be certain that some aspects of the world were independent of each other in an extremely strong sense. It would be required that no theory could possibly unify the two sorts of phenomena in such a way that considerations from that theory could bear epistemologically upon the acceptance of individual statements about the two realms. If such a theory was imaginable (even if we did not possess it) then we could imagine evidence from the two realms supporting the theory which in turn bore upon an individual judgement about one realm. And this imagined structure has brought the individual judgements from the two areas to bear upon each other. The impossibility of such a theory could come about in either of two ways. It might be that we knew ourselves to be infallible with respect to the two subject matters. In this case a unifying theory might exist in the sense of a compendious or illuminating overview. But such a theory (in effect a mere conjunction) could not, because of the infallibility, play any epistemological role. On the other hand we might have confidence in the impossibility of any linking theory on the basis of some scientific or metaphysical compartmentalization of things. But it seems extremely implausible to suppose that either the infallibility or the compartmentalization condition is fulfilled.

The important upshot, as far as the attempt to restore determinacy of meaning is concerned, is that we should accept some version of the Quinean thought that our beliefs face the world *en bloc*. Let us now go back to our rational candid babbler. We may establish that some particular fact which impinges on him is causally relevant to the production of some particular utterance. But if the babbler is, as imagined, rationally conscientious then the explanation of his making that judgement will involve his background view of the world. He judges as he does in part because, for example, there are no elements in his view which lead him to reject the judgement which the current confrontation prompts him to. And what explains the absence of such elements? Both the nature of all the actual encounters which led to the beliefs he does have and also the absence of some encounters which, given his cognitive nature, would have led to the formation of disruptive beliefs had they occurred.

The non-holist supposes that the description given in the last sentence, fixes some totality of causal information which, in theory if not in practice, one could imagine assembling and which, if possessed, would single out some causal factors from others as the ones proper to supply intentional content. But it is far from clear that these suppositions are correct.

One sort of worry arises from the idea that we can find a

principled limit to the number of standing negative conditions to be taken into account. Identification of an utterance as expressing a given thought involves the idea that the maker of the judgement would respond appropriately to a variety of new juxtapositions, challenges, and so forth. But how are we to list in advance what they all are or what the appropriate reaction is, given that we are ourselves enmeshed in the middle of the development?[9]

A second difficulty has to do with the identification of falsehood. Not every utterance can mean even one of its causes, unless our subject makes no mistakes. So, given that we are aware of the possibility of error, we cannot ever move from causal information to assignment of meaning without some extra premise about the tolerability of imputing error. Where is this to come from? Will it be non-holistic? The answer is far from clear.

A third difficulty is marginally more concrete than the highly abstract considerations marshalled so far and gives more sense of the problems encountered in moving from causal to intentional. It poses the question of whether we could even be sure of distinguishing indexical statements from non-indexical theoretical ones on the basis of causal information, not itself employed under the constraint of a holistic story.

Suppose that we have securely identified sentence types and tokens, and also their negations. An indexical type will then, it seems, be one, different tokens of which are happily accepted as having different truth values. So it is supposed we can observe a group of persons oscillating between asserting a sentence and its negation and decide that the sentence must be indexical. Having got this clear we then move to identify causes and so content. This is the usual story. But how do we know that we have got even the first stage right? Perhaps the persons are changing their minds frequently about some theoretical matter. Suppose they are gazing at a screen on which two slowly growing lines are exhibited. They utter affirmative and negative tokens of a type according as the lines converge or diverge and we establish that the positions of the lines are causally relevant to their utterances. Does it follow that they are talking about the position of the lines? Might they not be expressing changing theoretical views about whether or not the moon has a magnetic core, according as the results of some analysis gradually unfold?

One might object here that we have forgotten the condition that our candid babblers must voice all their thoughts. If things were as I have suggested, would there not have to be utterances other than those I have mentioned to which we could assign an observational and indexical role? Can we make sense of the idea of someone 'seeing' the composition of the moon in a screen display without that observer being aware of and voicing epistemologically inter-mediate links of an observational kind? We may well be able to make sense of 'seeing' things other than what is (in some sense) present and causally effective; this would be a consequence of allowing (at least some) observations to be 'theory laden'.[10] But the currently imagined case seems to go even further than this.

Concession of the force of this objection however leaves us able to construct an analogous problem. What of somebody who utters pairs of apparent indexicals, one of which supports the other? Can we be sure that both are really indexical? Might not one be an indexical and the other a theoretical view whose plausibility changes in step with the acceptability of the indexical? It seems that it must be features of how things pan out, from the point of view of coherence etc., in the rest of what he says, which would enable us to decide between the two views. And what entitles us to think that these features will be non-holistic?

The thrust of all these considerations taken together is to suggest that causal considerations will indeed be highly relevant in the assignment of meaning but that they do not play a role alongside and independently of holistic constraints. Rather they are them-selves among the U-predicates we use to support our attributions of P-predicates. As such they serve as grist to the holistic mill and not as the desired independent check on its results.

I am far from claiming that the arguments of the past few pages show that this is so, only that it is a hypothesis which we cannot dismiss. And if it were correct then we seem to have no defence against the conclusion that meaning ascriptions of their nature cannot be guaranteed to obey the law of non-contradiction and hence to the conclusion that meanings are not real and that there are no facts about them.

6

The Slide into the Abyss

6.1 THE INCOMPATIBILITY OF REALISM AND MEANING SCEPTICISM

How should we respond to the conclusion of chapter 5? It offers us scepticism about meaning – not in the sense of claiming that there is something to know which we do not know but in the sense of claiming that there are no facts to be known. This position is the same as that recommended by Quine, but generalized to all sentences and reached by a different route. Psychology, history, literary criticism and everyday talk of thoughts and feelings are thus revealed as (mere) pattern construction rather than fact discovery. But other investigations are, for anything we have so far said, still to be credited with finding how things really are. To make this contrast is not necessarily to think psychology etc. unimportant, still less to suppose them dispensable. But it is certainly to view them as something sharply different from investigations in the natural sciences. And given the honorific status of words like 'fact' and 'real' it is difficult to avoid the implication of some kind of downgrading.

Two questions now arise. Should we accept this view? And does Wittgenstein follow something like the route mapped out in chapter 5 to reach it? I wish to suggest that we should answer 'no' to both. On the second question, as I remarked in the Introduction, we certainly do not find in Wittgenstein any explicit drawing of sceptical conclusions about meaning such as we find in Quine, nor do we find claims that only the natural sciences describe the real. But on the other hand we do find attacks on a certain conception of what facts about meaning could be like (the negative arguments so forcefully expounded by Kripke). And the materials for some argument like that of chapter 5 may seem to be provided. There are many passages in Wittgenstein where he stresses that when we see a gesture, words or facial expression as 'full of meaning' this is bound up with its occurrence in a context.[1] Thus 'holism' of some kind there certainly seems to be in Wittgenstein.

But (as I shall try to suggest in the next chapter) on examination this holism proves to be even more all embracing than the version we have discussed so far. That version emphasized what a person could coherently be said to believe, given that he or she believed such and such else. It thus had to do with the existence of suitable patterns among things which are to be taken as representing the world. And its central theme is that the things a person takes to be the case must hang together in a certain way. But on Wittgenstein's view to see what someone means by some utterance I may need to see not just what else he or she takes to be the case but also what he or she is trying to do, what he or she takes to be important and why; it is only in grasping these things that I can understand even his or her most austerely descriptive words.

This introduces a very important theme – the interpenetration and interdependence of description and project, of theoretical and practical, to which we shall return. This broadening of the scope of possible considerations needed for understanding does not, I shall suggest, leave the indeterminacy of meaning even more firmly rooted. Rather it moves us on to a different conception of 'realism' from either the mirroring or the pragmatist one – and to a different conception of epistemology – which ultimately allows us to escape from the sceptical conclusion of chapter 5. But before we can begin to examine this alternative vision we need to turn to the first question I mentioned above, namely the acceptability of the position now arrived at. In the remainder of this section I shall argue that no kind of realism can live happily with the sceptical view of meaning we have arrived at; in the next section I shall contend that realism is not easily dispensed with.

In the mosaic-construction story, and equally in the story about interpretation of language, we took it for granted that we, the picture builders or interpreters, were seeing Lisa in her landscape or thinking about the world around us. What we do is tell a story about how we might go about assigning meanings to items other than our own utterances or states. We give an epistemological and methodological account, from which certain ontological conclusions are supposed to follow.

But what happens if we try to think through the application of these conclusions to our own case? Here we return to a theme touched on briefly in section 4.3. Suppose for example I say 'There is a tree over there'. Application of the conclusion of chapter 5 to this utterance tells me that I have made a noise which someone else (or I myself if I had enough ingenuity) could perhaps with perfect defensibility take to mean not that there is a tree over there but something quite different – that the moon is spherical.

I am now driven to exclaim 'But I don't mean that the moon is spherical. I mean that there is a tree over there.' Our theory however tells us that this is itself just another piece of noise-making to which, in turn, various different meanings might be assigned. 'Assignment of meanings' cannot itself be taken to set up some connection between noises and something other than noises, because the noises that are used to do the assigning cannot themselves be allowed to have connections with non-noises which the original subjects of interpretation were denied. All that 'assignment of meanings' can do is to set up correlations between noises.

We arrive thus at a (temporary) resting place in which we say to ourselves: 'The notion of meaning has been revealed as incoherent; there are really nothing but noise-makings, which in turn provoke other noise-makings. But none of these noises have any properties beyond their non-representational ones. The truth is that the idea of there being items (or performances or states or activities) which point beyond themselves, things in virtue of the occurrence of which we are in touch with or open to the nature of something other than ourselves, is an illusion.'

But this conclusion cannot provide a very satisfactory stopping point. In enunciating it we seem to ourselves for an instant to have got the real truth about how things are. We have plumbed the depths and there is some melancholy satisfaction, even a sort of thrill, in having got to grips with the human condition, however illusion-ridden and unfortunate it turns out to be. However a moment's reflection upon what our conclusion says (or at least seems to say) puts any such feeling of satisfaction or stability in jeopardy. Our understanding of the conclusion (whatever 'under-standing' is allowed to be, even if it is just a disposition to move on to some other utterances under the stimulus of this one) drives us on to say that if the conclusion is 'right' (whatever that now comes to) then its enunciation cannot have the status of 'being the truth about how things are' which we hoped for it. The more defensibility the conclusion has, the less any such defensibility ('truth') can amount to. In particular it cannot amount to that representation of what is independent of us, belief in which is the hallmark of the realist of whatever variety.

A central thread of these remarks is that there is something extremely strange about assigning a high semantic status ('really true', 'limning the true and ultimate nature of reality' or what not) to some class of utterances, and a different and lower status ('no fact of the matter') to utterances which report, or would prima facie be taken to report, the features of the first sort of utterance – their meanings – in virtue of which they were suitable recipients of the honorific-seeming label. The suspicion arises that the disparage-ment of certain supposed properties of the vehicles ('they do not really have one meaning rather than another') must carry over to disparagement of what one might attempt to do ('truly describing the real world') by use of the vehicles.[2]

I want to argue now that we can make this charge stick a little more firmly by showing that an adherent of indeterminacy about meaning cannot with confidence defend the law of non-contra-diction, even for those statements about which he says that there is a fact of the matter as to their truth or falsity. He thus cannot deliver even the minimal demands of realism.

Let us remind ourselves of what the principle of non-contra-diction says. It is the claim that when I know that each of two incompatible utterances could be equally and fully defensible then I cannot take it that those utterances are to be realistically con-strued. This is not to say that I take it that I can always know without any difficulty or reflection whether any given incompatible sentences could both be fully defensible and so whether realism is the right construal of them. That would rule out the possibility of intelligible philosophical dispute about controversial cases. What it is to say is that reasons for thinking that the principle of non-contradiction does not hold in a particular case are *ipso facto* reasons against realism in that case. The greater the likelihood that non-contradiction fails, the greater the implausibility of realism.

To get the argument under way we now need to note an important feature of interpretation as described in chapter 5. It is this: Although I must make my subject come out as having a set of opinions which is recognizably a view of the world I share with him, there is no bar to attributing to him what I take to be false opinions. Putting things in the translation idiom, I do not always have to map things to which he assents onto things to which I assent, or vice-versa. More particularly, there is no bar, in the methodology as sketched, for supposing that in some cases I might not find two acceptable translation schemes, which translate a given sentence of the other person into two sentences of my language *which I take to be incompatible and to be subject to the principle of non-contradiction*. For example, there might be a sentence of the other's language which I can translate defensibly either as 'The moon is spherical' or as 'The moon is a flat disc'.

Remembering that the indeterminacy claim is applicable to my own case also, let us imagine that my own set of utterances is an example of what has just been described. So when I say 'The moon is spherical' I can *either* translate myself as speaking familiar English (let us call it English 1), and take it that I mean that the moon is spherical *or* I can take myself to be speaking another language, call it English 2, in which what I mean is that the moon is a flat disc. (You may object that this is an implausible claim about our actual utterances. Yet even if this is conceded, and it is not clear that it should be, the objection will turn out not to help as much as might be imagined. We shall return to it below.)

Now what the indeterminacy of meaning thesis tells us is that 'is a speaker of English 1 who says "The moon is spherical" and believes that the moon is spherical' is one predicate applicable to me; it also says that the predicate 'is a speaker of English 2 who says "The moon is spherical" and believes that the moon is a flat disc' is also applicable to me; and finally it asserts that there is no fact of the matter as to which description is really true of me; both are equally and fully defensible.

At this point we shall make a further assumption, which must be allowable, namely that when I utter 'The moon is spherical' what I do is 'right' and fully defensible. The assumption must be allowable because all parties to this dispute are agreed that *some* utterances are 'right' and 'The moon is spherical' seems an uncontroversial candidate. At the moment we are all claiming to understand rightness in a realistic way, and, on my contention – which the believer in indeterminacy claims to be able to endorse – this implies that the utterance is subject to the principle of non-contradiction.

What does this 'rightness' have to do, if anything, with the language I am taken to be speaking? The advocate of indeterminacy is in trouble whatever he says. He could maintain that whether I am speaker of English 1 or of English 2 bears directly on this assessment. I might, for example, be right *qua* speaker of English 1 but wrong *qua* speaker of English 2. But if this is the line we take then one could hardly say that the two descriptions of me are merely different notations for the same facts. Or to put the point another way, if we say that I am right *qua* speaker of English 1 and wrong *qua* speaker of English 2 and, at the same time, say that there is no fact of the matter as to which language I speak, then we have already thrown in the realist sponge as far as the moon is concerned. For what we have said implies that there is no fact of the matter as to whether I am right or wrong and hence no fact about how it is with the moon.

So to avoid this and to maintain, as he thinks, his right to be a realist, the advocate of indeterminacy ought to hang on to the idea that my rightness is not bound up with the (non-factual) question of which language I speak but is independent of it. Then the difficulty with being a realist comes out another way. The claim now is that I can properly be taken as speaking English 2 and saying in it that the moon is a flat disc and that my utterance is correct. Now, by anybody's lights it must be agreed that if it is 'all right' to do what we properly describe as 'saying that the moon is a flat disc in English 2' then it is 'all right' to do what we would describe as 'saying that the moon is a flat disc in English 1'. Changing the language in which I express my views (whatever account we give of what that amounts to) cannot change the views from right to wrong.

But the effect of this admission is disastrous. The advocate of indeterminacy now has no grounds for finding any fault with a person who utters those sentences of English 1 which we would take as expressing the bizarre beliefs which are attributable to me *qua* English 2 speaker but utterer of all the sentences I now utter. In short, the advocate of indeterminacy has got into a position where acknowledging the full defensibility of 'The moon is spherical' as said in English 1 is no bar against acknowledging the full defensibility of saying 'The moon is a flat disc' *in the very same language.* And now we have lost grip on our supposed commitment to the law of non-contradiction with respect to these utterances about the moon in that language, and with it we have lost the right to claim to be even minimal realists about the shape of the moon.

But what of the objection that this is all irrelevant because the imagined alternative translations are not plausibly forthcoming? This may seem a forceful riposte. The claim of indeterminacy is not that I can take an arbitrary utterance, assign it any meaning I like, and then be certain of finding a translation scheme which will vindicate the assignment. In the case of the mosaic we admitted that certain particular sets of elements might in fact determine or rule out given roles for a particular piece. So the same may be the case for interpretation of sets of utterances. And if our actual sets of utterances are not such as to allow for interpretation of 'The moon is spherical' as 'The moon is a flat disc', then my argument seems to lapse.

One reply would be to remark that access to this fact about limitations on interpretation may be pretty difficult to obtain. Indeed it is far from clear that we could tell a story about how we could be reasonably certain of it. For the mosaic, we have a finite and small set of elements to play with; there is some sense in the idea of a full and systematic survey of all possibilities or arrangement. But how would we do anything similar for utterances (especially if we cannot even be certain that we have rightly distinguished indexicals from non-indexicals, as suggested at the end of chapter 5)? But let us waive this point and allow that we can have reasoned confidence that our actual utterances about the moon, together with the other things we say, form a set which resists the kind of translation imagined above.

Does this help to restore a respectable sense of commitment to realism? It does not. What is required to undermine the argument is to make plausible the much stronger claim that there could not be *any* set of utterances such that both (1) there is in it a sentence which is suitable to be interpreted as meaning that the moon is spherical and also (2) it is as a whole so structured that it is possible to set up an equally good rival scheme in which that sentence is interpreted as saying that the moon is a flat disc. And what grounds have we been supplied with so far on the basis of which we could rule out the possibility of such a set of utterances? The epistemological task is far more demanding than the admittedly tough one we contemplated in connection with our actual sets of utterances. It is difficult to see how one could so much as begin to go about trying to show the non-existence of the specified sort of set. One might be tempted by a line of argument starting in a priori fashion from something we take ourselves to know about the meaning of 'The moon is spherical', for example that it is incompatible with 'The moon is a flat disc'. Such an argument could proceed via contraposition of the considerations I have urged to the denial of the existence of the relevant sort of set of utterances. But this approach is emphatically not available to the proponent of indeterminacy. What he can allow himself to know about meaning must be established through examination of patterns in sets of utterances and not the other way around.

But if the existence of a set of utterances of the type described is an epistemic possibility, indeed even a probability (given only the kinds of data we can imagine ourselves to have on the holistic methodology of chapter 5) then our confidence in the propriety of a realistic construal of remarks about the moon must be correspondingly weak. And an exactly similar argument can be run for any set of incompatible sentences we please, rendering realism an unattractive position right across the board. In as much as we have not proved the existence of sets of sentences of the kind described, minimal realism remains an option. But, given that minimal realism looks so epistemologically precarious, it would surely be desirable to give an account of what we are up to in our judgements, and what success in making them amounts to, which does not require the truth of realism. From the perspective of the position sketched, it looks much more certain that our judgements are well-founded and that some of them are 'right' than it does that any of them conform to the conditions of minimal realism. So there is now strong pressure to find an account of 'being right' and related notions which cuts them free from the marginal looking concern of whether a 'realist' construal is defensible. This is also something which is strongly indicated by the earlier move which separated the question of whether some utterances is right or not from the question of what it is to be taken to mean. Realism remains on the books, perhaps, but concern with its truth, in general or in the particular case, appears a profitless enterprise.

What might an alternative account of judgement and its concerns be like? It would very plausibly take the form of a general version of pragmatism, and it is unclear that there is any other option. The difficulties that have been raised for the combination of indeterminacy claims about meaning with realism are closely related to the arguments advanced in section 4.3 against the coherence of a possible Quinean position combining realism about the subject matter of underdetermined theories with claims of indeterminacy of meaning for sentences of those theories. In both cases the trouble arises from attempted combination of the position about approval and condemnation of sentences implicit in the realism with the position on approval and condemnation which the indeterminacy claims involve. The way out for Quine was, I suggested, to embrace an explicit instrumentalism, and it is the analogous move that we now need. Since Quine left observations and logic untouched by the indeterminacy, their realism is similarly left untouched by his instrumentalism. But our current claim about indeterminacy, being that much more general, brings with it a correspondingly generalized form of instrumentalism and denial of realism. Thus the claim will be that what we do in thinking is aim at the formation of some workable, coherent and useful body of judgements. We do not have a body of given data to systematize; each potential new judgement is rather to be assessed by its coherence with what is already there. And any already accepted judgement is assessed, if we need to, in similar fashion.

It may be, one might add, that we get temporary configurations of judgements in which some of them appear as incompatible and as subject to the principle of non-contradiction. If such a configuration occurs then it will give its users grounds for claiming to be, temporarily and in a modified sense, 'minimal realists' about the subject matter of those judgements. It may also be that these speakers are, through lack of imagination, under the impression that certain of their sentences are such as to be always subject to the principle of non-contradiction. Perhaps this gives rise in them to the idea of 'describing the real nature of a determinate independent world'. But, says this view, such a metaphysical reading of any of our judgements or utterances is always a gratuitous and epistemologically ill-founded extra, from which it is better to refrain; in any case it has nothing to do with any feature of the judgements which really matters to us.

In summary then, the thrust of the arguments of this section has been to suggest that denial of realism about meanings (on the grounds given in chapter 5) leads on to downgrading of the importance of realism about any subject matter whatsoever. (Another line of thought to the same conclusion can be constructed from a generalized version of the epistemological holism we examined in section 5.4. Without pursuing this in detail, we can see that the idea that every judgement gets its epistemological status from its coherence with all remaining judgements, is likely to lead to the idea of generalized fallibilism, which in turn leads to the idea that commitment to non-contradiction in the case of any particular judgements can never be more than a matter of provisional convenience.

We contemplated at the start of this section a stable position which combined realism about the subject matter of the natural sciences with non-realism about the subject matter of the (broadly speaking) human sciences. But such a position has proved untenable. This does not yet provide reasons for supposing that there is something amiss with meaning scepticism. The question now is whether thoroughgoing pragmatism is something we can live with. I wish to suggest in the next section that it is not.

6.2   THOROUGHGOING PRAGMATISM

By 'pragmatism' I understand the view that we choose what

concepts to have and what judgements to make. The choices are made in the light of the expected usefulness of the judgements, given the rest of the scheme of thought; and any current feature of the scheme is conceived of as open to modification.

The appearance of the notion of *choice* may seem odd in this context, particularly if we have arrived at this position by the epistemological route. That route asked us to accept some thesis about what form evidence always had to take. But how do we get from the thought that justification is always a matter of coherence to the idea that judgements and concepts are chosen? There is a link here which is worth examining.

To see it we need to consider what account a pragmatist is to give of the pressures which lead us to modify and improve our scheme of thought. What is it for a scheme to be useful, to succeed or fail? On the earlier explicitly instrumentalist view discussed in chapters 3 and 4 we had 'recalcitrant experiences' in the form of the subject matter of infallibly known datum statements. These provided pressure to modify the scheme by which we systematized and predicted them. But lacking experiential data, what account are we to give now?

Wright offers the only plausible answer.[4] We have 'recalcitrant experience' in a revised sense appropriate to pragmatism, he suggests, if we find ourselves spontaneously inclined to accept an inconsistent body of judgements. To see how this might work let us draw a rough and ready distinction between observational and theoretical judgements, not on grounds of the supposed complete certainty of the former or of their conceptual independence of the latter, but simply on the grounds of what is and what is not explicitly arrived at inferentially. Observation statements are those which present themselves non-inferentially to nearly all of us as acceptable and which we are agreed in wanting to preserve – although of course we can reject some of them on holistic grounds. Tension in a system of thought then appears in the following schematic form: we find ourselves inclined to assent to two observation statements, say P and not R. But our theory T, together with its underlying logic L, entails that if P then R.

This now is where the choice comes in. We have to decide which element to alter. No particular adjustment is forced upon us. If it

were we would be back in the realm of the given. All that is
required is removal of the tension, but this can be achieved in
various different ways. How do we choose? According to the
pragmatist we do so in the light of expectations about which move
would minimize future tensions, i.e. future occurrences of recalcitrant experiences. (Or at least this is one important consideration
guiding choice. Some kinds of pragmatism would allow in other
factors, e.g. the pleasantness of having in some particular element.
But we shall not pursue these complications.)

One may still find the talk of choice odd. Why speak of choice
and action when judgement of probabilities is all we need? Why not
just recognize that possibly not P and possibly R but most probably not T? In effect the pragmatist can concede this. He builds in
recognition of these possibilities as proper and continuing responses to the tension, in as much as he knowingly holds himself
ready to discard the statement that P or not R if at some future time
that seems the advantageous thing to do. But the choice he insists
on is that of putting down some one thing rather than another as an
assumption which (for the time being at least) we are going to work
with. 'Working with' an assumption has two faces. It is a matter of
exploring a theoretical formulation but also of a policy of fixing
non-theoretical courses of action. (These two things, exploring a
theory and acting upon it, do not necessarily go together. I can
explore one theory while acting on another. But it would be odd
were I to act upon a theory which I did not explore.)

So the pragmatist's only difference from the more purely epistemological holist (who wants to talk only of probability) is that the
pragmatist (plausibly) adds in the idea that, confronted with
differing world views, all of which are defensible in differing degrees, we will have a non-epistemic decision to make about which
of them to take seriously – i.e. about which of them to use as a
basis for action, both practical and more purely investigative.

For the thoroughgoing pragmatist then, everything, including
the very idea of there being incompatible judgements obeying the
law of non-contradiction, is up for grabs. There is no feature of
current practice which he is not prepared to contemplate abandoning; and his taking seriously what he does now take seriously is, he
says, the outcome of choice.

But is everything up for grabs *simultaneously*? Even the hardiest pragmatist might boggle at this since it asks us to contemplate a choice made by a conceptless (and hence goalless and information-less) creature. So the Neurath boat picture is surely a better image. Everything is up for grabs but piecemeal. The pragmatist thus admits that in order to conduct any intellectual operations of assessement and choice we must make some assumptions and adopt some procedures. But any given assumption or procedure can be asked to justify itself and it will do so by appealing to its advantages, compared to its rivals, in contributing to the effective functioning of the whole. So the 'facts', in the light of which we make choice of further 'facts', are there only because we have chosen to put them there.

There is, however, something incoherent in this view when we follow it through. A central point in seeing why this is so is the following. It is taken for granted (and rightly so) that we are not able to choose what to believe in the sense of making up some world entirely to suit ourselves. Pragmatism is not the fantasist's or self-deceiver's charter, telling us each to build a world to fit our heart's desire. It is in the business of giving an account of recogniz-able human intellectual endeavour. Here, all too clearly, things sometimes go badly wrong. Things turn out other than we would wish them and we recognize that they have done so. Constraining forces thus operate upon our belief system; there is something, independent of us and not subject to our choice, to which we are endeavouring to accommodate ourselves. Our pragmatic choice cannot then be seen as freedom to ignore 'external' pressure en-tirely; it must rather be read as freedom over which adjustment to make in response to that pressure.

To see the incoherence in thoroughgoing pragmatism, let us now return to the notion of recalcitrance as Wright sketches it and follow through the ingenious line of argument he develops.[5] The situation was that we found ourselves inclined to assent to both P and not R while already being committed to a theory T together with a logic L which entails that if P then R.

Initially one might suppose that the choice was between T, P and not R. But the pragmatist will deny that these are the only options. 'What about adjusting L?' he will say. So we have a list of four things to choose from in making our adjustment – T, P, not R and L.

'But is this really all?' enquires Wright. We seem to be taking it as absolutely unquestioned that L in application to T yields that if P then R. Let W be the claim that T entails that if P then R when we use logic L. Might not acceptance of *that* be our mistake? Perhaps we are wrong in thinking that we are in a situation where experience is recalcitrant! So now we have five things to choose from, T, P, not R, L and W.

At this point Wright perceives a problem for the pragmatist which he sets out as follows. According to the pragmatist, choices are to be made in the light of the expected amount of recalcitrance they will produce. But whether or not some experience is recalcitrant – i.e. prompts us to tension-inducing observation statements – has now itself become a matter of hypothesis and so of choice. In accepting or rejecting W we render P and R recalcitrant or not recalcitrant for T with L. And the advice on how to choose any hypothesis is to see how much recalcitrance it would produce. So the injunction to choose a system which minimizes recalcitrance becomes an injunction to choose a system which minimizes what the best system says is recalcitrance. And, Wright remarks, this is 'hopelessly impredicative' and can yield no methodological advice at all.[6]

How should we respond to this? It is clear that (at least some of) the kinds of judgements we are interested in at the moment are, broadly speaking, judgements of logic, necessity or conceptual connection. They are judgements in which we lay out fundamental links between linguistic moves, in virtue of which the truth or falsity of some can be brought to bear on the truth or falsity of others. Before we continue by discussing Wright's view of the difficulty we may note that we are in a position to rule out one style of theory about these problematic judgements, namely a crudely construed projectivism. This sort of theory says that our judgements of necessity represent a reading onto the world of some psychological facts about the limitations of our imaginations.[7] What seems attractive here is the replacement of metaphysically and epistemologically problematic ideas with the unproblematic notion of an ordinary, unmysterious and merely psychological fact. But the more the theory emphasizes how commonplace and everyday it is to find that some people are stymied when asked to imagine this or that, the less it can provide a satisfactory explanation of how there can be pressure on a system of thought, pressure to which it ought to respond. The projectivist's view is that when we are forced to abandon one of our judgements, all that is going on is that, because of our imaginative limitations, we find ourselves psychologically unable to maintain a certain conjunction of beliefs. But if this is conceived as a *mere* psychological fact, it amounts to saying that there are no real constraints on the system, only supposed constraints which we cannot imagine not to be there. And the implication of this is that, if we could unshackle our imaginations, we might have our heart's desire.

Sometimes, of course, this is the right picture. Suppose I am confronted with a green fruit which I unhesitatingly, through limitation of imagination, take to be sour; I am just unable to conceive how a green fruit could be other than sour, but, all the same, it is in fact sweet. My limitation here may well prevent me getting what I want, namely a sweet fruit. But this structure can hardly be extended to all cases. Suppose I desire that this bare floor should be carpeted. Can we make sense of the idea that it is just limitation of imagination which prevents me recognizing that this bare floor is, perhaps, at this very moment, carpeted? Is it merely a limitation on my imagination that I take it that bareness and carpetedness are incompatible? To put the point more generally, is it just limitation on our imaginations that when we think that p we find that we cannot at the same time take it that not p? If this were so then indeed, for all we know, we have our heart's desire but have, unfortunately, failed to realize it.

Let us return to the difficulty for the pragmatist posed by the need to give an account of the nature and justification of judgements like W. Wright's response to the difficulty is to say that the consistent pragmatist cannot allow that W is up for pragmatic judgement. 'Such statements admit of totally convincing proof. We must take seriously the idea of proof as a theoretically uncontaminated source of rational belief.'[8] It is not entirely clear what Wright means by this. It is not anything as strong as that we must credit ourselves with infallible access to a priori truths. The thought seems to be more that a proof supplies some prima facie support to a statement like W, support which although defeasible has its strength independently of the empirical considerations which might oppose it. Whatever the details, Wright's wording strongly suggests that he thinks that the difficulty uncovered for the pragmatist is a methodological or epistemological one, which requires correspondingly some epistemological or methodological solution, a solution which tells us about the kinds of warrant various statements may have and when we are entitled to rely on them.

Now there may be something defensible in the suggestion of epistemological privilege, and we shall return to the matter below. But it seems misapplied as an answer to the current difficulty. In the case outlined, W has been framed precisely so as to be the judgement of whether or not recalcitrance is now being manifested in the system. According to the pragmatist programme that pressure which is to guide us in shaping our system (i.e. the appearance or non-appearance of recalcitrance), is exerted or not exerted precisely as we accept or do not accept W. Hence if we try to regard the choice of W itself as to be guided in this way, we discover that we have no independent source of pressure. The problem then for the pragmatist is to give an account of what he is doing or trying to do in debating about W. What would it be for W to be right or wrong? What are the standards of success here? These are the conundrums that face the pragmatist. He cannot give his usual answer, that the standard of success is minimizing recalcitrance, because to do so would lead to his losing touch with the idea of constraint and hence to his moving off into the realm of wish fulfilment.

This problem of making sense of what counts as right or wrong in accepting W is not solved by providing reason to regard W as methodologically or epistemologically privileged, even if such were forthcoming. A methodological privilege might resolve the circularity question of how actually to proceed in assessment, by bypassing the question of whether or not to assess W; but it leaves the question of what W's rightness consists in as obscure as ever.

A move that would resolve the difficulty here would be to recognize that the question 'Is my system in trouble or not?' has to be taken in a realist spirit. And it is quite unclear to me that there is any other move that would restore coherence to the story. A realistic treatment of the question seems to be what is implicit in the idea of constraint. A constraint the operation of which one can choose at one's convenience to recognize or disregard is no constraint at all. To put it simply, there may be something right in the picture of an indefinitely malleable system. But even given that, the pragmatist has presented it to us as a system for doing something, for coping with what impinges on us. (And if we extend the range of things which the system is supposed to do for us beyond that of enabling us to predict, the fundamental idea of the system having to deliver something remains.) Can we then abandon the idea that there is a source of pressure on the system independent of our choice? Only, I think, at the cost of abandoning the attempt to give an account of something, however attenuated, which is still recognizable as rationality and intellectual integrity. These virtues have to do with facing up to the possibility of failure in thought. So they can only have as much substance as we can give to the idea of there being such success or failure.

If we feed this thought back into reflection on how one would decide on some judgement like W we see that it does not enjoin us to give any particular epistemological privilege to apparent proofs. It certainly leaves open the possibility that a person should rationally abandon a proof that he or she finds psychologically compelling upon non a priori grounds. But the thought does enjoin us to hang on firmly to the idea that a proof is either valid or not. We will thus need a distinction between a posteriori considerations which are clues to the invalidity of a proof (even when the flaw has not yet been detected) and considerations which rationally, but in fact mistakenly, lead us to doubt the validity of what is actually correct.[9] It may well be that it is something along these lines that Wright has in mind with his notion of a 'theoretically uncontaminated source of rational belief'. To hear his remark this way is to take the lack of contamination (of the a priori by the theoretical a posteriori) as having to do with the content of the belief in question rather than with any epistemological mode of investigating it. 'This proof is valid' remains the same thought, has the same correctness or incorrectness conditions, through all the varying epistemological contexts in which it might occur. This is something we cannot say, on the pragmatist story, about other judgements, because their correctness consists only in forming part of the most convenient total system.

The conclusion that I would like to stress at this point is that the difficulty we have found with thoroughgoing pragmatism constitutes a problem for the indeterminacy of meaning. The first section of this chapter argued that indeterminacy of meaning seriously undermined the defensibility of even minimal realism. At that point it seemed that the position reached might be acceptable if we could make sense of thoroughgoing pragmatism – because pragmatism seemed designed precisely as a theory which jettisons the need for realism. But the suggestion now is that even pragmatism requires at its foundation some realist element. And it is quite unclear that, if we accept pragmatism as springing from the indeterminacy of meaning, we could possibly be entitled to make the repair to pragmatism which would incorporate this essential strand. Modified pragmatism, made coherent by inclusion of a realist treatment of the question of whether the system as a whole is coping or not, presupposes that we are able to identify those thoughts of ours in which we address the question of how the system as a whole is faring; and it presupposes also that we are justified in treating them in realist fashion. Given indeterminacy of meaning, we have reason to suppose that these conditions are not fulfilled. How are we to identify the sentences which mean 'My system is in trouble' and 'My system is not in trouble'? And why are we entitled to assume that they will not succumb to the same argument which showed us, in the first section of this chapter, that indeterminacy of meaning left us unable to defend minimal realism with respect to 'The moon is a flat disc' and 'The moon is spherical'?

6.3   WITTGENSTEIN AND PRAGMATISM

In this section I would like to indicate a further difficulty for thoroughgoing pragmatism which has to do with the idea of 'taking for granted'. I shall argue that the category of the 'taken for granted' needs to be divided into two and that the items in one of the subdivisions are 'taken for granted' in a more profound sense than those in the other. On this more profound sense a certain sort of justification for what is thus taken for granted is neither available nor called for. Wittgenstein's ideas in *On Certainty* have sometimes been seen as importantly similar to the thoroughgoing pragmatism discussed above. One suggestion of this section is that they differ precisely in recognizing this contrast between kinds of 'taking for granted'.

The usual pragmatist story stresses that it is not committed to the absurdity of claiming that we can think without using some concepts and assumptions; but it emphasizes that any elements on which we rely in one deliberation can be questioned and holistically justified in another deliberation, provided that we take some other appropriate things as (temporarily) fixed. Any part of our boat can be inspected and, if need be, reconstructed provided there is enough of it left to keep us afloat while we work. So far we have seen no reason to question the viability of this story. The point emphasized above was that in our assessment of W we had to think of the question in a realist way; but that says nothing directly about how in practice we handle the assessment of such a claim as W. And in a particular case it seems enormously plausible that what we would actually do is what the pragmatist recommends, namely take for granted various other matters, both logical and non-logical, and balance them as best we can to come up with some verdict.

The strength of this view is its openness to the idea of our making radical changes in the way we look at things, changes which, from the point of view of many earlier users of the system, are extremely hard to assimilate and may seem quite unintelligible. It is clear that, psychologically speaking, any thinkers will have some very deeply entrenched elements in their thought system. These will manifest themselves in part in the form of unquestioning reliance on certain principles of inference. It may seem to the thinkers that the identity of their concepts is bound up with recognizing these principles. And they may also suppose that these concepts are indispensable elements in any system. They will take it that those principles of inference that are bound up with their concepts are used in the assessment of other judgements; these principles are the tools employed in gauging the degree of support that other judgements have; but they are not themselves supported in that fashion.

If they are questioned, their defenders are liable to fall back on saying that they are obvious, that they are grasped intuitively or something of the kind.

The pragmatist would like to unsettle this, and to deny that there is any significant difference in the kind of support different elements have. It is a matter of degree, of depth of entrenchedness, not of kind. He will point to cases (replacement of the 'square of opposition' view of quantificational inference by the Fregean one, the laying out of coherent non-Euclidean geometries, Einsteinian insights into the notion of simultaneity, etc.) where such unquestioning reliance has been shown mistaken. When a particularly deeply entrenched principle is overthrown, we may, if we like, say that a concept has been abandoned and a new one adopted, rather than say that an opinion about an existing subject has been changed. But nothing of this importance hangs on this distinction, says the pragmatist.

It is possible to view such fundamental changes as upheavals which are perhaps causally but not rationally explicable. The pragmatist however will not be sympathetic to this. His view is that, with hindsight at least, we can see justification for change in the increasing amounts of recalcitrance in the old system and in the way the new system eliminates or drastically decreases it.

It is at this point that the question I wish to focus upon appears. Suppose we agree with the pragmatist in seeing even the most fundamental changes as instances of rational adjustment of the system in view of the pressures on it. The abandonment of old certainties is justified by the range of difficulties that have been encountered in continuing to try to incorporate them. It may seem to follow from this that we could, as things now stand, provide a parallel justification for hanging on to fundamental features which are *not* now diagnosed as sources of difficulty. If certain occurrences would provide justification for adjustment of some fundamental principles (and so of the concepts that are thereby defined), does not the fact of their non-occurrence provide our justification for currently keeping the principles entrenched? It may be that we find difficulty in formulating descriptions of these non-occurrences. But it looks as if this is merely lack of imagination on our part. Thus it may seem that these negative facts provide positive support for the fundamental principles of the system. And if this were so then the pragmatist would be right in seeing every element of the system as justified in the same way, namely in the light of certain considerations which favour it rather than its rivals when we engage in the enterprise of testing that particular plank of the ship.

This is a mistake. It is true that within the everyday parts of our scheme positive and negative facts stand on a par for justificatory purposes. It is the fact, for example, that there are no fingerprints on the glass which leads me to suppose that the burglar wore gloves. But we cannot extrapolate from this case to the limiting one of conceptual stability. It we are to imagine providing similar justification for fundamental principles in terms of the hypothesized non-occurrences we must suppose ourselves equipped with some vocabulary for describing those non-occurrences. That vocabulary will in turn be individuated by its own associated fundamental inferential principles. And what is the pragmatist to say about our (temporary) acceptance of these while we specify the facts? Presumably the same, namely that it is justified by the non-occurrence of the happenings which would show them to be inappropriate elements of a conceptual scheme. And so on, down an infinite regress of vocabularies and schemes.

We might avoid the regress by supposing that the questioning of schemes takes us round in a finite circle, or that we arrive at some one ultimate vocabulary in which all basic evidential facts are to be described. But to suppose either of these is in effect to return to instrumentalism and thus to betray the most central tenet of thoroughgoing pragmatism. But it is equally unacceptable (and not only to the pragmatist) to suppose that any thinker, however imaginative, is capable of working through the infinite series of negative scenarios which would be required to provide positive justification for staying with our current conceptual scheme.

The conclusion is that it is not a mere superficial psychological fact, for example about the limits of people's imaginations, that we are brought to a standstill by the request to justify certain of our concepts and their attendant principles. To suppose that we were never at such a standstill is to suppose that our minds responded easily to every one of an infinite number of requests to skip on from one conceptual scheme to another. This indefinite flexibility of mind (which we here imagine to be exercisable without even the stimulus of actual puzzles and adverse circumstances which require to be dealt with) is as incompatible with recognition of our finitude as is the idea that we have already traversed the infinite series.

To say this is not to say that there is some one definite part of our conceptual scheme for which it is impossible for anyone to perform the imaginative feat of conceiving of occurrences which would lead us to want to change it. It is to say, rather, that we cannot make sense of thinking except as proceeding in accordance with at least some principles and assumptions which the thinker 'takes for granted' in the sense of being nonplussed at the request to justify them and being unable to muster any positive evidence in their support.

We may, of course, on identifying such principles in our thought, point to such things as that they are fundamental for us and that we would hardly know how to carry on thinking at all if we were denied the use of them. But this is not the same kind of justification as that which we are able to supply for other elements in the system, elements for which we can think of alternatives and can formulate descriptions of the circumstances in which we would adopt the alternatives. Talk of 'coherence' and 'holism' may disguise this difference. But what we do on becoming aware of the status of fundamental assumptions is not to *decide* to keep them fixed because they seem useful or to judge that are correct because all the evidence speaks in favour of them. It is not a move of the same shape as choosing some basic elements of a theory to hold steady or take for granted for the time being. That kind of taking for granted, which goes with justification, requires ability to envisage alternatives. But in this case there are none envisageable. The conventionalist moves on necessities and fundamental principles, moves which are congenial to the pragmatist, are in consequence empty posturing. Rather naturalism (in one sense of that term) is the outcome. What honest appraisal brings us to do is recognize a fact about how we conduct our thought, and recognize also that we cannot but acquiesce in it.[10]

One final important point which needs to be made here is that when we look at our own patterns of thought, among the principles we find ensconced are many which underpin minimal realist styles of thought about all sorts of subject matters. We find, for example, that we are equipped with the ideas of ranges of different and incompatible properties (position, shape, colour, temperature, material composition . . .). These are some of the basic tools in terms of which we articulate our experience and their use brings minimal realist practices along with it.

The kinds of ideas I have been discussing in the past few paragraphs are closely related to those which Wittgenstein raises in *On Certainty*.[11] Some have seen Wittgenstein as a thoroughgoing pragmatist and there are indeed important negative themes which he pursues in common with the pragmatist, most notably opposition to mirroring realism. (The grounds of the criticism however are different, and we shall see more of this in the next chapter.) Both Wittgenstein and the pragmatist reject the idea that the world demands certain concepts for its correct representation. But Wittgenstein differs from the pragmatist in his view that we come in the end to recognition of facts about our practices and not to decisions. He is also at pains to stress that this is not a blemish in our thinking, the intrusion into it of unwarranted and dogmatic assertion. For that criticism to be in order it would have to be possible for us to do better, to cease to be so dogmatic. But there is no such possibility.

There may still however be worries about (so to speak) the metaphysical status of our fundamental principles. Are they, for example, the recognition of truths? If so can we use them to underpin minimal realist practices not merely psychologically but also metaphysically? We shall return to this in section 9.4.

6.4 EMPIRICISM AND PLATONISM

One might be struck by the fact that, in practice and by and large, we have no difficulty in understanding each other, even in cases of radical interpretaion. We just are not faced with competing interpretations in the way in which the arguments of chapter 5 suggested that we might be. There are indeed cases, for example those explored in the novels of Henry James, where we become aware that our everyday psychological labels are crude and that insistence on getting a yes/no answer in their terms ('Does he love her or not?') would be misleading. But these situations are ones which spur us on to develop subtler forms of description and in so doing we have the sense that we represent more accurately what is determinately there. Further interesting questions may then arise about exactly what the propriety is of describing people's beliefs, feelings and aspirations in terms which they themselves might not (or not without a good deal of prompting) acknowledge, and about what further complications of human interaction become possible with the developing complexity of our self-descriptions. But again none of the subtle reservations raised by these lines of thought have anything to do with the indeterminacy worries generated by the mosaic comparison. And in many everyday cases we would find it absurd if such subtle reservations were entertained.

What use, however, can one make of the fact about the practical determinacy of meaning ascription in arguing against the indeterminacy thesis? What I want to suggest now is that if one is a mirroring realist it is highly unlikely that this thought can be of any help in re-establishing our right to talk about the facts of what people mean.

This is because the mirroring realist will, in all probability, be a modal realist of a Platonist sort as well as a realist about the sense data, physical objects or whatever else he takes the world to consist of. That is to say that he is committed to the view that states of affairs are possible or necessary independently of our views about whether they are possible or necessary, and independently also of whether we have so much as thought of them. So the mirroring realist takes it that, independent of him and his thoughts, either there is or there is not an alternative equally defensible translation, i.e. a possible way of matching sentences which observes all the appropriate constraints. If there is such another scheme then its mere existence, even if entirely unsuspected by us and beyond the reach of our imaginations, will nevertheless do its malign work of unravelling our entitlement to realism about meaning (and hence about anything else).

The claim that the mirroring realist is also likely to be a Platonist modal realist may seem odd. That it is coherent to combine

mirroring realism with such modal realism (as in a rationalist style
of system) seems plausible. But should it not also be feasible to
separate the two? And is this not what empiricism (the form of
mirroring realism we are primarily considering) actually does? The
empiricist is one who supposes that we acquire concepts and
knowledge from confrontation in sense perception with the facts. It
seems immensely plausible to suppose that we cannot have that
kind of confrontation with supposed modal facts. Hence the empiricist turns to conventionalism, or so it is supposed, to explain our
use of modal concepts.

This story is, of course, partly right from a historical point of
view. The logical positivists did indeed turn to what they called
conventionalism, but their resort was half-hearted. The conventionalism advanced, for example by A. J. Ayer, is *modified* and not
radical conventionalism.[12] On the latter every individual necessary
truth is separately adopted. There are not logical discoveries, no
logical compulsions, revealed to us on reflection. But on the former
we make certain decisions, e.g. on what rules we shall follow in
using the words 'all', 'not' etc., and in consequence find ourselves
committed to certain other uses of these words which we had not
explicitly anticipated; we discover, in other words, that doing what
the initial rules prescribe necessarily involves doing what certain
other, derivative, rules demand.

But, as Dummett remarks, 'this account is entirely superficial
and throws away all the advantages of conventionalism'.[13] His
point is that the modified conventionalism leaves entirely unexplained the nature of the truth: 'Necessarily, if you follow this rule,
you will follow that other rule also.' And it leaves unexplained
(from an empiricist point of view) our access to this fact. These
matters are conceived, by the modified conventionalist, in a modal
realist manner.

But is this just an accident of what these particular empiricists
said? Can we make sense of an empiricist style mirroring realism
which in a thoroughgoing way repudiates any taint of modal
realism, but allows talk of necessity as an upshot of conventions? I
do not think that we can.[14] Let us consider how such a theory
would have to be articulated.

Such a view will say that there are no facts about how things must be but there are facts about how they are. What then are we doing when we use modal terms? We are expressing decisions. The decisions will be, for example, to hang on to any statement of a certain form come what may, or to accept a statement of one type as unimpeachable warrant for making a statement of some other type.

But if there are no modal facts to underpin these decisions, how are they to be defended against the charge that carrying them out might lead us astray? If the realist thinks, as he does, that there are facts and we have epistemological access to them apart from these decisions, then the decisions can do nothing except introduce some short cuts and rules of thumb into the process of acquiring judgements. There may be room for tightening up vagueness by convention. But leaving that on one side, either the nature of the judgements already guarantees certain truth–value links – in which case modal realism is conceded – or it does not – in which case deciding to treat some proposed links as absolutely firm is pointless foolhardiness. What this suggests is that radical conventionalism is only fully at home in a pragmatist setting, where *all* of our judgements are open to choice and so can be jerrymandered to fit the chosen necessities. Radical conventionalism thus makes an uncomfortable ally for empiricism, conceived in a robustly realist way.

What then are we to make of the, at first sight plausible, claim that experience teaches us only what *is* the case and cannot yield the concept of what *must* be the case? The conclusion to which the argument points is that this does not stand up to serious pressure, when empiricism is allied with the mirroring realist metaphysics and when perceptual confrontations are conceived of as those events in which the nature of the world impresses itself upon us. There are indeed certain sorts of necessity (e.g. the synthetic a priori, or physical necessity) for which the empiricist claim can be defended. But the idea that no notion whatsoever of any necessity is derived from experience is in tension with the empricist idea that it is *facts* which are revealed to us in confrontations. The idea of a fact involves the idea of a property being instantiated. But how are we, in any realist and non-pragmatist spirit, to conceive of a property which does not, of its nature, enter into relations of exclusion or inclusion with other properties? Such relations between properties reveal themselves as necessities in the world of instantiations. Moreover we see that the empiricist does have an account to offer of how we come to know them: awareness of them is impressed upon us as a component of that awareness of fact which experience gives us. Experience shows us the universals as much as the particulars.

Can the upright empiricist Dr Jekyll reject this unwelcome conclusion that he has all along been a Platonist Mr Hyde as well? One way of doing so is to play down the conceptual and to play up the sensory element in empiricism. But on this tack empiricism loses plausibility as an account of thinking and loses also its attractive role in the mirroring realist story of how we come to know the true nature of the world. So is there perhaps a coherent view which combines the empiricist and the realist elements but which is neither conventionalist nor modal realist? Could such a view not simply repudiate the idea of necessity altogether?

A move to sketch such a theory would be to say that all positive features revealed to us in experience are simple and mutually compatible. Hence all relations of exclusion or involvement among them are discovered a posteriori. One might enquire what these features are. It is remarkably difficulty to specify any which fit the bill. But waiving this objection we may allow that the move does indeed do away with a good deal of Platonist machinery. However, it does not quite satisfy the requirements of disposing of all modal notions. What is to be said, for example, about negation?

There are two lines the empiricist could take here. He could say that 'not F' and 'F' are independent simple characters; the presence of the phoneme 'F' in 'not F' is just a coincidence. The lack of co-occurrence of F and not F is a very well supported empirical generalization and not a logical truth at all. If the empiricist says this then, for him, no remark is incompatible with any other. But what sense can we now make of the idea that what is going on is description of how things are in an independent and determinate world? Certainly this empiricist position no longer fits our requirements even for minimal realism.

On the other hand the empiricist could say, much more plausibly, that in grasping what it is for something to be F (and even if one does not grasp anything about any other property G or about relations of exclusion or inclusion with G) one does grasp that there is such a thing as not being F; and one also grasps that being F and not being F are incompatible. But this thought supplies us with the modal notion of incompatibility, that which is necessarily not so. From this, together with the view that no simple property is incompatible with any other simple property or its negation (which we conceded above in talking of compatibility) we can generate a rich and determinate modal structure. (It is, or course, closely akin to that of the *Tractatus*).

The upshot then is that the link between mirroring realism and modal realism seems to stand. And in consequence the mirroring realist is in no position to resist the indeterminacy of meaning arguments presented in chapter 5. From our current perspective we need to emphasize how two factors work together to generate the indeterminacy conclusion. The first is the one we have spent most time expounding, namely that meaning ascription is justified by holistic considerations. The second is equally important. It is the assumption that determinately either there is or there is not a holistically acceptable alternative interpretation of the utterances of a given person. This assumption is the one to which the current version of mirroring and modal realism commits us. If we make this assumption then the question of whether we are entitled to think of our meanings as determinate, turns into the question of whether we can prove that there are no acceptable alternative interpretations. But this, as I emphasized in section 6.1, is a daunting task which we have no idea how to carry out. Hence our seeming loss of right to be confident that we do determinately mean something in our remarks and that we can know what we mean. The actual unavailability of alternative translations and the practical workability (indeed indispensability) of a realist practice of meaning ascription is now represented as a mere psychological or sociological observation. Given the idea of a totality of metaphysical possibilities, epistemologically independent of us, and the envisaged methodology of meaning ascription, the actual success and importance of meaning talk all go for nothing, metaphysically speaking. The next step (as I argued in section 6.1) is the loss of a right to take a coherent realist stance about anything and the emergence of thoroughgoing pragmatism as the only option. But (as I argued in section 6.2) this in turn proves unattractive. We need an account of our thinking which allows us at least those repairs to pragmatism which make it coherent. But we cannot effect these repairs when we still recognize the force of the arguments for indeterminacy of meaning.

Can we extract ourselves from this imbroglio? There are many routes out from this uncomfortable position, as many as there are disputable assumptions that I have made on the way into it – and they are not a few. One route would be to try to defend thorough-going pragmatism against the charge of incoherence, or to deny that importation of realist elements is the only way of making it coherent. Another would be to try to uncouple the linkage I have endeavoured to set up between realism about the objects of our thoughts and realism about the content of those thoughts. The idea I offered (at the start of this chapter) was that there is bound to be tension in a philosophical position which endeavours to maintain any robust form of realism (i.e. something more than mere Quinean disquotationalism) about the natural world while denying correspondingly robust realism about the semantic properties of our thoughts. I do not claim to have proved this in full generality however, only to have made it plausible by examining some cases. So one might find a way out by showing the combination to be, after all, defensible.

Even supposing that these moves are not attractive, many paths remain open. If we start with a mirroring realist view of the subject matter of natural science and wish to preserve it, then our concern must be to give an account of mind and meaning on which they have reality of this kind. One could achieve this by denying the claims about holistic constraints on meaning ascription. And another move, even more attractive perhaps, would be to admit them but to reject the arguments offered in section 5.4 for saying that these holistic considerations could not be supplemented by causal, determinacy restoring, facts. To pursue these programmes is to endeavour (by talk of functionalism in philosophy of mind, teleology and natural selection, etc.) to produce a naturalized theory of mind. The upshot of success in such an enterprise would be the defensibility of mirroring realism all across the board, for natural and semantic facts alike. And given the extremely sketchy and inconclusive nature of the arguments advanced in section 5.4 I am in no position to deny the viability of these philosophical programmes.

But what if we are, all the same, dubious of the chances of success by this road? What if it seems likely to us that mind and matter, subject and object, rationality and causality, will not lie down together in the required way? And what if we combine this scepticism with a commitment to the reality of the natural world and also commitment to the linkage of realism about objects of thought with realism about content? Are we now stuck in an impasse? I wish to suggest that there is a crack through which we can slip – namely the denial of mirroring realism. My suggestion above was that mirroring realism, via its generation of commitment to the totality of epistemologically independent metaphysical possibilities, is an important underpinning element in the move from remarks about the holistic nature of meaning to indeterminacy claims. If we could somehow rid ourselves of the need to take seriously these shadowy, unimaginable, but (it seems) theoretically possible other interpretations, then there might be no bar to combining the holistic story about meaning with the view that our remarks, by and large, determinately mean what we take them to mean.

I have concentrated here on the modal and metaphysical elements in the mirroring realist position and our need to be rid of them. It is worth remarking that were we to see how to satisfy that need, certain epistemological consequences would follow. If we can, so to speak, ignore the possibility of an arrangement or interpretation other than the one that we normally take for granted, that is tantamount to allowing us to be confronted epistemologically by an utterance-*qua*-element-of-such-and-such-a-pattern rather than by mere uninterpreted noise.[15] To put this the other way round, the idea of the need to take the other arrangement seriously brings with it the idea that we must separate the secure datum that so and so uninterpreted utterance occurs from the less secure hypothesis that it can be placed in such and such a pattern.

This epistemological presupposition of the indeterminacy arguments (one which explicitly acknowledged by Davidson)[16] suggests another respect in which mirroring realism, in its naturalist version, is powerfully influencing the development of the ideas. Such naturalized mirroring realism brings with it empiricist sympathies, and preconceptions about what kind of fact could impress itself upon us or reveal itself to us. Meanings, when regarded as residing in patterns, clearly are not the kind of thing which could do the required impressing. Hence they have to be seen as inferred or constructed.

Another corollary of the shift in outlook sketched above would be a need to refine and recast all the remarks we have made about the methodology of meaning ascription. We would have to distinguish views on the kinds of consideration that judgements of meaning are answerable to if doubted, and reflections on how, in their holistic commitments they differ from those of natural science (about which the discussions of chapter 5 are largely right) from the idea that we go about interpreting our first language by assembling data on uninterpreted utterances (on which chapter 5 is wrong). All of these themes could well have been more fully represented in an alternative approach to the outlook we are about to explore.

Let us return to our main theme: How are we to be realists without mirroring? How could ignoring these possibilities be other than epistemological irresponsibility? It is to the Wittgensteinian treatment of these questions that we now turn.

7

The Dissolving Mirror

7.1 WITTGENSTEIN'S HOSTILITY TO MIRRORING REALISM

Mirroring realism is now the focus of our discussion. I suggested in chapters 3 and 4 how attraction to it, in its empiricist form, might issue in a Quinean version of meaning scepticism. It was perhaps not surprising to find sceptical theses about theoretical meaning issuing from premises which themselves explicitly concern our limited ability to acquire concepts and knowledge. The argument of chapter 5 is of interest in part because it starts from something so much less controversial. It does not involve, explicitly, mirroring realism and even less does it involve a particular empiricist form of it. It seems to invoke only some pre-theoretical, commonsensical, idea of realism about the ordinary material world, together with some ideas about the contrast between concepts used for describing it and concepts used for describing the psychological and semantic. But the idea floated at the end of the last chapter was that mirroring realism, appearances notwithstanding, is one of the crucial assumptions in generating the indeterminacy conclusion of chapter 5 and hence the difficulty which that precipitated us into in chapter 6. Undoubtedly other assumptions are also important in enabling us to derive the conclusions. Hence there are many possible routes out of that difficulty to be explored. Philosophical reflection can resemble a giant maze with decisions about promising paths needing to be made all the time. The interest of the path we shall enter is, I shall try to suggest, that it resembles the one followed by Wittgenstein.

What evidence have we that Wittgenstein was hostile to mirroring realism? First there are some remarks which are most naturally read as explicit statements to that effect: secondly, we can detect in his writing some powerful arguments directed against the intelligibility of the idea; and thirdly, if we take rejection of this form of realism as the end of a thread and follow it through, we find the whole tenor of Wittgenstein's thought becoming more comprehensible and many difficult ideas fitting into place.

The first kind of consideration will not get us far without the others. But let us remember the following:

> If anyone believes that certain concepts are absolutely the correct ones and that having different ones would mean not realizing something that we realize – then let him imagine certain very general facts of nature to be different from what we are used to and the formation of concepts different from the usual ones will become intelligible to him.[1]

> One is tempted to justify rules of grammar by sentences like 'But there really are four primary colours'. And the saying that the rules of grammar are arbitrary is directed against the possibility of this justification, which is constructed on the model of justifying a sentence by pointing to what verifies it.[2]

> Do I want to say, then, that certain facts are favourable to the formation of certain concepts; or again unfavourable? And does experience teach us this? It is a fact of experience that human beings alter their concepts, exchange them for others when they learn new facts, when in this way what was formerly important to them becomes unimportant and *vice versa*.[3]

> We have a colour system as we have a number system. Do the systems reside in our nature or in the nature of things? How are we to put it? Not in the nature of numbers or colours.
> Then there is something arbitrary about the system? Yes and No. It is akin both to what is arbitrary and to what is not arbitrary.[4]

> Yes, but has nature nothing to say here? Indeed she has – but she makes herself audible in another way.
> 'You'll surely run up against existence and non-existence somewhere.' But that means against *facts*, not concepts.[5]

I want to say: an education quite different from ours might also be the foundation for quite different concepts.

For here life would run on differently. – What interests us would not interest *them*. Here different concepts would no longer be unimaginable. In fact this is the only way in which *essentially* different concepts are imaginable.[6]

What is the vision of people, thought and language from which these remarks spring? Let us consider some of the themes treated in the *Philosophical Investigations* up to section 242. The later elements of this sequence of sections, from about 138 onwards, are sometimes known as the 'rule following considerations' and have been much discussed. A certain consensus (which I do not at all desire to undermine) has emerged upon at least one of the things which is brought to our attention here. The point in question is a negative one and has been expounded very clearly and elegantly by Kripke.[7] Let me summarize these ideas briefly, for the ground is fairly well trodden.

Suppose we consider the questions 'What does this person think?', or suppose we are faced with the challenge of defending the attribution of some particular thought to him or her. In either case we are inclined to look for something that having a certain thought consists in. We try to find some item the occurrence of which in or to the person, the existing of which in some relation to the person, fixes it that the person must be having a certain thought (expressing a certain meaning). The kinds of items we look for, although they may be very various – sequences of marks, noises, pictures (which are external to the person), images, formulae before the mind's eye and feelings (which are 'internal') – all have something in common. This is that we can conceive of their existence as consisting in the exhibition of certain determinate, intrinsic, non-representational properties over some area of space–time (or mental quasi space–time). There is, so to speak, clearly a 'what it is like' for these things to occur and it is this which makes us confident that there is such a thing as their occurring (or not occurring) which we could, in epistemologically favourable circumstances, establish. It is also the case that in virtue of their possession of such properties the things in question are fitted to enter into causal or quasi causal explanatory relations. Our looking for these kinds of items in answer to the original questions about thought is bound up with the dominance of scientific modes of understanding and our disposition to assume that we can find an account of thinking closely analogous to the kinds of account which science has given us of the constitution and workings of the natural world.

Our search, however, is doomed to failure. The sort of thing which we are determined to find always turns out on closer inspection to be a vehicle of meaning rather than meaning itself. Moreover in these cases it is *not* a vehicle suited to carry only one meaning but one capable of varying interpretations. Whatever kind of item we consider – a diagram, image, formula, picture, feeling, etc. – we always find that we can suppose that it occurs in whatever relation to a person is appropriate to its nature but that the person carries on using it, responding to it or whatever, in a way which shows that he or she did not mean by it that thought which we had intended it to pin down. Something other is required for meaning than the mere presence to or in the subject of the item itself. This is most obviously true of the external items, but Wittgenstein takes us through a variety of inner items and shows us that it is true of them too.

But it would be wrong, I suggest, to see the implications of these ideas as bearing only on the question of how or how not to conceive of 'meaning' 'understanding' or 'thinking' as states of persons. The moral is not merely, to put it crudely, that 'understanding is not having an image before the mind's eye' or something of that shape. The remarks about formulae, images and the like follow on from discussion in the earlier sections of *Investigations* (1–138 roughly) of ostensive teaching, of the role of examples and of the phrase 'and so on' in explanation of meaning. They thus follow on from discussion of the need for some response from the pupil which the teacher should not suppose to be made inevitable by the circumstances of teaching and the examples he presents. This phase of Wittgensteins's investigation bears upon mirroring realism and we can, with a backwards look, see it as a version of the later thought.

What Wittgenstein's considerations show is that we cannot make sense of the idea that being confronted with some set of objects or chunk of the world should force possession of a certain concept upon a person. We do indeed develop our concepts and make our judgements as the outcome of such confrontations. But sets of items we can be confronted with will clearly, in many cases, fall under many different concepts. A set of objects cannot of itself determine that one rather than another similarity shall be noticed and so cannot force extrapolation of the set one way rather than another. This may look at first sight a very different type of consideration from the earlier ones about the insufficiency of formulae, mental imagery and the like to constitute meaning, but it is the same fundamental thought at work. If the items themselves were capable of forcing an extrapolation then, in the extreme case, I could bring *them* along to be my formula or image, which of itself carried my meaning.

There is something initially strange about the idea of the world, or part of the world or a set of objects in the world, (other than the small, easily recognized subset of items which make natural languages) constituting some sign or formula which carries meaning. But in an only slightly extended usage this clearly is a defensible way of looking at things. The not-obviously-linguistic world (or some part of it) can be the sort of thing we bring attention to when we try to determine or convey to one person what another person thinks. 'What is she thinking?' someone asks. I might in response just nod in the direction of some happening in the environment. Or I might say 'He thinks this one is like those', pointing to some objects. Ostension cannot but play an important part in concept acquisition and hence it can continue to serve the role of concept identification within the practice of a community which has already learnt the language. The points that Wittgenstein stresses about the indispensable role of the nature of the learner in acquisition reappear in the other context as points like the ones about the possibility of alternative employments of formulae, images and the like.

Now mirroring realism is, in effect, the claim that the world, if properly attended to, does determine one and only one (set of) thought(s). If there were a way that things are in themselves then there would be such a thing as thinking that things were that way. That thought would be, so to speak, the correct reading of the item which is the world. We can see Wittgenstein, then, as saying that the world does not in itself carry any message. It does not as it were say 'I'm like this'. It cannot carry a message, any more than formulae, images or pictures can.

The view put this baldly might be thought to have sceptical implications. It might be thought, for example, to be committed to the idea that the world is an indeterminate mush upon which we impose form. It might be thought that even minimal realism could not be preserved. This is a matter to which we shall return at several points in the chapters that follow.

Relatedly, but more subtly, it might be thought that the view I am ascribing to Wittgenstein involved clear cut commitment to the idea that there are alternative ways of 'reading' the world and so alternative conceptual schemes. We have, after all, both in the considerations about formulae and in the considerations about the role of samples in learning, stressed the seemingly real possibility of alternative responses in the user or learner. Thus some version of the realism-threatening relativism which we mentioned in section 2.4 appears to be looming.

It is important however to make a distinction here and to attend more exactly to what the consideration of formulae and samples shows. We may in particular cases draw attention to the fact that formulae or samples can actually carry different meanings. But what this makes vivid is that the formula, or set of samples, is itself inert; it has no life as a sign unless it is read, i.e. used in a certain way. Reflection on these cases leads to the thought that this is a quite general matter. What someone is thinking is never a question of the existence of some item that he or she stands in some relation to, but always a matter of what life that person is living, and hence of a role that the item plays in the life. Concepts are explicable and defensible only as elements of a whole which must also include projects, actions etc. This goes for the placement of a creature in the item which is the world just as much as for the placement of the creature *vis-à-vis* a formula or set of samples. Stress on the alternative readings is merely a heuristic device, a step towards this realization, not something which itself is to be unthinkingly extrapolated to all cases.

So, given this interlocking of concepts, lives and interest as a starting point, the question 'Is there a way that the world is in itself?' comes out as the question 'Is there only one way that a person could live an intelligible life in which he or she dealt rationally with this world?' Or, better, it comes out as 'Is there a large common element in all such lives? And must fully rational lives converge upon one account of the nature of the world?' To claim that mirroring realism is not a good metaphysical picture is *not* to claim that we see that the answers to these questions is 'No' – i.e. the claim is not that of relativism. Rather it is to point out first that one is entitled to mirroring realism only if one can make out a clear case for a 'Yes' answer, and it is to suggest, secondly, that we cannot make out such a case because the question does not have the kind of sense which would enable us to give a clear cut answer. We may come to think that we cannot make much of the idea of a 'form of life' different from our own without thereby coming to think that we see that ours is the only possible one. We shall return to these matters in chapter 9.

7.2 EXPLANATION AND THE ABSOLUTE CONCEPTION

The line of thought concerning the interdependence of concepts and interests which is opened up in the preceding section requires much more exploration. But before we turn to that directly we can get more light upon some aspects of the problem by discussing a recent defence of the central idea of mirroring realism. This defence is offered by B. A. O. Williams in his attempt to clarify a notion he calls 'the absolute conception'. Williams' claim is that we can make sense of the idea that some of our beliefs represent the world 'in a way to the maximum degree independent of our perspective and its peculiarities'.[8] And he makes another claim also, namely that this conception is bound up with our idea of knowledge in such a way that commitment to the possibility of knowledge is commitment to the intelligibility of the absolute conception.[9] This is an interesting claim from our point of view because what it proposes is, in effect, a move directly from minimal realism to mirroring realism; it insists that the latter is implicit in the former.

We started out by considering mirroring realism primarily in the form of sense datum empiricism and I suggested (in section 2.3) that this is the form such realism is likely to take when we demand some one-by-one certifications of concepts and judgements. But the form of realism proposed by Williams cuts free from all the sensory and atomist limitations of that scheme by withdrawing any demand for one-by-one endorsement. For Williams, to certify a concept as reality-representing, we look to the explanatory role of judgements employing it. Here are some quotations which summarize the view:

> We can select among our beliefs and features of our world picture some that we can reasonably claim to represent the world in a way to the maximum degree independent of our perspective and its peculiarities. The resultant picture of things, if we can carry through this task, can be called the 'absolute conception' of the world. In terms of that conception we may hope to explain the possibility of the conception itself and also the possibility of other, perspectival representation.[10]

And at another place we find this:

> That possibility, i.e. of forming the absolute conception, as I have explained it, depends heavily on the notion of explanation. The substance of the absolute conception . . . lies in the idea that it could non-vacuously explain how it itself and the various perspectival views of the world are possible. It is an important feature of modern science that it contributes to explaining how creatures with our origins and characteristics can understand a world with properties that this same science ascribes to the world. The achievements of evolutionary biology and the neurological sciences are substantive in these respects.[11]

The advantages of this view over the more crudely empiricist versions of mirroring realism are considerable. The 'absolute conception' is seen as something that we strive towards, not something handed to us on a plate. The striving towards it, and the measure of whether we have attained it, take the form of reflecting on what explains what within our view of ourselves and the world.

An objectionable feature of the older empiricism is the conception of thought as something passive, to which the knowing subject makes no contribution. The theme of some Wittgensteinian criticism of this (as we have seen in the first section of this chapter) is firstly that the nature of the subject must make some contribution to the content of the thoughts that spring from a given series of confrontations, and, secondly, that the subject's contribution needs to be thought of as, in some sense, bound up with activity.

It may seem that Williams' version of realism can accommodate what is correct in these responses. His view is that we start out with some set of representations of the world which are (or may well be) 'perspectival'. That is to say that they involve concepts which we exercise only because of our peculiar interests, sensory equipment etc. Williams does not thus suppose that we can make sense of our mind being a *tabula rasa* which from the start forms uncontaminated judgements. How thought gets under way, so to speak, is only comprehensible by bringing in a large dose of activity, interest and the like. But we also, Williams implies, come to develop an interest in representing things 'in a way to the maximal degree independent of our perspective and its peculiarities'. And in pursuit of this interest we reflect upon our representations, perhaps come to have some new ones, and so arrive at something we can defensibly take to be (at least nearer to) the absolute conception.

It looks as though we do not at any stage in description of this development have to make play with the suspect notions of a self-extrapolating set of objects, passive thinkers or signs which can be correctly read only one way. So we may seem to have driven a wedge between the ideas about meaning which Wittgenstein has shown to be nonsensical and the defensible idea of there being a way that things are in themselves.

But on closer inspection it is far from clear that Williams' notion should satisfy the Wittgensteinian. It is an assumption of Williams' approach that there is such a thing as an interest in how things are in themselves which makes intelligible the formation of one set of concepts, those of the absolute conception, rather than another and merely 'perspectival' set. But the Wittgensteinian may well respond that the supposed 'interest' is purely formal and cannot contribute to commending one extrapolation rather than another. Mere interest in 'the truth' without any specification of subject matter is of doubtful intelligibility as a value.[12] And as soon as we put in some specific subject matter – whether it be the origin of the universe or the growth of my neighbour's marrow – which makes the curiosity comprehensible, we shall find that we are employing particular concepts, the role and importance of which in our thought the Wittgensteinian will wish to relate back to our interests, practices etc. That the concepts of fundamental physics have some interesting differences from those of everyday human and social life is undoubted. But that the interest which drives us to construct the concepts of physics is that in 'pure truth', rather than an interest itself rooted in that life, is not an unquestionable datum.

A further worry could be put this way. If a certain idea makes no sense, namely the idea of being a passive *tabula rasa* upon which the unambiguous sign imprints a judgement, then it makes no sense either to suppose that each of us should strive to become a *tabula rasa* by selecting among our beliefs so as to remove the contamination or limitation of our perspectives and interests.

In order to get any further we need to look more closely at what Williams means by 'explanation'. Can he supply an account of a sort of explanation which would validate the claim of a notion to be part of the 'absolute conception' and lay to rest the Wittgensteinian worries?

His references to evolutionary biology and the neurological sciences suggest on first reading that it is some substantive account of what it is to think this or that (something of the kind which functionalist accounts in the philosophy of mind aim to supply) which Williams has in mind.[13] The idea could be developed like this. We find that, as science progresses, we are able, at last, to give an account of what it is to have thoughts, of what thinking consists in. We find that the explanation calls upon only some of the concepts which previously we unreflectively used; the others turn out unnecessary and the supposed 'thoughts' in which they were exercised are revealed by science to be not central cases of intellectual actions or states but to be characterizable in some other way. For example, one might claim that thinking that something is square is explained as a state caused by confrontation with square things and apt itself to lead to behaviour appropriate for dealing with square things. 'Square' is thus vindicated as part of the absolute conception, since mention of squareness is invoked in the account of what it is to think about it. On the other hand thinking that something is wicked is explained as having a certain feeling and producing certain behaviour on confrontation with certain things – where all of the items in question are characterizable without mention of wickedness. Our propensity to have the reaction to the items is itself explained (perhaps) as a result of natural selection and/or social conditioning. 'Wickedness' is thus thrown out of the absolute conception.

But this bold and simple strategy is not what Williams has in mind, as is clear from a variety of considerations. One is that he explicitly expresses sympathy for Quinean and Davidsonian themes (akin to those discussed in chapter 5) which he takes to be incompatible with any 'reductive' and functionalist style of account such as that proposed above.[14]

Another reason for thinking that the above misrepresents Williams' strategy is that he acknowledges the force of the 'shapelessness' objection (advanced, for example, by McDowell) against projectivist accounts of ethical notions.[15] Williams thus concedes that the items grouped together under one of the concepts he wishes to label 'perspectival' may not have any neat set of 'absolute' features in common. What is common, what makes it intelligible to group them together, can, he admits, only be grasped by someone who sees the world from the relevant point of view (or at least has sympathetic insight into what that would be like). So what is called for (and all that is available) to attain understanding of such perspectival concepts is insight into the possibility of these various points of view. But this insight, although according to Williams facilitated by possession of the relevant absolute concepts, will not necessarily be the kind of thing which enables us to carry through the imagined kind of reductive manoeuvres.

And a third consideration, of a more structural but still weighty kind, is that Williams just does not attempt to provide himself, or to cite others as providing, the sort of substantive philosophy of mind which would be required to made the above strategy work. This would be a serious oversight were his 'explanations' designed to have the form suggested. But they are not. We can get a much more coherent and interesting reading by pursuing another line.

On this second strategy, the focus is not on the act of thinking but rather upon the *contents* of thoughts and how they are seen as knowledge advances. The idea is that such advances reveal certain notions to be 'merely perspectival' and hence as not to be taken as representing how things are in themselves. But these same advances presuppose, and have to be seen by us as presupposing, that we have at least the idea of other notions which resist any such relegation. Let me quote the crucial and exceedingly condensed argument in which the vital moves are made. (I have inserted numbers at certain points, for ease of later reference.)

(1) Knowledge is of what is there *anyway* . . . (2) Suppose A and B each claims to have some knowledge of the world . . . Now with respect to their supposed pieces of knowledge A's and B's representations may well differ. (3) If what they both have is knowledge, then it seems to follow that there must be some coherent way of understanding why these representations differ, and hence how they are related to one another . . . (4) A story can be told which explains how A's and B's can each be a perspective on the same reality. To understand this story, one needs to form a conception of the world which *contains* A and B and their representations . . . (5) But this process, it seems, can be continued. For if A or B or some other party comes in this way to understand these representations and their relation to the world, this will be because he has given them a place in some more inclusive representation . . . If this is knowledge, then we must be able to form the conception once more of how this would be related to some other representation which might equally claim to be knowledge; indeed we must be able to form that conception with regard to *every* other representation which might make that claim. (6) If we cannot form that conception, then it seems that we do not have any adequate conception of the reality which is there 'anyway' . . . But that conception appeared at the beginning as basic to the notion of knowledge itself. That conception we might call the absolute conception of reality. (7) If knowledge is possible at all, it now seems, the absolute conception must be possible too.[16]

It will be noted that Williams does not in this passage give the characterization of the 'absolute conception' as that which represents how the world is independent of the peculiarities of observers. But we may justifiably take that to be the right interpretation of the phrase here. This is both because he elsewhere uses the same words explicitly with that sense and equally explicitly with reference back to this argument,[17] and also because (as we shall see) it is the interpretation required by the internal coherence of what is claimed.

What is going on in this argument? It starts at (1) from a claim which is very plausibly a version of something like our minimal realism – namely that certain of our thoughts we take to be of things independent of those thoughts. To claim to have knowledge is to claim (in part at least) that such a thought is correct and in claiming knowledge we do not suppose that this correctness is derived solely from the nature of the thought. On the contrary, we think of it as dependent on how it is with things which are there 'anyway', i.e. things independent of the thought. But, as stressed at (2), I must recognize that my thoughts may differ from those of others who also claim knowledge of this independent reality. Now, if I see some representation of mine as knowledge then I will take it that any seemingly incompatible representation can either be shown up as simply erroneous or shown not to be really incompatible. This is what is asserted at (3) and again our earlier thoughts in chapter 2 chime in with it. To admit that my representation and the incompatible one could both be right is just to admit that neither is a thought about what is there 'anyway', i.e. neither is deserving of realistic interpretation. Williams does not stress the notion of incompatibility. But its importance is implicit in his notion of mere difference. If I suppose that what I think is a correct representation of what is there anyway, then any differing representation presents a problem, namely 'Why is it not the same as mine, since mine is of what is?' If the question does not worry me it will be because I already have what Williams next speaks of, at (4), namely the wider representation in which both of these differing ones are accommodated, for example a view of 'what is' in which it has various different parts, only some of which I have detailed information about.

Let us now pause in our examination of the argument to consider what happens at the point where representations seem to clash and

then we arrive at some resolution. It is essential to Williams'
position that sometimes at this point one of the representations is
revealed as being merely perspectival. That is, we say to ourselves
'Earlier we might have taken it to represent what was there anyway
but now we see that it does not; it merely represents how things
seem to us because of some peculiarity of our situation.' But what
form does this insight take? How do we deploy the resources of the
wider view of things we have now arrived at to enforce this
judgement of the status of our earlier concepts? Remember that this
is not to take the form of the functionalist or projectivist style of
story which we earlier contemplated.

Williams himself offers the realization that A and B are in
different places as a very primitive example of how one might come
to understand how representations could differ.[18] And it is presumably from this primitive case that he derives the word 'perspectival'. So meditating on it should give us the clues we need.

Suppose, then, that A and B speak the same language (operate
the same system of representations) and A claims 'It is raining'
while B says 'It is not raining'. Their representations are different
and incompatible so they cannot rest content with the view that
both, just as they stand and without any further setting or explanation, embody knowledge. A and B then reflect and come to enlarge
their (explicit) representation of the world by the idea that there
are different places in it. Perhaps they add place-marking elements,
whether indexical or of some other character, to their vocabulary.
The representations using these notions are now accepted as absolute (or nearer the absolute) and the earlier ones are thought of as
perspectival. The 'explanation' that A and B offer for their previous
way of talking might go something like this: 'We used to talk in a
way which took no account of the possibility that we might be in
different places; we, as it were, "took it for granted" that we were at
the same place.' Let us note that this explanation deploys the new
conceptual apparatus to illuminate the content of what was previously said. It operates in an interpretive or rationalizing mode. It
does not purport to offer any reductive account of what it is to
think.

The 'perspectivalness' of the previous representations, on the
view sketched, consists in their 'recognisably and diagnosably

coming from a point of view'[19] in the sense that their use has built into it a certain assumption. 'Use' must be read here as invoking the role of the representation in the whole system. It is the system, rather than the particular element in it, which, in its limitations, embodies the assumption or point of view. The structure of the range of remarks which the language or system provides for has no place in it for marking the possibility which has now thrust itself upon the speakers.[20]

Now that we have in hand this picture of what perspectivalness is and how it manifests itself in unexpected disagreement, let us return to Williams' argument. We have seen how, if I make a knowledge claim, I take it that a prima facie incompatible knowledge claim can be shown to be either erroneous or not incompatible. This can come about in various ways. The other's knowledge claim, if not simply discredited as false, may turn out to be perspectival and mine will already have the resources to explain why it is different; or perhaps the reverse is the case; or perhaps both claims will be seen as perspectival from the wider view we shall then command. But such a commitment to the possibility of vindication of knowledge is open-ended – as Williams remarks as (5). He expands on this by claiming that we must be able to make sense of every possible challenge from rival knowledge claims having been successfully negotiated. We must thus, he concludes, be able to make sense of the idea of a way of conceiving of things which cannot itself be regarded as perspectival from any more inclusive standpoint.

This is Williams' way of puttings things, but we may add the following gloss. The suggested 'absolute' way of conceiving of things would have to be one which could not be seen as taking anything for granted. The nature of the subject who judges (e.g. the fact that he or she seems not to countenance certain possibilities) does not have to be grasped by anyone who is to understand that person's representation. The representations can thus be taken as providing an account of how the world is in itself.

Williams' argument then concludes at (7) by drawing attention to the conditional claim: in making sense of knowledge at all we commit ourselves to the intelligibility of the incorporation of every worthy (i.e. not simply false) knowledge claim into one, unique, unified and perspectiveless picture. So if we can make sense of knowledge at all, we must be able to make sense of the absolute conception.

Is the argument persuasive? There seem to be two points at which one might have qualms. The first is the move from the open-endedness of the commitment in the making of a knowledge claim to the supposed intelligibility of an endstate of having incorporated all knowledge claims in one unified picture. The idea of knowledge may well involve the idea of ability to negotiate success-fully with every challenge that arises. But why need we suppose that there is some given totality of challenges with which it is intelligible to suppose oneself having negotiated? Williams, as we have seen, claims that if we cannot make sense of this then we 'do not have an adequate conception of the reality which is there "anyway"'. But then perhaps in this sense of 'adequacy' we neither need nor can have adequate conceptions.

This leads to consideration of a second questionable assumption, more deeply buried in the argument but even more fundamental. This is that a knowledge claim which negotiates a challenge by admitting itself to be 'perspectival' has thereby been shown to be in some sense at fault. The idea is that it has been shown to be less than we were striving for, less than we implicitly claimed to have in having knowledge; perhaps the fault is merely that of some kind of incompleteness, but a falling short of some sort there is. This is the idea that fuels the first questionable move. The assumption is that in having the idea of knowledge we have a certain ideal, namely that of the 'faultless' representation, where the possibility that there is another representation which differs from this and is not ex-plained by it is taken to be a fault. A representation can only fulfil the ideal we have in having the conception of knowledge if there are no further worthy rivals for it to negotiate with. So in having the idea of something faultless we must have the idea of the non-existence of rivals. And knowing ourselves to have knowledge would involve knowing that there are no more rivals to be defeated or negotiated with.

But the idea that there is a fault here is *part of*, not separately motivated from, the 'absolute conception' idea itself. If one sup-poses that there is a 'how things are in themselves' and that every knowledge claim is a move in an intelligible project of getting a picture of it, then indeed revelation of perspectivalness will be discovery of a fault. But if one thinks that making a claim about what is so is always an aspect of (is only intelligible in the context of) some life-involving project – a project *not* revealingly characterized merely as 'discovery of the truth' – then what counts as fault in a representation will be bound up with what the life and its projects are.

Wittgenstein draws attention to the idea that an activity may be fully defensible although it is not everywhere bounded by rules. This is a prominent theme in the early sections of the *Investigations*.[21] It may seem that Williams can acknowledge whatever truth there is in this. He does not want to condemn perspectival representations in the sense of urging us not to have them or even in the sense of denying that they can ever rightly be classed as knowledge in some sense. So, for Williams, languages are not everywhere bounded by rules; there are, quite properly, ones where the participants are not equipped to deal with every possibility.

But Williams' conception does clash with the Wittgensteinian one in this, that Williams thinks that the full ideal of knowledge is bound up with the idea of a language which *is* everywhere bounded by rules – i.e. a language which is equipped to describe every possibility. If there were a possibility which it could not describe – which its speakers would be at a loss to deal with – then the views expressed in that part of the language are, for Williams, merely perspectival.

But Wittgenstein is not merely concerned to point out that many of our perfectly acceptable linguistic practices are not everywhere bounded by rules (e.g. the case of the disappearing chair).[22] Nor is he saying that there is a given totality of possibilities which our language will always, but excusably, fail to articulate in every detail.[23] He is, I suggest, trying to get us to see that the idea of the given totality of possibilities makes no sense. Any linguistic move at all has presuppositions because it is bound up with, and its sense is dependent on, a context of interests and acitivities – interests and acitivities which, in turn, only make sense given other empirical facts. We do not make sense of the idea of a totality of possibilities because that would require us to get some overview of the totality of ways life could intelligibly be lived. And although we may mouth this phrase, it does not have for us the kind of sense which would enable us to do substantive philosophical work with it.

It may sound as if an unacceptable form of pragmatism was here being recommended. For example it may sound as if it were being suggested that the making of a statement was always a move in some limited pratical project and that its 'truth' could amount to no more than its turning out effective in securing the desired goal. I shall try to suggest, in section 8.1 that this is not so.

7.3 KRIPKE AND NORMS

In order to understand meaning more fully we need to bring in projects, interests, values or the like. That was the theme of the first section of this chapter. But how exactly do they enter an account of meaning?

One theory is that which is offered by Kripke.[24] Or if not offered by him it is at least a plausible reading of what he says which has been adopted by some.[25] This theory constitutes a move which we might make in response to the negative claims, about the insuffic-iency of formulae, images etc. to constitute meaning, although it is also bound up with the exact form that the diagnosis of insuffic-iency takes. The view is that those negative conclusions are essen-tially linked to the fact that meaning is a *normative* notion. When we realize this, we can devise a sceptical solution to the sceptical paradox, a solution which shows what the role of attributions of meaning is in the context of a language-using community.

I shall argue in this section that the proposed theory is unattrac-tive, first because meaning attributions are not 'normative' in the sense required and, secondly, because if we accepted it we would be back in a version of the unfortunate position examined in the first section of chapter 6, namely of endorsing a form of meaning scepticism which undercuts the realism which we had thought to preserve about things other than meanings.

Suppose we are considering some speaker and we say of her that she means addition by 'plus'. When we do this are we describing something? Is there some fact which makes our remarks true or false? This is the question that Kripke asks us to consider.[26] We then examine various candidates for what her meaning addition by 'plus' might consist in. We may find items, (formulae, brain states or whatever) which cause or causally contribute to utterances of '125' in answer to the question 'What is 68 plus 57?' Now someone's meaning something by 'plus' surely (helps to) explain why she speaks as she does. So it seems that we have in these brain states, formulae or whatever plausible candidates for what it is to mean.

But, says Kripke, 'the relation of meaning and intention to future action is *normative*, not *descriptive*'.[27] One central point here seems to be this. Given that she does mean addition by 'plus' (and also of course 68 by '68' and 57 by '57') and that she is asked 'What is 57 plus 68?' then she *ought* to reply '125'. This is the correct, the true, thing to say.

It is worth stressing that the strategy here (as I am interpreting it) requires us to deny the link between meaning and utterance in the form in which the alternative, causalist, theory assumes it. The fact that someone means something by a certain noise does not (according to Kripke) imply that she will or is likely to say a given particular thing in answer to some question. Meaning is no guarantee against mistake. That is what seems to be implied by the remark that the relation of meaning to future action is 'not descriptive'. If the relation to action were both descriptive and normative then it would be open to someone who thought that meaning consisted, for example, in the occurrence of some causally efficacious item to argue that all his theory needed was supplementation by some further element which captured the desired normative features. Kripke's contention is that items which contribute to causal explanation of noise-making are not merely an incomplete analysis of what it is to mean but could be no part of the analysis at all.

Kripke's emphasis on future action in his initial exposition has misled some commentators into thinking that cross-temporal linkages of some sort are the crucial issue.[28] But he could just as well have said that the relation of meaning to current action is normative and not descriptive. The point has to do not only with language but with thought more generally. Attributions of content of any kind can be said to be normative and not descriptive. If I say of someone that she is thinking that the tree is about to fall, I have not said anything descriptive (about the imagery going on in her mind or what not) but I have made a commitment about the conditions under which her judgement will be true, right and what she ought to have judged.

Let me emphasize once again that there is much more to be said on this issue of whether a causalist, or broadly functionalist, account of mind of the kind Kripke attacks can give an acceptable underpinning to whatever notion of the normative is required. But we are proceeding here upon the assumption (to which I am very sympathetic) that Kripke is right in rejecting such approaches.

We have, as we have seen, a trio of terms for appraising utterances and judgements, when they are regarded as meaning-bearers. We can say that they are what one *ought* to say or judge, that they are *correct* or that they are *true*. Each of these terms can be used to express the key 'normative' idea we are trying to capture. The naturalness of 'ought' in this context sets us off on a line of thought in which we hear 'normative' as meaning 'evaluative' and where we take 'evaluative' in the sense of the traditional fact/value distinction.

By the 'traditional' distinction I mean the one grounded in Hume's style of consideration.[29] The key elements are these: Motivation to act always involves desire (pro-attitude, feeling) as well as belief. A clear line can be drawn between belief on the one hand and desire (attitude, feeling) on the other. That is to say that given any mere belief it is always possible, i.e. intelligible, i.e. coherent and not irrational, to take up various different attitudes to the state of affairs the belief is about. To apprehend that things are thus and so (or might be thus and so) is never of itself a motive to action. There must also be the (at least in theory) separable matter of whether one cares about things being thus and so. No caring about anything is logically required by the fact apprehended. Consequently any intentional state, however prima facie belief-like, which does necessarily provide some motive for action must contain a desire (feeling, attitude) component as well as the belief component. So any prima facie descriptive remark which is such that in accepting it one necessarily allows that one has some reason to perform an action cannot be entirely fact-stating. It cannot be expressive merely of belief but will also express some desire, feeling or attitude.

As Blackburn has argued, we are not committed by this outlook to some crude 'Boo–Hurrah' theory about evaluative utterances.[30] We do not need, on acceptance of this view, to reform our linguistic practice of treating these utterances almost exactly as we treat fact-stating utterances. We may talk of them as 'true' or 'false' and operate as though the laws of non-contradiction and excluded middle held for them, we may include them as premises in arguments and so forth. But acceptance of the view does involve supposing that there is some highly reflective philosophical standpoint from which we can distinguish the real facts from the secondary or projected ones, the seeming presence of which in the world is the result of the interaction of the value-free world with our affective natures.

Suppose we hear Kripke's remarks about what someone 'ought to say' (given what she means by 'plus' and so forth) in this light, how do things then unfold? Perhaps like this: In saying 'she ought to say "125"' I am not describing any real fact about her. Rather I am expressing my approval of her now uttering '125'. Why do I have a pro-attitude towards her uttering this noise? Because it is what I myself feel impelled to say and I like other people to keep in step with me. I like that because it makes me feel at home in the world and enables me to do various of the other things I like doing.

The remark 'she ought to say "125"' is entailed by 'she means addition by "plus"' together with some other statements. What entails an evaluative statement must be in part evaluative itself. So unless the extra premise not concerning meaning, i.e. that 68 plus 57 is 125, is evaluative (which seems implausible) then the 'means' statement itself must be evaluative. What attitude or feeling does it express? It expresses my willingness to dignify this other person as a mathematician of sorts. It shows that I regard her as a creature whose utterances in context like this – where someone has asked 'What is 68 plus 57?' – matter to me. I have the attitude of taking seriously whether she is in step with me or not. I welcome her into the linguistic community.[31]

But will all this do as a coherent story about meaning? (We are not here concerned directly with its accuracy as a representation of Wittgenstein. But many commentators have made telling points against supposing Kripke's argument, whether or not this is quite the right reading of it, it to be acceptable in that role.)[32] The problems with accepting it are first that the premise is false and, secondly that the conclusion self-undermining.

For the first of these claims I have argued elsewhere.[33] The central point is that, whether or not we accept the Humean account of evaluative (i.e. action-guiding and practical reason giving) vocabulary, it would be wrong to put 'true', 'false' and 'means' in the same bag with 'amusing', 'noble', 'kindly', 'cruel', 'betrayal', 'boring' and so forth. To say that a remark is true, or that some course of action would lead to acquisition of a true belief is not an action-guiding or reason-giving comment. I do not come to understand *why* someone made a remark or pursued some course of action simply by learning that the remark was true or that the action led to acquisition of a true belief.

We are often led to think the opposite by concentrating on cases where a context of interest in some particular subject matter, a context requiring remarks or beliefs about it, is already set up. This is what Kripke's imagined question does. But if we imagine cases where there is no such context then it becomes plain that truth as such has no evaluative pull. There are many true sentences that I could insert into this book. I could for example write next what I ate for breakfast this morning. But you are hardly likely to find my doing so intelligible if I tell you that I just could not resist enunciating this truth. There are many facts that I could learn by observing the colours of the book jackets on my shelves. But I am not all the time struggling with some temptation, albeit very tiny, to go and learn those facts. Why we find it intelligible to make certain remarks and pursue certain enquiries has to do with the subject matter involved and with values bound up with talking and knowing about that subject matter, not with the evaluative status of truth in itself.

It is a good thing that we can thus resist embarking on the path suggested because the conclusion that meaning is itself a projective notion directly undermines the idea that there are any facts (or at least any of which we can have knowledge) which can intelligibly be contrasted with the pseudo and merely projected facts about values, truth and meanings. The difficulty the position encounters here is closely akin to that which we explored in the first section of chapter 6. We are told that the 'real' truth about meaningful speech is that it is social noise-making accompanied by various patterns of feelings of satisfaction and dissatisfaction in speakers and hearers. The noise-makings, and whether or not the noises are the same as the ones I feel impelled to produce, are the assertibility conditions, the skeleton, upon which my projection of feelings of like or dislike builds the phenomenal body of apparently meaningful language use. This is the story. But how can I (or you) apprehend a fact in the manner required by the attemptedly realist part of this picture, if the states such as thinking and speaking which at first glance we took to be that apprehension turn out to be mere noise-making accompanied by feelings of satisfaction? I have cut off the branch on which I hoped to sit.

Suppose that we push on, accepting the consequence of thoroughgoing projectivism about meanings, we then arrive at projectivism about the facts which that (apparent) meaningfulness (seemingly) allows us to apprehend. So the end point is a thoroughgoing transcendental idealism in which an interaction between an unknowable subject and an unknowable something else results in states in which we (seemingly) apprehend a world of things and persons. And we cannot even say this with a confident sense that, however mysterious, this is how things really are. The content we (seem to) discern in that very remark is, by its own lights, only a figment.

Let me here reiterate that I am not sure that the line of thought I have traced here accurately represents the one followed by Kripke. It could be said that I have imported talk of 'liking' and 'approval' where Kripke speaks only of primitive dispositions to give answers and to respond to training. Hence, it may be argued, there is little firm evidence that Kripke's 'normative' is to be heard as a Humean 'evaluative'. I would also like to acknowledge that Kripke is importantly right in his initial attack on the dispositionalist or causalist account of meaning and in his invocation of 'norms' at this point. The two crucial claims here would be these: first, that talk of meaning is appropriate only for items which play a role in the life of creatures for whom some things, including on occasion their own utterances, are in various ways important, valuable and cared about; and secondly that the idea of something being important to a person, mattering to him or her, cannot be explained in terms of causes and dispositions. This is one of the points where battle might be joined, were we to pursue the issue raised at the end of chapter 6 concerning the feasibility of naturalized account of mind.

However right Kripke is in the general thrust of his claim here, and however unfair to him the more detailed interpretation of the course of the argument which I have offered, the important point for the line of argument in this book is that the notions of meaning and value should not be tied together in the way set out in that detailed interpretation. And a further important point is that, on the view I recommend, there will be something wrong about Kripke's argument, whatever its details, namely that it issues in a *sceptical* thesis about meaning. The strategy I am pursuing is that of bringing interests, values, forms of life and so forth into the discussion of meaning as a way of loosening the grip of mirroring realism and hence finding a stance from which we can happily acknowledge the *reality* of meaning (and very probably of value too – although that is not a theme I shall pursue).

8

Interpretations and Misinterpretations

8.1 SPEECH ACTS AND LANGUAGE GAMES

The last chapter introduced the idea that Wittgenstein is hostile to mirroring realism and attempted to sketch the grounds for that hostility. It also endeavoured to disarm a counter-argument on behalf of mirroring realism and to forestall one misinterpretation of the proposed meaning-interest link. But many questions remain. Some concern the nature of the interconnection between concepts and interests on the Wittgensteinian view; others are about whether any non-mirroring view can rightly claim to be realistic at all. The aim of this chapter is to explore these issues and to clarify the Wittgensteinian position further, in part by distinguishing it from tempting but ultimately misleading views with which it may be confused.

The mirroring idea offers us the thought that there is one way that the world is in itself and which (some of) our thoughts strive to capture. A proposal to abandon this way of looking at things is liable to be seen as recommendation of the idea that 'there is nothing determinate out there' – that the world is a kind of mist, upon which we project shadows which we then mistake for pre-existing figures. Recoiling from this picture, while still striving to respect the insight that the world cannot enforce any classificatory scheme upon us, we might hit upon the idea of crediting the world with immense richness of characteristics, rather than with none at all. What was wrong with the mirroring picture, we say, is that it assumed just one nature for the world; the truth is that it has indefinitely many.[1]

Given this idea we seem to have no difficulty in saying what the role of our interests (values, projects) is in the business: they determine what facts, or what sorts of fact, are of concern to us, what conceptual net we shall use. Our fishing with a net of a certain mesh fixes that there are some fishes we shall not catch, but it does not create the fish that we do catch. To put it less metaphorically, our interests make certain aspects of the world of importance to us and others of no relevance. But the aspects that we do notice are there all right and we need have no qualms about realistic construal of our thoughts about them. The sort of example one might use to illustrate the idea would be the familiar one of the Eskimos and their recognition of many types of snow. Their interests require them to use snow as a building material; consequently they mark all kinds of differences between types of snow of which we are oblivious.

I do not want to suggest that this kind of explanation can never be given or that it is not illuminating. What it provides, however, is a causal or quasi-causal account of why certain concepts are possessed. We may agree that having certain interests (in building shelters) is likely to lead to acquisition of certain concepts (of different kinds of snow and their properties) if the agents and their environment are of certain kinds. But the relation between interest and concept remains contingent and external. We have not been given any reason to suppose that the same features of snow could not be noticed by someone with very different interests. So possession of the interest is not in any sense constitutive of possession of the concept; the interest explains possession of the concept but not in a way which gives us deeper insight into what it is to have that concept at all.

We should note also that there is nothing in this story to prevent us supposing that we can set aside the practical interests which make our familiar concepts useful to us and ask, disinterestedly, what further features things have which we have so far failed to notice. We might hope to get some sort of schematic view of a greater range of properties and to locate our own conceptual scheme among various others which we see would be appropriate to creatures with different interests. An enterprise of this shape may be intelligible. But if we ask what metaphysical picture goes with it, it is clear that mirroring realism is not ruled out. The theory offers us the facts that creatures have interests, the fact that they have concepts and the fact that the world includes such and such a range of properties, and it knits them together in an explanatory way. But there is nothing to prevent us from conceiving of these things themselves on the mirroring model; that is how things really are (we think) and we have become aware of it through our ability to grasp how things are in themselves.

To understand Wittgenstein's vision better we need, I suggest, to move to something more radical than this. Perhaps one of his own starting points, the comparison of a judgement to a move in a game, will help us.

Let us consider something like making a bid in bridge. In order to understand what is going on one needs to grasp that making a bid is a particular sort of element in a whole complex pattern of manoeuvres. What would be a good or bad bid (and what counts as making a bid at all) is seen only when one sees the structure and objectives of the whole set up. The bid may be assessed in various dimensions, as sensible, exciting, successful and so forth. The possibility of such assessments is implicit in the structure of the activity. But it would be odd to assess the bid as true or false or to think of it as a factual claim.

Compare with this my measuring a sofa, writing down '4ft 6ins' on a piece of paper, carrying out a similar operation on a space of wall, comparing the written marks and finally moving the sofa into space. One might say analogously that 'measuring', 'noting the result' and the like can only be understood as elements in the complex whole. The objective is to fit the sofa somewhere in the room; judging that it is 4ft 6ins long is a move which is assessable in various dimensions ('justified by the rules of measurement', 'actually leading to a successful placing of the sofa' etc). And even if one of these dimensions is labelled 'being true' (says this line of thought) that should not blind us to the fact that what is really at issue is success in the enterprise.

Contemplating an example such as this, or Wittgenstein's 'five red apples' case,[2] it may seem that what he is recommending is a 'speech act' account of the ways of talking under discussion. This 'speech act' manoeuvre is one that we are familiar with from the discussion of such things as the emotive and prescriptive theories of ethics or the suggestions of Austin.[3] What is distinctive in such theories is the idea of taking some philosophically controversial word ('ought', 'true', 'responsible' etc.) and denying that it has a descriptive role. Philosophers, it is said, have spent many years trying to understand what facts one could be describing by the use of such words and how we could provide a respectable epistemology for them; but we now see that these attempts were all misguided and doomed to failure, because the role of the words is to be conceived differently; the essential thing to realize is that in uttering them we are making moves in some complex social activity and the question of whether such moves are right or wrong should not be construed as the question of whether they are true or false.

Perhaps, then, Wittgenstein is proposing a wholesale extension of this policy to every expression of our language, not just those that have proved philosophically controversial? Number words, colour words, temporal and modal expression, psychological vocabulary – to understand any of these we must grasp what language games their use is embedded in, we must see what moves we make in uttering sentences containing them.[4]

There are serious things wrong with this proposal, as we shall see, namely that it yields an unacceptably non-realist story and, worse, that it is incoherent. But before considering these objections we should note that there is something very importantly right in the idea. This is the prominence it gives to the idea that the meaningful employment of any linguistic item requires a great deal of stage setting, in terms of circumstances and kinds of objectives, a stage setting which, in that employment of the item, is just taken for granted.

It is worth meditating on this further, for it is one of the important corollaries of the thought in section 7.1 and one which we again and again shy away from or fail to get into focus. Consider a person who, as the outcome of some confrontation, makes a judgement of the form 'This is F'. If we are not meaning sceptics then we take it that this judgement invokes a standard of what is to count as the same which places the confronted item as a member of one extended grouping rather than another. The judgement is in order as a judgement, not in the sense of being true but in the sense of having a content and being assessable as true or false, provided that there is such a standard.

But what is required for such a standard to exist? On the mirroring view all that is needed is that 'F' be a label marking one of the ways things can be, i.e. picking out an independent, built into the nature of things, property. Whether or not a classificatory rule has this status is not a contingent matter. So there are no contingent facts the existence of which is required to underpin the respectability of 'F' as a predicate. The use of 'F' runs no risk of turning out to be radically flawed because of the non-existence of such facts. On the Wittgensteinian view of section 7.1 by contrast, every concept is bound up with a way of living and with the possesion of certain interests which inform that way of living. The viabililty of a concept will thus be dependent on whatever is required for that way of life to be pursued and for its interests to be continuingly defensible. And it is difficult to see how this could fail to involve a ramifying set of contingent facts, which then constitute a needed stage setting for the use of the concept 'F'.

Suppose then that we recognize some unavoidable entanglement of concepts with stage setting, does this have the consequence that any linguistic move is to be seen as (really) an action, as opposed to a judgement of the truth? This is the way that the 'speech act' idea chooses to spell out the idea. I want to argue now that such a view is incoherent. For it to work it is required that an account of various assessment conditions for a given utterance should be available in terms not invoking the utterance to be explained. For suppose this were not so; suppose for example that in talking of the success conditions of the utterance 'The sofa is 4ft 6ins long' one had to invoke the condition that the sofa is 4ft 6 ins long. Clearly here we have lost any leverage for saying that the utterance is to be given a 'speech act' construal. Let us imagine that this pitfall has been avoided and that we do have some independent specification of what counts as success of various kinds. What story are we now to tell about the linguistic moves involved in giving this account of success? Imagine, for example that I say a bid in bridge is successful provided that such and such a number of tricks is secured by the bidding player and his or her partner. This certainly avoids (and plausibly in this case) any risk of precipitation back into some idea that making a bid is producing some sort of statement. But what am I doing in saying of some bridge players 'They made such and such a number of tricks'? The natural thing is to construe it as a description. But then the theory is not fully general. And if we endeavour to make it fully general by finding some further language game in which that 'description' is a move, we are embarked on an infinite regress. Let us spell this out in more detail.

The original speech act theories, as proposed by the emotivists, prescriptivists and Austinians, had built into them a contrast between content-giving, sense-giving or 'phrastic' elements on the one hand and mood, force-indicating or 'neustic' ones on the other; they also had built in a contrast between assertive and non-assertive force. Particular 'speech act' theories were offered within this framework and involved trying to re-locate suspect items from the 'sense-indicating' box into the 'force-indicating' one. But what we seem to be asked to do under the present proposal is different from these piecemeal manoeuvres. We are asked to put *everything* into the 'non-assertive force indicator' box.

One might suppose that the incoherence here lies in the fact that notions like 'force' require the intelligibility of 'sense'. But this objection is not a serious one. It is true that some force notions do require sense as a contrast – for example the idea of assertive force requires the idea of the content of what is asserted. But not all force notions have this feature. (Consider the force of 'Hello'.) What we are being asked to do (on this construal of Wittgenstein) is to construct a grammar in which every sentence is built up from force-determining elements and has, as a consequence, a complex force, i.e. suitability for performance of some appropriately complex move.

So far so good. But the incoherence emerges, the infinite regress appears as vicious, when we ask ourselves how we are to conceive of what we do when we set out the conditions under which these linguistic items are to be used and the conditions under which the moves made by them succeed. In giving these conditions we seem to ourselves to state circumstances which, among other things, provide reasons for making the linguistic moves we are trying to explain. But giving the conditions is, of course, just itself making more linguistic moves. These moves themselves must, if the theory is right, be regarded as actions which we choose to do in the light of circumstances which make them appropriate or not. So we now have a picture of ourselves choosing whether or not there will be justifying reasons for some other action. And our current action of so doing will turn out to have reasons in favour of it only in the light of certain other moves which again we must choose to make. And so on.

The difficulty we have arrived at here is a close relative of (indeed perhaps another incarnation of) that which we encountered with thoroughgoing pragmatism in section 6.2. There the insurmountable problem was that of combining the idea that every feature of our world is put into place by our choice with the idea that the choice could be thought of as constrained. The upshot was that the idea of constraint on choice (and the linked idea of rational motivation in choice) requires the notion of fact. It requires it both to give substance to the idea of that in the light of which the choice is to be made and to give substance to the idea that something hangs on the choice – that it could turn out to be wrong as well as right. The earlier debate of section 6.2 took place in a rarefied atmosphere. We talked of the advantages of adopting theoretical positions, of recalcitrant experience and the like. Now we are talking about more mundane activities like shopping, arranging furniture and playing bridge, but the fundamenetal point carries over. We are invited in both cases to see 'making a judgement' as an action, something done by choice, the success or failure of which is to be assessed accordingly. But the inadequacy of this pragmatist stance is shown in the fact that we can think of certain of the things we do (in a broad sense of 'do') as motivated and constrained choices only if we see certain others in a quite different way, namely as recognition of facts.

We should mention one more consideration against the 'generalized speech act' proposal. As applied, for example, to the case of measuring the sofa, it hopelessly falsifies what is going on, from a phenomenological point of view. It just is not the case that I suppose that whether or not the sofa fits at the end of the day (given, of course, certain results of the other measurement and the comparison process) is of crucial importance in determining whether or not I judged correctly when I wrote down '4ft 6ins'. I do not conceive of myself as doing something (like making a bid in bridge) which has its sole significance from its role in this sharply bounded, if complex, set of transactions. On the contrary I take it that I am finding out how things are in themselves, that I am discovering which is 'there anyway'. Of course (one will add) this information may be useful and having it guides me to the satisfaction of my desires. But what it is to have the information and whether it is correct is independent of these particular desires and whether they get satisfied. The phenomenology, in other words, is such as to make the mirroring conception eminently satisfying.

If, then, we are to find any distinctive and defensible Wittgensteinian view on the interdependence of concepts and interests we need to find a way of rejecting a mirroring or 'absolute' conception which does not precipitate us into the absurdities of the thoroughgoing pragmatist or speech act view.

Some commonsense observations may help us here. Our lives do not segment into self-contained episodes of action. That is not to say that we all have a 'life plan' to which every particular action is tightly subordinated; all kinds of inter-relations, both strong and weak, may hold between all kinds of projects conceived at various levels of specificity. But typically we do have various long-term aims and persistent interests, even if they are only vaguely characterized; particular actions are often seen as means to, or elements of, or instances of, some more general enterprise. Another obvious feature of human experience is memory and the cumulative nature (up to a point) of our stock of abilities and elements of our picture of the world. We suppose ourselves to learn something on one occasion, a fact or a skill, which we may be able to apply on another.

It is the combination of these two features which makes the 'speech act' reduction of 'this sofa is 4ft 6ins long' so implausible. It is not whether it now fits the space (given the other results) which is the standard of 'truth', because I may well remember the dimensions and use the information on other occasions in the course of other projects. (Suppose, for example, that the space and the sofa measure the same, but the sofa fails to fit the space because the other pieces of furniture bordering the space expand between the measurement and the attempted fitting. Even though the fitting went wrong, I get the dimensions right, and may be able to use the

information elsewhere.) We can make the same point more generally about the possession of concepts exercised in the judgement.
My grasp on the concept 'four' does not consist simply in my ability
to go through some circumscribed set of manoeuvres of measuring
and fitting sofas. Once I have acquired numerical notions I am in a
position (if other things are propitious) to embark on all sorts of
projects, counting apples, measuring the distance to the moon and
so on.

What can I now say about this 'and so on', about the nature of
those other occasions on which I shall use the information about
the length of the sofa or exercise my grasp of the concept 'four'? On
the one hand there is something that tempts us in the mirroring
direction. It is that there seems to be nothing I can say of a general
character except that those situations will fit the given description,
namely will be ones where the information comes in useful or the
concept is exercised. I certainly cannot give any reductive 'speech
act' account because that would be to imagine, absurdly, that I can
foresee in detail the future course of my life and that it will consist
just of the repetition of some limited number of self-contained
activities; I cannot now lay down limits to the way in which my
information and concepts will interact with other similar items, nor
can I foresee the nature of the projects in which the resulting ideas
will play a part.

On the other hand there is something else which can be seen as
pointing another way. I find on reflection that there is at least one
more thing that I can say about these future activities, namely that
they will be like this one, in which I measured and attempted to fit
the sofa. To have the concept 'four' or the knowledge that the sofa
is 4ft 6ins long is to have a flexible and openended capacity for new
kinds of undertaking. But it is precisely *kinds of undertaking like this*
that it is a capacity for.

The mirroring conception imagines that judgements can, so to
speak, 'float free' from their historical and psychological origins in
training rituals and particular practical contexts. And in one way
they can. The child learns to say 'all gone' as a move in a
parent-satisfying and milk-drinking ritual. But he or she does not
understand what 'all gone' means until the words lose their tight
connection to this particular context and the child acquires the

ability to recognize of all kinds of things on all kinds of evidence that they are 'all gone'. But judgements and concepts cannot 'float free' from their roots in the sense that we can fully justify and explain them by pointing solely to the world which they are (on this view) designed to mirror. If we ask 'why do we have these concepts?' and attempt an answer by trying to show that the world of itself requires that we do then we run into the difficulties outlined in section 7.1, namely those of supposing that the world is a gigantic sign with only one interpretation and that we can make sense of having or aiming to have the content of our thoughts fixed by that inert item.

So we come finally to saying something like this: 'Possession of such and such a concept is exercised paradigmatically like this, at such and such a point in so and so kind of enterprise; we have the concept, and it is the right one for us to have, because it is part of our being able to do such things; if you doubt this, try to imagine what human life would be like if we did not undertake this sort of enterprise in this sort of way; you will find that you cannot make much of it.'

To say this is to invite ourselves to 'assemble reminders', to do 'the natural history of human beings', and it is to suggest that it will be a help to use certain simple 'language games' as starting points for reflection.[5] The upshot of pursuing the line, however, is not that we get some vantage point from which the overall layout of human thought can be surveyed and on which it turns out to be pragmatically rather than mirroringly describable. The central thing we need to hang on to is that the interdependence of concepts and interests is not to be spelt out as the *priority* of interests over concepts. That way lies incoherence (as in the 'speech act' view) or re-importation of another version of the mirroring view (as in the 'Eskimo and snow' view first canvassed in this section). The interdependence is genuinely that. And it manifests itself in the fact that 'assembling reminders', getting a sense of our language games and their not now foreseen ramifications, is the form that grounding and justifying our concepts will take. But none of this will supply us with materials for constructing reductive accounts of the content of any judgement or of what its correctness will consist in. Suppose that we wish to find out whether the sofa is more than four feet long. Our Wittgensteinian reflections on length, number, measurement, furniture and so forth do not tell us that what we are *really* trying to find out is such and such else. It offers us no substitute focus for our thoughts when we ask questions about or investigate the state of the sofa. And, relatedly, if we enquire what is demanded for it to be correct to claim that the sofa is more than four feet long, the reflections tell us that all we can say is that it is necessary that the sofa be more than four feet long.

Despite these reassurances about reductivism and the continuing defensibility of certain truisms about truth, is there nevertheless a threat to 'realism' in the view proposed? This is an outstanding question about which something needs to be said. There are two points to stress. The first is that there is nothing in what has been said to commit us to the idea that our judgements are unconstrained; in other words we have not been precipitated back into the situation threatened by thoroughgoing pragmatism where we lost grip on the idea of pointfulness in utterance, of succcess or failure to be faced. The second closely related point is that there is nothing in what has been said which requires us to deny the idea that there are certain elements of our thought that we take for granted (in the manner outlined in section 6.3), that these involve operation with the law of non-contradiction in many areas, and that our practices, in consequence, satisfy the demands of minimal realism.

Our situation then is this. We are not in a position to determine the success of our enterprises. We propose things to the world, but the world disposes. The central point that we have emphasized, in rejecting the mirroring view, is that the proposals (the concepts in terms of which all our judgements and actions are to be characterized) come from us and that their nature cannot be understood or our possession of them defended by pointing to the world. But this fact, that the proposals are ours, does nothing to soften or limit the fact of our non-omnipotence. This observation seems to protect one very important element which distinguishes realist from idealist stances. And we need to note also that the proposals or questions we put to the world are highly specific because they arise in the course of projects, thoughts and actions which have already a detailed and taken-for-granted structure. Moreover they are frequently posed on the unquestioned assumption that the answers are subject to the principle of non-contradiction. It is answers to these kinds of questions, success or failure of projects conceived in these highly specific terms, which the world, by and large, delivers back to us. It may be that we need to revise our mininal realist practices in particular cases. But the view under consideration offers no encouragement to the idea that wholesale revision is desirable or even intelligible. It may be felt that all this is not enough as a defence of a claim to be realistic. But the Wittgensteinian will then want to pose a challenge to the opponent, namely to articulate more clearly and intelligibly what is missing. The suggestion will be that any such attempt at articulation will fall back into the difficulties of the mirroring view outlined in section 7.1.

8.2   WITTGENSTEIN AND ANTI-REALISM

The object of this section is to consider whether we should see Wittgenstein as an 'anti-realist' in the sense explored by Dummett, Kripke and Wright and to say something about the arguments for anti-realism.[6] There is no agreed view offered by all those sympathetic to anti-realism, but the central idea is hostility to the view that our understanding can outstrip what we are capable of getting evidence about. We must *not* say that understanding a sentence involves grasping that it describes some state of affairs (has the obtaining of that state as its truth condition) when this state of affairs is one whose obtaining or not obtaining is, we acknowledge, something upon which we can get no epistemic handle.

Where we go (or suppose Wittgenstein to have gone), having got this starting point, is far from clear. Are there some base statements, which are 'decidable' and can quite unproblematically be allowed to have truth conditions, using which we can give some systematic assertibility conditions theory of meaning? Did Wittgenstein favour such a thing? Or did he (mistakenly) get his anti-realism mixed up in an abandonment of the sense/force distinction and so lose the chance of a systematic theory he should have pursued? (This last is Dummett's view.)[7] Does the idea of a base class require that its members be indefeasible? If so then perhaps there are no such statements. Did Wittgenstein recognize this and so move on from anti-realism to some form of idealism, to the view that our thinking it makes it so? (This is a possibility Wright canvasses, although he is by no means totally hostile to the base class idea.)[8]

All these exceedingly difficult questions are, fortunately, ones with which we need not concern ourselves. We need only ask what the connection is between the core anti-realist thought outlined above and the hostility to mirroring realism sketched in section 7.1, and elaborated in section 8.1. Is the former a corollary or natural ally of the latter? Are they independent? Or are they (as I shall try to show) opposed? My suggestion will be that we have got Wittgenstein seriously wrong if we see 'anti-realism' as any central strand in his thought. His concerns are, it seems to me, quite other. And the rejection of mirroring realism, far from entailing anti-realism, provides a perspective from which the fundamental anti-realist arguments are seen to be unpersuasive. To see Wittgenstein as an anti-realist is to see him as, at some level, in sympathy with empiricism, whereas, if section 7.1 is right, he invites us to make a radical break with that way of approaching things.

Before we embark on the discussion let us be quite clear that the issue now to be considered is quite different from that of the defensibility of what I have called 'minimal realism'. That position insists upon the lack of a guaranteed move from what we think to be the case to how things are. But the 'realism' we are now considering consists in the denial of a guaranteed move from how things are to be the possibility of our knowing that they are so. Both views insist upon separation of the ontological from the epistemological or psychological. (This is perhaps the hallmark of any 'realism'.) But the epistemological end is different in the two cases. In one it is thinking or being convinced that so and so, in the other it is possibly knowing that so and so. And the direction of dependence denied in the two positions is different. It may be that the two forms of realism are importantly connected. But to show this would require a radically different set of arguments from any considered in detail here. For the rest of this section 'realism' and 'anti-realism' will be used in the Dummettian senses unless there is specific indication to the contrary.

The anti-realist position is supported by a variety of arguments. As elegantly assembled by Wright in a recent discussion, there are at least three main strands: considerations having to do with acquisition, with manifestation and with normativity.[9] The first line of thought presses the question 'How is a person supposed to arrive at a conception of a verification transcendent or unevidenced state of affairs when (obviously) all he or she actually experiences are detectable or evidenced states?' The second poses the challenge of making intelligible how one person could know, or even reasonably conjecture, of another that he or she associated verification transcendent truth conditions with some sentence of the language. The claim of the manifestation argument is that we cannot give any defensible account of this. And consequently, even if the acquisition problem can be dealt with, the manifestation considerations show that such grasp of verification transcendent truth conditions could not be invoked as a central element in any account of the workings of a public language. The normativity argument claims that meaning is normative, in that grasp of it involves grasping a set of constraints to which use can intelligibly be designed to conform and, it adds, grasp of supposed verification transcendent truth conditions could provide no such constraints. In all of these, but most particularly in the second and third, we are supposed to find some distinctively Wittgensteinian elements – emphasis on publicity and on a link between meaning and use. And it is here that we are supposed to see Wittgenstein as probing deeper than traditional empiricists, although arriving at conclusions which would not be uncongenial to them and on the basis of arguments not totally different. One slogan in which these thoughts are presented is 'understanding is a practical ability'. Wright formulates matters this way and takes it be roughly equivalent to the Dummettian 'meaning cannot transcend use'. Both slogans clearly have some Wittgensteinian resonances.

How should we respond to the three arguments? I would suggest that they are not equally powerful. If the manifestation challenge could be met then the acquisition problem, although it might still demand treatment, would hardly be enough on its own to undermine claims to a 'realist' understanding. The normativity argument also seems less than compelling and I shall discuss briefly why this is so.

Wright starts this argument by making some plausible claims about intention – namely that the notion gets no grip where the agent knows that he or she can have no rational beliefs about how to achieve the supposed end or about whether it has been attained or not.[10] Let us agree that these things are so. What then follows about verification transcendent sentences which are admitted to be such? All that follows is that a rational agent will not intend to assert one. Wright takes this to be in tension with the idea that meaning is normative and places some constraint on correct use. But this dictum can be taken in two ways. Uncontentiously it claims (among other things) that if S means that p then an assertion of S will be correct if and only if p. This truistic conditional connection (If I were to assert S then it would be true iff . . .) is not unsettled by the discovery that rationally I have no way of finding out whether S and of so putting myself in a position to assert it. We have a tension only if we take the dictum about normativity in a stronger sense and tie it in with views about understanding being a practical ability – namely as saying that grasp of the meaning of a sentence must involve grasp of an intelligible project of asserting that sentence. But why should we say this? To deny it is not to deny that understanding is practical in the sense of having some actions in which it can manifest itself; there are plenty of things that I can do in virtue of my understanding of a verification transcendent sentence – e.g. lament that we will never be in a position to assert it, judge that another foolishly has asserted it, employ it in hypothetical reasoning, and so forth.

If I am right in saying that the acquisition and normativity arguments are, for various reasons, marginal then it appears that the manifestation argument is the central one. The challenge is to set out some account of what it could be to grasp verification transcendent truth conditions, given that we accept that grasp cannot transcend use and must be a practical capacity manifestable in action. Let us suppose that someone has no grasp of verification transcendent truth conditions for a sentence but has instead grasp of some suitable and complex set of rules for varying responses to detectable conditions. If the set of rules has been properly chosen it seems that there could be no difference between what this person does and what someone with the verification transcendent grasp does; each reacts the same way to all the detectable differences in the world. So, practically speaking, they do just the same things. And if meaning cannot transcend use, must not the use, and so the meaning, be the same?

The first move to make in questioning this persuasive line of thought is to ask how we should understand 'meaning cannot transcend use' or 'understanding is a practical ability', if we regard them as summarizing some Wittgensteinian line of thought. There are two ways in which the idea can be interpreted, only one of which points in the anti-realist direction.

There is a way of hearing the slogans in which they express something which need not be controversial and may seem unexciting. Suppose someone understands that a sentence S means that p. Then he or she will, *ipso facto*, have the ability to use S to assert that p and to use suitable relations of S to ask whether p, express the speculation that p, claim that if p then q, and so forth. Moreover someone who has these abilities to assert that p, ask whether p etc. by S and its relations understands that S means that p. 'Understanding' is an ability word; there is no gap between possession of the ability to do the actions described and understanding the sentence. Pointing out this linkage – although it indicates something which may seem obvious to us now – is by no means useless. What it stands opposed to is the idea that understanding is something (like a categorial base) from which an ability flows, something which explains or underlies the ability. The point now being stressed is that understanding is not something of this character, but the ability itself.

I do not want to suggest that these last remarks are entirely clear. What it is to 'explain' an ability, and how we are to conceive of abilities are important questions. But it is surely plausible to suppose that the line of thought opened up here does not necessarily tend in the direction the anti-realist wants. We are invited to ask why we have ability concepts, whether they are different from dispositional ones, how abilities might relate to categorical bases and the like. It is not obvious that all plausible answers to these questions constrain us to views about limitations on the intentional content that an item, whether it be an ability, like understanding, or an act, like speaking, can be said to have. In particular it is far from clear that verification transcendent truth conditions will have to be expelled from among the admissible intentional contents. My suggestion would be that this unflamboyant interpretation is the correct reading of Wittgenstein. Philosophically exciting consequences follow, in virtue of further links the slogan may have to the themes pursued in section 7.1 and in the first section of this chapter – namely to ideas about the failure of mirroring realism and the interdependence of concepts and interests. But it has yet to be shown that any of these move in an anti-realist direction.

This interpretation, however, will not do for the anti-realist. He wishes to get more mileage out of the idea of 'use' or 'practical ability' than is here allowed for. Let us consider the passage in which Wright poses the difficulty.

> The argument is directly that the realist misdescribes what understanding a statement of the relevant sort consist in, or better that he *overdescribes* it, finding it to involve more than there is any warrant to suppose . . . According to the realist, understanding a statement of one of the relevant kinds consists in knowing that a certain sort of potentially evidence transcendent state of affairs both suffices and is necessary for its truth. How can that account be viewed as a description of any *practical* ability of use? No doubt some one who understands such a statement can be expected to have many relevant practical abilities. He will be able to appraise evidence for or against it, should any be available or to recognize that no information in his possession bears on it. He will be able to recognize at least some of its logical consequences and to identify beliefs from which commitment to it would follow. And he will, presumably, show himself sensitive to conditions under which it is appropriate to ascribe propositional attitudes embedding the statement to himself and others . . . But the headings under which his practical abilities fall so far make no mention of grasp of evidence transcendent truth conditions. Is it the realist's view that such mention is somehow there implicitly? If so, let the implication be brought out.[11]

The challenge is to set out the *practical* ability involved in understanding some S to mean that p, with imagined evidence transcendent p. But the thrust of the earlier remarks is that we answer that challenge by citing exactly the same things as we would for non-evidence transcendent content. We say, that is, that understanding that S means that p is to have the ability to remark on others' assertions that p, debate on what would follow if p, and so forth. Why are these not enough? Are these not practical efforts we have described? They are intentional activities, carried out purposely under certain descriptions. Is this not enough to make them 'practical'? From Wright's point of view, something vital has clearly been left out: 'the headings under which his practical abilities fall so far involve no mention of grasp of evidence transcendent truth conditions', he says. But they do, says the realist. Whether or not the proposition that p is evidence transcendent, exercising the practical ability to recognize its expression by others, reason with it, etc. must involve grasp of the proposition that p – i.e. of the evidence transcendent state of affairs, if that is what the proposition specifies.

Clearly the ships are passing each other in the night here. What is the worry which the realist's apparently bland rejoinder ignores? Note the recurrence in Wright's exposition of evidential notions; one who understands is 'able to appraise evidence' and 'sensitive to conditions under which it is appropriate to ascribe propositional attitudes'. What this strongly suggests is that, for Wright, something counts as a 'practical' ability only if it issues in actions which are done under descriptions showing them to be responses to, or productive of, observable aspects of the world. Wright's 'practical' is not just 'intentional' or 'purposive' but something closer to 'makes a detectable difference'. Wright's worry is how one could justifiably get from a description of what is done which calls only upon responses to and changes in detectable states of affairs to another description which involves imputing grasp of what it would be for a state of affairs to obtain undetectably. But the realist does not accept this starting point. For him, the practical activities are *from the start* recognized and described in terms which impute such grasp.

How should we respond to this dispute? Before considering this question, I shall pause to say something about Wittgenstein's use of the term 'criterion'. The matter is relevant because it is clear that Wittgenstein's linkage of meaning with use is importantly bound up with his taking 'use' to be the criterion of meaning. His remarks to this effect form some of the evidence for an anti-realist interpretation. But is there any clear indication in the way Wittgenstein uses the 'criterion' idea that such a reading is correct? I shall suggest that there is not.

Let us look at the uses of 'criterion' in the text of the *Philosophical Investigations*. We may first extract all those cases where he speaks of use (or application or the like) as the criterion of meaning, since they are the ones whose interpretation is under scrutiny. We may also set aside cases where he asks what the criteria for such and such are (without supplying an answer) or remarks that the criteria are more difficult to fix than one would imagine or the like. We are left with a handful of cases in which he gives examples of criteria not directly concerned with meaning. I quote them here:

344 Our criterion for someone's saying something to himself is what he tells us and the rest of his behaviour.

377 What is the criterion for the sameness of two images? . . . For me, when it is someone else's image: what he says and does.

542 'But the point is, they felt to him like the words of a language he knew well.' – Yes: a criterion for that is that he later said just that.

625 'How do you know that you have raised your arm?' – 'I feel it'. So what you recognize is the feeling? And are you certain that you recognize it right? – You are certain that you have raised your arm: isn't this the criterion, the measure, of the recognition?

633 'You were interrupted a while ago; do you still know what you were going to say?' – If I do know now, and say it – does that mean that I had already thought it before, only not said it? No. Unless you take the certainty with which I continue the interrupted sentence as a criterion of the thought's already having been completed at that time.

What does it mean for me to look at a drawing in descriptive geometry and say: 'I know that the line appears again here, but I can't *see* it like that'? Does it simply mean a lack of familiarity with operating with the drawing; that I don't 'know my way about' too well? – This familiarity is certainly one of our criteria. What tells us that someone is seeing the drawing three-dimensionally is a certain kind of 'knowing one's way about'. Certain gestures, for instance, which indicate the three-dimensional relations: fine shades of behaviour. (Part II, p. 203.)

Let us assume there was a man who always guessed right what I was saying to myself in my thoughts . . . But what is the criterion for his guessing *right*? Well, I am a truthful person and I confess that he has guessed right. (Part II, p. 222.)

One thing which is striking about all of these is that there is not a single one of them in which the item cited as a criterion is a mere piece of behaviour; all of the criteria are actions, what people say or do, or (in two cases) their being certain. So a behaviourist view of Wittgenstein, with 'behaviour' somehow neutral between bodily movement and action, receives no support at all.

But what is really important, for our current purposes, is that none of the items cited as a criterion has a clearly less problematic or less complex intentional content (from the anti-realist point of view) than the item for which it is said to be a criterion. In all cases, the criterion is a contentful item whose content is the same as, or at least out of the same conceptual basket as, the content of the item for which it is criterial. Thus the criterion for the mind-reader's getting my thoughts right is that I say that he did so; the criterion for seeing a drawing in a certain way is that I make gestures which indicate three-dimensional relations.

If we transfer the structure of these models to the meaning and use case we will have the thought that the criterion for someone meaning that p by some sentence is that he (for example) uses it to say that p. In other words we have a version of the (from Wright's point of view) bland meaning/use link and a correspondingly non-committal sense of 'practical'.

What this interpretation will seem to leave completely opaque is what epistemological use 'criteria' can have. Criteria are things by which we judge of other things. Whatever kind of items they are taken to be, and whatever account we give of knowledge, this seems to be clear. They must therefore be epistemologically available when the things for which they are criteria are not. This is the thought which pushes one in the direction of giving prominence to the detectable and provokes suspicion of the evidence transcendent. But what is involved in being 'epistemologically available'? As with the question about 'practical ability' we can either give this question an unexciting seeming answer or offer something more controversial.

On the unexciting front we may note that some things are not (directly) available epistemologically because they belong to the wrong category of item to be observed. Dispositions and abilities fit this description. Having them is a 'state' in some broad sense, but not a state being in which involves the exhibition of some observable appearance. They can thus be epistemologically accessed only via some exercise or realization, which will take the form of an occurrence or episode. Such occurrences or episodes are of the right category to be observed. But nothing we have said so far requires that the occurrences or episodes be describable in terms of concepts independent of that of the state for which they are criteria.[12]

The anti-realist would like to suppose that Wittgenstein goes beyond this 'grammatical' style of remark. The idea would be that what is observed should be available to inspection. And in terms of his notion of what sort of things could be available for inspection some characterizations of events (e.g. those which invoke the notion of the disposition of ability it manifests) will seem question-begging. But worries of this kind, for example about how I could possibly *tell* that a certain gesture indicates a three-dimensional relationship perceived in a flat picture, do not seem to pre-occupy Wittgenstein at all. We have, then, no evidence that he thinks of the epistemological availability of criteria in anything other than the first and extremely non-committal sense.

The upshot of the reflections of the past few pages is that, as far as interpretation of Wittgenstein is concerned, it is far from clear that we can pin anti-realist thoughts on him. But of course this leaves the plausibility of the anti-realist position on its own grounds unexamined. And it is to some brief remarks on this that I now turn.

Let us go back to the thought that understanding is possession of a practical ability and to the centrality of the manifestation challenge. The realist thinks that one finds out whether someone understands S to mean that p (where it may be verification transcendent whether p) by seeing what actions he does with the sentence S. If he uses it to speculate whether p, express the view that someone else would like it to be the case that p and so forth, then we have the relevant evidence to say that he does so understand it. The anti-realist objects that one cannot just observe that someone expresses the speculation whether p and so on, where it is evidence transcendent whether p. All one can do is see that S is used in so and so detectable circumstances.[13]

Could the undermining of mirroring realism provide any support for the realist? One might argue that the idea of what one can 'observe', what can be 'manifested', to a person is crucially unclear. What is observable to a given person will depend upon the conceptual apparatus which that person brings to the business of observation. The beauty of the music or the brilliance of a chess move might be apparent to the expert but unobservable by the beginner. So, one might say, why should not grip of verification transcendent truth conditions be apparent in someone's use of language, when the interpreter is himself or herself equipped with the relevant 'realist' concepts?[14] Is this not the nub of the anti-mirroring view – that the thinker's nature and equipment contribute vitally to the content of any thought arising from a given confrontation?

Put thus baldly, however, the thought will not move the anti-realist at all. From his point of view the important thing is that *we all agree* that the sentence whose meaning is in question is such that no evidence bears on its truth or falsity; we *agree* that it has verification transcendent truth conditions (if that is the right way of speaking at all). How, then, can all these remarks about different things being verifiable or observable by different people provide any grip on what ability someone has in virtue of understanding a problematic sentence – a sentence which is on all hands admitted to be unfitted for the expression of the outcome of some verification process? Surely, the anti-realist will urge, anything that a person does with such a sentence could be explained without postulating grasp of verification transcendent truth conditions, namely by saying that its user has grasped some (complex) set of rules for its use under evidenced conditions. To suppose that there is something else going on is to move unwarrantably beyond what we can properly defend on the data available, because (to stress the truistic) it must be admitted by everyone that, as far as the circumstances of utterance are concerned, we can only detect what is detectable; and so, it seems, all we know about the utterance is that it occurs in such and such detectable circumstances. Thus it may seem that the rejection of mirroring realism – read just as the idea that approaching the same situation with different concepts will yield different judgements – is quite powerless to ward off the manifestation challenge.[15]

But this underestimates the disruptive potential of the rejection of mirroring realism, while at the same time slightly misrepresenting its central theme. In the current context its importance lies not just in the thought that what you see in a situation depends upon the conceptual equipment you bring to it. The importance is rather this: Once we have rejected mirroring realism then we have nothing pushing us in the direction of empiricism, no reason to be attracted to the idea that we have concepts only of things which can reveal themselves to us or impress themselves upon us. In consequence we need have no predisposition to sympathy with the root idea of anti-realism, namely that there must be epistemic constraints on ideas of meaning and truth. The acquisition challenge entirely loses its force. We do not get our concepts from anywhere, in the sense of extracting them from, or having them supplied by, presented instances. There is thus no difficulty in principle (mirroring view and attendant empiricism having been jettisoned) in supposing that we have concepts of which we see that we can never apply them categorically in rational assertive judgements.[16] Possession of such concepts is a matter of having the interests and living the life in which they have their role. And now we see that the manifestation challenge loses its force as well. Knowing that someone, oneself or another, has such concepts is a matter of knowing that the person has the relevant interests and lives the relevant life. And why should this be supposed insuperably difficult?

The anti-realist may not be much impressed by this last rhetorical question. He will demand to know what it could possibly be about how people talk and act which, if someone know of it, would show him that the subject grasped evidence transcendent truth conditions. He will reiterate that all that is there to be seen are responses to detectable conditions, responses which could be explained more economically by grasp of assertibility conditions.

What he shows by this protest is that he takes it as obvious that claims about meaning, if epistemologically respectable, must be based on, explicable as rationally derived from, data about uninterpreted utterances observed when occurring as responses to observable circumstances. If one were a mirroring realist (particularly of an empiricist kind) this view about how judgements of meaning are to be established would be natural, indeed perhaps mandatory. On that view one supposes that all our notions are derived from situations in which the relevant properties or relations are instantiated and impress themselves, directly or indirectly, upon us. Meaning is such a notion and is a matter of some kind of correspondence-style relation between labels and features of the world. So how could one establish that it obtained except by observing both relata in the required configuration? At the thinker's end of the relation all one can establish is that an assertively intended response occurs. The burden of determining the content of the response falls entirely onto the world.[17]

But if this whole 'trying to label the independently given facts' picture of meaning is the wrong one then the conception of evidence about meaning to which it gives rise will be the wrong one too. My suggestion is that it is implicit attachment to this picture which provides much of the motive force for anti-realism. Once we have got free of the temptations of this picture, we see that nothing has yet been found in the rival non-mirroring account of what it is to have a concept (including the account of what it might be to have the concept of meaning) to give us any reason to suppose that there is some special difficulty in crediting people with grasp of verification transcendent truth conditions.

Let me admit at once that the above considerations are entirely negative. They have been aimed at undermining a possible source of support for anti-realism and not at establishing a positive case for realism. The anti-realist is still perfectly entitled to ask for an account of a form of life in which the notion of the verification transcendent plays an important part, and no such account has been supplied. My own hunch is that there are two ideas which are fundamental to our way of looking at things which do indeed give Dummettian realism an important place in our view of the world. These are, first, the idea of the world as separate from us and, second, the idea of the dependence of our awareness of any item in it upon the, only contingently related, existence of other things of the same kind. (For example my awareness of the tree over there is dependent upon the existence of light rays and the non-existence of intervening objects. My awareness of the existence of Napoleon is dependent on the existence of certain pieces of paper with ink on them, etc.) It is difficult to see how these two ideas could be prevented from combining to deliver the idea of the undetectable event, undetectable because of the non-existence of the requisite links between it and us. It may be that in this area there is an argument from the 'separateness' of the world invoked in minimal realism to the claims of Dummettian realism. But I shall not pursue these difficult issues here.[18]

There is however one extreme version of Dummett-style realism which a Wittgensteinian will certainly oppose. This is the idea (called by Putnam 'metaphysical realism') that *if* we had got a complete and, from inside, perfect world view, which satisfied all demands on world views (experimental adequacy, elegance, simplicity etc.) *then* it would nevertheless be intelligible to suppose that it was false.[19] The problem with this 'realist' thought is not that, on reflection, we see that there can be no sense in the idea that such a perfect theory was false. If that were so then we might, at this limit, have to abandon even our minimal realism and admit the coincidence of the ontological fact of what is and the epistemological fact of the perfection of the theory. The problem with the idea is however much simpler; it is that we can make no real sense of the antecedent. The idea of a theory which meets and could be known to meet all possible demands presupposes the idea of a totality of demands on a theory – both of kinds of demand and of members of each kind. But it is entirely mysterious how one could give substance to any such notion.

9

Interests, Activities and Meanings

9.1 PROOF AND NEW CONCEPTS

In the earlier part of this chapter I shall make some suggestions about Wittgenstein's views on the philosophy of mathematics. The point is not to provide a full account of these matters – which would require a much more extended treatment – but to give a little more substance to the schematic ideas about concepts, interests and their interdependence and thus to put us in a better position to appreciate Wittgenstein's views about necessity, possibility and 'other forms of life'. This in turn will stand us in good stead when we return, in the final section, to the question of realism about meaning.

Let us start by considering one of the puzzling things that Wittgenstein says in the *Remarks on the Foundations of Mathematics* (hereafter RFM), namely that a proof creates new concepts.[1] This is a thought to which he returns throughout the period 1937–44 spanned by the writings in RFM and so seems to represent something important for him.[2] He also uses the notions of decision and invention in this context, speaking of the mathematician as an inventor and introducing the idea of the discovery of a proof as winning through to a decision. Another well-known strand in his thought on mathematics is hostility to Platonism – the idea that in doing mathematics we are doing a sort of natural science where, using some special faculty, we peer into a crystalline realm of abstract objects forever fixed in necessary relations to each other.

The conjunction of this anti-Platonism with the talk of new concepts and decisions has led many commentators, very naturally, to the idea that Wittgenstein is some kind of conventionalist, probably a radical conventionalist, about necessary truth.[3]

The direct textual evidence for this is far from conclusive. If we consider the way Wittgenstein wishes to invoke the decision idea, we find that his wording is, predominantly, oblique and suggestive rather than directly assertive. For example 'It would *almost be more correct* to say, not that an intuition was needed at every stage, but that a new decision was needed at every stage.'[4] Or '*Why should I not say*: in the proof I have won through to a decision' (my italics)[5] So he does not say, baldly and *in propria persona* that all or even some judgements are made at will or are the outcome of decisions. Rather he invites us to play with the notion, misleading though he implies it is, as an antidote to some other even more unfortunate picture of the matter. It is important also to remember and set against these passages other remarks where he is speaking baldly and *in propria persona* and where he links the idea of compulsion and rule-following, e.g. 'If a rule does not compel you then you aren't following a rule', or 'When I say "I decide spontaneously" naturally that does not mean I consider which number would really be the best one here and then plump for . . . '[6] This latter remark shows clearly that it cannot be decision in any ordinary sense, a decision where one is aware of alternatives, that he has in mind.

Let us note also that conventionalism can be seen either as an empiricist response to the epistemological and metaphysical problems of necessity or (and as I suggested in section 6.4 more defensibly) as a component of a thoroughgoing pragmatism. But I have tried earlier to suggest that Wittgenstein is neither an empiricist nor a pragmatist. And if these earlier interpretive moves were in the right direction then we have further reason not to take the talk of 'decision' in a direct conventionalist way.

What then is going on with these invocations of decision? Clearly it is in line with our earlier proposed reading to see them as expressions of hostility to mirroring realism. Wittgenstein is, in them, emphasizing the element of activity (spontaneity, practice, form of life) in concept-use. Thus taken they fit in well with the line of thought sketched in section 7.1. Passages where Wittgenstein talks of the limits of empiricism and of the difficulty of combining empiricism and realism also make good sense in this light.[7]

But if conventionalism is not what Wittgenstein is after, what are we to make of his hostility to Platonism and of his talk linking proof and change of concept? On one reading, that favoured by Crispin Wright, the hostility to Platonism is an implication of a general scepticism about the notion of meaning. On this view the rule-following discussion (together, perhaps, with other considerations of the kind mentioned in section 7.2) gives us a picture in which we see that there could be no such thing as the fact that a person meant one thing rather than another at a given time. So, in particular, it makes no sense to suppose that there is such a thing as 'grasp of a concept' which could commit one to recognizing necessary or conceptual truths about a certain subject matter.

But from the point of view I propose this is not at all an attractive line of interpretation. My theme is that Wittgenstein's rejection of the general mirroring realist outlook allows us to defend a (more sensible and minimal) version of realism about meaning. It is a welcome fact, then, that the meaning-sceptical reading is (as Wright notes) in serious tension with the other element mentioned above – namely the idea of proof as modifying concepts.[8] If all talk of determinate meaning is illegitimate how can we make sense of the idea of change of meaning? On the view of Wittgenstein which sees him as a radical sceptic about meaning he is not entitled to the idea that there is anything to be changed.

So let us look afresh at anti-Platonism and at the idea that proof modifies concepts, starting with the latter. There is, of course, something paradoxical about it, however we read it. It seems to deny that we can understand some mathematical conjecture perfectly well, look for a proof of it, find one and thus prove exactly that statement which we set out to prove. If the proof changes the concepts – i.e. the meanings of the words in which we express the object of our interest – then we have not proved what we set out to but some other statement instead. The paradox is made particularly acute – indeed so acute as to be intolerable – if we suppose not only that proof of a sentence alters its meaning but also that the meaning it had before the proof was found remains available to be expressed by some other sentence. For now it looks as if any attempted proof of a statement was bound to miss its mark. We are going to prove a proposition different from the one which we set out to prove, even if, at the end of the proof, we express it by the same words as we used to express our original proposition. And the originally questioned proposition remains unproven but still available to be wondered about. This story leaves it totally mysterious how the proof is supposed to shift the meaning of the sentence – given that we can still entertain the original conjecture. How could the proof force us to abandon this meaning? And should we not have rejected as invalid any step of the proof which tempted us to alter our understanding of some word or construction?[9]

The paradox however does not become intolerably acute unless we make this extra assumption – and we need not make it. Our 'concept' of something may be altered, colloquially speaking, when we learn something new about that thing. And our earlier concept of the item, i.e. our body of information about it, no longer exists as the same total body, because it has been superseded by the new body. For Platonism, a mathematical investigation tells us more about the properties of numbers, shapes and so forth, and so, in the colloquial sense it modifies our concepts. If we have a view of concepts which is bound up with some sharp distinction between a priori and a posteriori truths then acquisition of empirical information about something will not count as 'modifying the concept'. But even on this second and restricted sense the Platonist can still make some sense of the concept-modification idea because the truths revealed by proofs do precisely alter, by addition, our range of a priori knowledge and the set of conditions recognized as necessary or sufficient for the application of a given word. So the Platonist might admit that mathematical formulae do 'mean something different' to me before and after the proof: my understanding after grasping the proof is deeper and richer; I have seen more into the nature of things; I have unfolded what was implicit in my previously grasped concept. It would not, of course, be congenial to the Platonist to say that the concept, regarded as the abstract focus of my somewhat confused thoughts, has changed. But my concept, in the sense of important structural features of my intellectual relation with that object, has been altered. Wright is struck by the appearance of incongruity in the idea that action in conformity with or dictated by a concept – e.g. following a proof employing it – should at the same time change the concept.[10] But the Platonist conception of 'unfolding' what was implicit is admirably designed to allow us to remove the appearance.

This interpretation is, of course, not available as a reading of Wittgenstein. He is hostile to the ideas of 'unfolding' and 'the implicit' which it employs. So how can we improve matters?

9.2   CONCEPTUAL CHANGE AND DETERMINACY OF SENSE

We have just considered two models of conceptual change – the absurdity generating one, where the original concept remained to be used, and the Platonist one. We are now in search of a third, which might provide some insight into Wittgenstein's views. I shall first consider a tempting interpretation. It is deeply mistaken but looking at it will provide some useful clues.

Let us start by setting in place an idea (which we shall later abandon as thoroughly unWittgensteinian), namely that of the fixed totality of metaphysical possibilities. As we have seen before (in section 6.4) this idea is very naturally found as an element in the mirroring conception of the world. On one view about thought (a view found in Frege and also in the early Wittgenstein) any respectable thought must be fully determinate. That is to say that, for any possible way the world might be, it must be the case that the thought would be true if things were that way or false if they were. In grasping a meaning, on this conception, we embody a function from possible ways the world might be to truth values. There is on this outlook only one conceptual scheme – the one which recognizes those features the presence or absence of which differentiates and defines the various possibilities. But we do not have to suppose that we now mark all those features explicitly with separate words in our language. The concepts associated with our words may represent complexes of simpler elements. Given this view, there is plenty of room for Platonistic unpacking of what is implicit, but no room for conceptual change of an any more radical kind.

However, one comparatively small modification of this story will give us an account in which a notion of conceptual change makes sense. Suppose we leave the set of metaphysical possibilities in place but abandon the demand that possession of an intelligible thought must involve ability to classify every possible way the world might be under one or other of the headings 'situation in which the thought is true' and 'situation in which the thought is false'. Would-be thinkers are allowed to be doing something respect-worthy as long as they are equipped to respond to a fair range of situations of the kinds they are normally confronted with, even if in other situations they would have to admit that they did not know whether their thought was true or false. Here we can allow for conceptual change because we can allow different thinkers, or the same thinker at different times, to embody different incomplete classificatory dispositions.

Before proceeding further I shall sketch a possible case of conceptual alteration which will give us something more concrete to think about and may help us in developing a view of the mathematical case.[11] Consider someone who has been taught the use of colour vocabulary but only on the basis of seeing objects in sunlight. He is now shown his familiar toy postbox, which he is used to thinking of as red, by the light of a sodium lamp and he is asked what colour it is. There are two ways he might respond. (There are many others as well, but I shall not discuss them, since their presence does not affect the argument.) He might say that the postbox was no longer red but had become white. Or he might say that it was still red but something was making it look funny.

We may reconstruct his puzzlement as arising from the fact that he has been used to applying colour vocabulary in cases where two features coincide. On the one hand we have the view that colour is a stable property of things and hence that how it was in the immediate past (provided it has undergone no causal process which could alter it) is adequate ground for attributing the same colour now. On the other hand we have the view that one can detect colour by looking. What the surprising experience shows is that these ways of ascribing colours can conflict. So we may say that colour ascription was earlier governed by two criteria, each treated as both necessary and sufficient; the speaker was thus not equipped to deal with those possible situations where the criteria diverged.

Faced with such situations, language learners may well be at first nonplussed. But various moves are made to encourage them (as we would describe it with hindsight) to associate the word with one criterion rather than another. And after a while the learners find themselves proceeding in step with the rest of the linguistic community. Given the picture of the total set of metaphysical possibilities, what has happened here is that the learners first had a method of dealing with situations where the two criteria were either both present or both absent but had no response ready for situations where they diverged. The teaching or training at the point of muddlement somehow alters the function their understanding embodies so that they are subsequently equipped to deal with a wider range of possibilities.

It is a corollary of the way we have described the matter so far that the training which resolves the muddle is not a matter of getting the child to think, in the sense of forming and testing hypotheses, in terms of concepts he already has.[12] *Ex hypothesi* he does not have the concepts to cope with the new situation and we have to supply him with them by some appropriate non-cognitive procedure. If this conclusion is found too offensive we can devise a hybrid scheme which combines elements of the original 'total determinacy of sense' model with our new 'partial function' model by speaking of *tacit* as opposed to *explicit* knowledge. On this hybrid view, we say that the child did have separate concepts of each of the two criteria but had also an inexplicit and deeply rooted theoretical commitment to their co-occurrence, so that the two concepts were not differently marked at the surface of the language. (The differences between the views may appear merely verbal. This outlook finds it natural to think of a concept as a disposition to produce a classificatory response. The dispute is them only about what kind of disposition is required – e.g. whether a second-level disposition to acquire a disposition is enough.)

It is worth noting that the sort of 'conceptual change' and 'conceptual difference' that we are trying to get a grip on in these models is not that which is sometimes discussed when the question of the possibility of different conceptual schemes is raised. The possibility canvassed in these other discussions is that of a kind of thinking which is so different from ours that no mutual understanding at all is to be hoped for. Various general arguments have been proposed (e.g. by Davidson), the thrust of which is that this is a seriously defective notion; attempts to defend relativism by its use need not, it is said, worry us.[13] On this line of thought, if we can make something of another creature's thoughts and offer defensible translations then that creature is operating with our conceptual scheme.

On the view of what it is to have different concepts which we are now exploring, this last mentioned connection does not hold. We can make something of the children's thoughts and translate their utterances. But the difference in their way of looking at things, the distinctness of their conceptual scheme from ours, comes out, we imagine, in the fact that none of these translations is entirely satisfactory.

Underlying this contrast is a methodological difference. Our sense that none of the translations is entirely satisfactory is bound up with the fact that we are prepared to recognize a greater variety of responses to circumstances than just whether those circumstances provoke assent or dissent to a sentence. We build in, for example, the idea that a circumstance might provoke an impulse both to assent and to dissent or, relatedly, that it might provoke a particular kind of surprise. The surprise is not just that of discovering that something one took to be the case is not the case but is more akin to bewilderment or just not knowing what to say. If we flatten out all this variety of response to mere assent or dissent we shall indeed end up with only two options – namely that those we seek to understand either have our conceptual scheme or have none (that we can make sense of at least).[14]

Let us return to the main line of thought and try the experiment of viewing Wittgenstein's claims about proof and new concepts in mathematics in the context of our above model of conceptual change.

The idea will be that at certain points in learning to use mathematical vocabulary a person may find himself or herself in a position where two criteria for the application of some description conflict; he will be confused and bewildered. The job of the 'proof' is to remove his uncertainty as to how to proceed by encouraging the association of the word with one of the criteria rather than the other.

Here is an example on which to try out this highly abstract schema. Suppose that I have learnt to use the numbers up to '20' by being taught how to count the members of groups of apples, beans etc., and to answer questions of the form 'How many so and sos are there here?' Sometimes I count two groups and then put them together and count the resulting larger group. When I put together groups of seven and four I usually get a group of eleven. Then one day a disconcerting thing happens. I count a group resulting from the putting together of groups of seven and four and the result is not eleven but twelve. What am I to say? Perhaps I say 'Here's a strange thing; seven and four do not make eleven in this case. I wonder if that happens very often?' This remark is not well received and I am told 'Nonsense! You must have miscounted.' And, perhaps by exhibition of this picture

$$\{ \text{III} \} \quad \{ \text{III} \} \quad \text{I} / \quad \{ \text{III} \} \quad / / \quad \text{I}$$

I am led to exclaim 'Oh I see. It must be eleven.'

Something has changed in me. But what? If I assume that I now mean exactly the same by '7', '4' etc. as I did before then I must have discovered something expressible in terms of those concepts. But I have not discovered empirically that, by and large, seven and four make eleven. So (it seems) I must have unearthed something that was all along implicit in my concepts – a relation that necessarily and antecedently held between the essences of seven, four and eleven.

But surely (says the old Platonist Adam in all of us) this is the right response! How could seven and four *not* equal eleven? What are the 'two criteria' which previously governed application of the numerals? Why should we not suppose that there is only one, the one we all understand, grasp of which remains constant?

Let us go back to the slightly easier case of colours to give ourselves a model to work from. Suppose that I have applied colour terms to something up to now on the basis of a good look at it in ordinary daylight. But I am already aware, let us suppose, of the possibility of making mistakes; I know that people can be inattentive and not look carefully enough; I know also that illness may lead them to perceive abnormally. So in reporting on the colour of a thing I am reporting on a public feature of the world. (I emphasize this in order to make clear that the question at issue here is not that of whether colour is only a feature of private experience. The issue concerns the possibility of different ways of thinking of something like colour, given already that what we think of is a feature of the world, accessible to other perceivers.) It is a corollary of this that what counts as a 'good look' cannot be something fully definable by reference to how things seem to me, what procedures I seem to myself to have carried out, etc. If I admit, as in the imagined state I do, that features of the world inter-relate in many complicated and as yet unknown ways (e.g. that I may suffer delusions from as yet unknown causes) then whether I have had a good enough look to pronounce definitively on the colour of something will only be as certain as whether I can rightly discount all sources of error.

Now for the first time I encounter a red object under sodium lighting and I have a problem. On the one hand my usual way of applying the 'good look' procedure yields one result – the post box is white. On the other hand I have, up to now, met with changes in the colours of things only when they were produced by fairly drastic or prolonged procedures (painting, boiling or ripening); colour has been a stable feature of objects. This current experience involves colour change (if that is what it is) of a very different sort from any I have previously encountered.

There are two ways of proceeding. One is to insist that the colour has not changed and to search for something to add to the list of possible confusing circumstances. The other is to leave the 'good look' conditions in practice much as before and to allow that the object has inexplicably changed colour.

Whichever of these courses I take I can still say 'One tells what colour a thing is by having a good look at it'. In that sense the 'criterion' for what colour a thing is has not changed. And neither the way that I would go about teaching colour words to someone else nor my judgements about earlier cases need be affected. These points are worth remarking on because some have seen it as a difficulty for the idea that our concepts get modified (e.g. by a proof) that earlier verbal forms of explanation and teaching by example are not impugned or replaced even after the concept is supposedly modified. The problem some have detected with this is that if a concept is modified then we would expect exactly these things, i.e. examples and forms of explanation, to change as well.[15] But on the view we are now exploring this problem is an illusion since the new concepts are acquired only via development of the old. The methods of initiation remain as before and also the verbal clarifications. The concept-developing procedure is itself a continuation of what was achieved by those methods; and in so far as it alters understanding it does so simultaneously for all the concepts linked together in the verbal statements of criteria.

Both of the two possible courses outlined are (as I have stressed before) moves in the public realm and involve treating colour as a publicly accessible property. But they nevertheless operate on different assumptions about what kind of objective property colour is. To take the first view is to treat colour as a stable and persisting feature of objects but one which may not be as easily detectable as we might like. Colour reveals itself when one can get a good look, but setting up the circumstances for that look may present problems. However, once one has established a colour one can rely on it staying the same in the short term, barring drastic treatment of the object. To take the second view is to treat colour as (comparatively) easily accessible. Taking a good look is something we are almost always in a position to do. But we pay the price in that what we thus detect cannot be guaranteed to persist.

Imagine that someone finds the first view natural. He may express himself in remarks such as these: 'How *can* a thing change from red to white without anything acting upon it?' (Note the appearance of modal terms.) He will find it difficult to hear the remarks of anyone who takes the second view in any other way than as expressing empirical mistakes or nonsense. Let us use 'white (1)' to express the first person's colour concept, and 'white (2)' for the second. Then the second person will say of the postbox in the strange light 'But it is white [meaning white (2)]; I see that it is' The first person will hear this as the false claim that it is white (1). And if the second person remarks that he does not see why colours should not change without cause the first will hear this as an expression of grotesque confusion.

The best we can do in the first vocabulary to suggest the second person's idea to the first is to stress that use of 'looks white (1)' in which it is used to report a public fact about an item, the same sort of fact as that we report about the two lines in the Müller-Lyer illusion when we say that the one looks longer than the other. This explanation will not give exactly the right extension for the second person's use of 'white' and will misrepresent his notion as a compound one, but it might push the 'white (1)' user in the right phenomenological direction.

Suppose then that we do, by this or some other means, give the user of the first conception some inkling of how the other is employing colour terms, how will he respond? His view well may be that, although there is here a consistent policy of application, one which he could himself follow, nevertheless there is no 'real' feature of the world being recognized. Part of what he is saying in expressing this view is that he cannot see how anybody could find it worthwhile to bother with the classification; he himself uses colour as a clue to the ripeness of fruit, the heat of the fire and so forth; the other man's notion, he thinks, has no such useful links; as far as he can see it is hoked up and arbitrary. But perhaps he could be persuaded to change his mind by being encouraged to take up painting or interior decorating. Or perhaps it could turn out that application of the other man's notion does, after all, provide useful clues to ripeness or heat.

Can we find for the mathematical case analogies to the things we have said about colours? Consider again my disconcerting experience with the groups of seven, four and eleven (or twelve). With reflective hindsight what description can we give of my puzzlement? I have mastered the use of number words where the criterion of application is careful counting of the whole group. Counting is what establishes number, just as looking is what establishes colour. But I have also another governing assumption about numbers, which has never yet clashed with the counting criterion, namely that number relations are permanent. Thus if seven and four ever make eleven then they always do. How am I now to respond in the disconcerting case? I could harden this permanence assumption into a rule, insist that there must have been a miscount and look around for an explanation of it.[16] Or I could allow that seven and four might sometimes come to something other than eleven.

We are not here to consider the easy ways out, like supposing that one of the objects has divided into two or another has been added between the countings that yielded seven and four and that which yielded twelve. Let it be agreed on all hands that these things have not happened – just as in the colours case we did not seek to make sense of the strange experience or the divergent responses to it by imagining that the two respondents had different views about whether or not someone had nipped up and painted the post box.

But if I deny the easy way out how can I intelligibly say that I had a groups of seven and four, put them together and got a group of twelve? If I say this do I not just reveal that I cannot have properly understood '7', '4', 'none have been added' and so forth?

It is essential to attend closely to what it is we are being asked to imagine here. Let us as before use '7 (1)', '7 (2)' etc. to express the putatively different numerical concepts manifested by the two different responses. The question is not whether we can make sense of the idea that 7 (1) apples and 4 (1) apples do not make 11 (1) apples. The answer to that question is that we cannot. But then neither can the person who thinks in terms of colour (1) concepts make sense of the idea that something should change its colour (1) without cause. This fact alone does not show that colour (2) concepts are unintelligible or (more importantly) are not a possible development of the colour concepts possessed before the strange experience. So the real question about the mathematical notions is whether there are number (2) concepts which can be regarded as possible extensions of the original, and (it is suggested) not fully developed, number competence.

The best route to grasping 'white (2)' was via the idea 'looks white (1)' – where the latter was understood as a public property about which one may be mistaken. One cannot make sense of something being red (1) and white (1) at the same time, but one can make sense of the idea that something which one knows to be red (1) should nevertheless look white (1). That is just what has happened in the case of the post box in the sodium light. The numerical analogue will be as follows: One cannot make sense of a group which contains exactly the sum of seven and four and yet also contains twelve. But we can make sense of the idea that group which we know to contain the sum of seven and four (from previous counting, together with the fact that nothing has been added etc.) should nevertheless yield a count of twelve. Perhaps it does so again and again. We make marks on the items as we count them to avoid double counting; we pin numbers on them; we cross-check on each other.[17] But they defeat all our attempts to get a sensible count of eleven.

How could this be? Perhaps, as we later discover, this particular group of objects makes the air around it shimmer so that it is difficult to fixate properly; one item always gets counted twice or marks and numbers on objects get overlooked or misread. Or perhaps the group exerts a hypnotic influence on anyone attempting to count it so that he or she always omits the numeral '6'. Or perhaps . . .

What we are searching for in trying to construct such stories is an explanation of why this group *yields a count of twelve*. And this is the property in which the user of number (2) concepts is interested. Those groups which from his point of view go importantly together from our point of view fall into two subgroups – namely those which yield a count of twelve because they contain twelve members and those which yield a count of twelve because they are bewitched, shimmering, hypnotic or what not. We are inclined to say that the user of number (2) concepts is mistaking shadowy and parasitic features of the world for what is really there. We cannot see what point there could be in so grouping items, since all the things we are interested in doing connect up (or at least so far empirically seem to connect up) with how many things there are in the group, specified in number (1) concepts, and not with how many things there seem to be. But we are invited to consider how things might appear to us if we had different interests or if the world were empirically different.

The suggestion about proof, then, is that what it does is provide a stimulus for us to develop the earlier numerical concepts (which have no provision for responding to cases where the two criteria fall apart) in the direction of number (1) concepts rather than number (2) concepts.

9.3　OTHER FORMS OF LIFE?

There is much in the above account which makes it attractive as an interpretation of Wittgenstein. It gives us an account of how 'proofs' can lead to the acquisition of new concepts and it seems to accommodate thoughts about how different empirical circumstances and interests would make possession of different concepts intelligible. But there is nevertheless something fundamentally wrong with it.

Let us remember that we have been proceeding all this time against the background assumption that there exists a given totality of metaphysically given possibilities. We have been speaking of different ways in which an ability to cope with some subset of the possibilities might be extended to bring a larger set within its scope. It is a clear implication of this that the sense of inevitability about a proof – the idea that it shows one what one *had* to say, – is illusion. This is so whether we take the view that concept development is a sort of learning (and use the contrast between explicit and implicit knowledge) or whether we think that conceptual development is merely a sort of non-cognitive training which somehow results in cognitive abilities. Either way there is a real alternative development to the one that actually occurred – even when that development is triggered by a proof. And a clearsighted person is, at least in principle and if he bothers to spend time in working it out, capable of coming to see what the alternative was. The proof has indeed induced him to adopt a certain way of using number terms. But it is clear that there is another way and his following this one rather than that other is a matter of choice and convenience, not of necessity.

All of this might seem to fit well with what Wittgenstein says about proof, especially if we concentrate on those passages which encourage a conventionalist interpretation. But there are serious grounds for doubt whether the whole story we have told does give the Wittgensteinian view. We saw earlier reason to doubt that he was a conventionalist. But even worse is the fact that if one thing is clear about Wittgenstein's views on meaning it is that he is not prepared to work with the idea of a given totality of metaphysical possibilities. The early sections of the *Philosophical Investigations* (where he discusses simplicity and complexity and whether rule systems need to be complete and the like) are not designed to provide materials for rejecting total determinacy of sense in favour of the sort of theory of 'permissible vagueness' which we have been discussing. Rather they provide material for throwing out the whole picture underlying the determinacy of sense view. These passages form part of the discussion of ostensive definition and related topics which, on the interpretation advanced earlier (in section 6.1) are in turn part of the rule-following considerations, the upshot of which is the rejection of mirroring realism. But the 'given totality of possibilities' we have been considering is precisely that defined by the combinations of the supposed 'real' properties. And if the conception of such real properties is an illusion then so too is the conception of the given totality which they contribute to defining.

One way of seeing the incongruity of the picture of Wittgenstein we have been trying to build up is to consider the following. As long as the 'total set of possibilities' is in place we may make room for 'proof' as a tool of some conventionalist type of choice for sharpening up not fully determinate notions. But the possibility of Platonist-style proof still remains in those cases where our concepts are adequately sharp. There is nothing in the picture to rule out the idea that sometimes we do embody a fully determinate function, for example to some conjunction of properties. If we did, then there would be room for an activity of reflective unpacking in which the implications of this were brought out in thought experiments and hitherto unrealized necessary connections noticed. This is surely not a Wittgensteinian position. To put things at their simplest, the idea of concept possession as the embodying of some psychic mechanism, in virtue of which a person is hooked up (perhaps in determinate ways as yet unclear to him or her) to some predefined set of possibilities is exactly the tempting misconception from which the Wittgensteinian reflections are designed to free us.

So something has gone badly wrong. We need, if we can, to

rescue what in the earlier discussion seemed illuminating for the understanding of Wittgenstein and to disentangle it from the unsatisfactory metaphysical setting.

One illuminating thing seemed to be the reflections on the kinds of circumstances and interests which would make other concepts appropriate. We should, I suggest, accept the cases roughly sketched as instances of what Wittgenstein wants to bring to our attention. He does wish us to entertain the idea that someone might, for example, respond to the carrying out of a counting procedure or to scanning through a proof by regarding them as some kind of experiment, rather than as pointing to necessities. And he wishes us to try to imagine how the world might look to such a person and what features of the situation he is noticing. But let us look again at the counting case and ask ourselves whether, or better, in what way, we can make sense of the supposed alternative. Let us pose the blunt question 'Is it possible to use number words in the alternative way indicated?' The idea of the 'given totality of possibilities' enjoins us to give to this, as to any other modal question, a clear-cut 'yes' or 'no' answer. Either there is or there is not a possible situation in which the facts and the interests combine to deliver the workability of the imagined concepts. (In following through this train of thought, we seem to be conceiving of facts and interests explaining concepts very much on the 'Eskimo and snow' model discussed towards the start of chapter 8. And if we were then right in rejecting that as an account of Wittgenstein's view then its reappearance here is another sign that we have been on the wrong track.)

Neither a bald 'yes' nor a bald 'no' gives a coherent interpretation of Wittgenstein. It seems right that he would like us to consider such imagined situations, other 'forms of life' and so forth. But what sort of upshot is this consideration to lead to? To suppose that he imagines it leading to either a clear 'yes' or a clear 'no' answer is to commit him to landing in a muddle. Thus if we say 'no' we are back with Platonism; the claim that there is only one possible development of the number system stands vindicated; in developing the system in the way we did, we discerned what we were already tacitly committed to. But if on the other hand we say 'yes' then we are back with the sort of conventionalist/Platonist hybrid we had above.

But what if we were to say rather that we just do not know whether such an alternative is possible or not? This claim of ignorance is indeed on reflection entirely plausible. What would be required to show the possibility or impossibility would be some rigorous proof that attempting to use such concepts was either bound to result in some sort of absurdity or contradiction or alternatively could never so result. But how could we have such a proof? An attempt to examine what it would be like to use these other concepts takes the form of trying to specify in non-question-begging ways a set of circumstances and interests which make them appropriate. But this involves us in reflections which ramify to embrace more and more of our interests, assumptions and practices, in ways that are less and less easy to handle formally. The hope of finding some uncontroversially acceptable demonstration of the coherence or incoherence of these alternative concepts dwindles away.[18]

But let us not just say that we are invincibly ignorant on the matter, for that is not quite right either. It is not that we are ignorant of something about which there is an answer; it is not that we finite beings cannot handle the complexities required to get an answer; if that were all that was amiss perhaps a computer could help us. The problem is rather that we do not know in enough detail what to do with the questions, 'What do you mean "*Could* people go on like this?"?', 'What do you mean "*like this*"?' The bewilderment which poses these counter-questions is not, however, a straightforward and clear-cut discovery that the question is nonsense and so could never be given any intelligible answer. That would precipitate us back into Platonism, since relegating the remark 'people carry on in this other way' to the realm of the clearly nonsensical is a close relative of relegating it to the realm of the impossible and would have the same effect.

Our bewilderment is also not the outcome of knowing of nothing one could do to answer any question posed in this form of words. In other contexts, e.g. where we knew what features of our current world view and practices we are required to hold constant or what sort of evidence is required for talk of 'possibility', we could arrive at an answer. Neither is the problem that, in this particular philosophical context we have no inkling at all of how to go about answering the question. The position is rather that we have enough grip on the question to set us off down a path which we soon realize we can not get to the end of.

Is asking the question pointless then? No. Posing it is one way of articulating our aspiration towards self-understanding, towards insight into our ways of thinking and whether they are all right or not. Wittgenstein does not want to deny us this aspiration or to prevent us pursuing the enquiries it leads us into. But my suggestion is that he supposes that working through the lines of reflection suggested will show us that what we end up with, and will find satisfying, will be awareness of the interconnectedness of our concepts, practices and interests. We shall become reflectively aware of the internal complexity and mutual dependence of the elements in our form of life – *not* aware of its advantageous placement in some (independent and given) array of 'possible forms of life'. Philosophy therefore 'assembles reminders' which 'enable us to command a clear view'; it *describes*, but in a way which satisfies whatever deserved satisfaction in the aspiration to *explanation*.[19]

The considerations set out above are the ones we need to bear in mind in considering whether rejection of mirroring realism commits us to a form of relativism which, in turn, undermines even minimal realism. The threat of a breakdown in minimal realism, which we saw (in section 2.4) to be implicit in relativism, recedes on the Wittgensteinian view (as I read it) because the putative 'other ways of looking at things' never acquire in our thought more than the shadowy and notional status which they have at the beginning of the process of reflection. We never answer the question 'Are there other conceptual schemes?' affirmatively in a way which would precipitate us into relativism. On the other hand, the intelligibility of the initial question which sets off the reflection, together with the non-availability of a clear negative answer, is enough to scupper mirroring realism. We are thus enabled to walk the tightrope between the two unsatisfactory options.

9.4   MODAL REALISM

So now, after all this, what account are we offer of mathematical proof? How are we to understand the idea that proof alters concepts? I would like to make some (sketchy and unsatisfactory) gestures in the direction of what I take to be a Wittgensteinian account.

The connections will go something like this: We must hang on firmly to the idea the possession of a concept is not being the container for some psychic mechanism linking one to the structure of the world. Rather a concept is an element in a way of living; it is that which we say someone has when we see that he or she is able to participate in that way of living. So a change in a concept is not a change in some disposition to respond to states of affairs, a disposition which is grounded in a state of one's mind. Rather it is a change in one's way of life. But, one might protest, any kind of change in things a person does – a change of job or of habits in eating – is a change in way of living. Why should going through a proof and accepting its conclusion (with whatever alterations in behaviour are consequent on that) be singled out as the sort of change to be labelled 'conceptual'? The answer will be that this sort of change is interestingly fundamental from a particular point of view. It is a change which puts a new rule into circulation. This rule is not some abstract object (e.g. an aspect of the supposed psychic machinery) but an actual formula which is used in a certain way. People who have accepted the proof and the formula which is its conclusion, have altered the range of descriptions they are prepared to give of what they do, the range of discriminations they see themselves as making and the techniques they have for making them. Thus the range of things that makes sense to them has altered. But no such alteration is to be seen as an unfolding of what was implicit before – when this is envisaged as some discovery about the totality of possibilities and the machinery linking us to it. We may always dislodge that picture by attempting, as we did in the seven, four and eleven case, to imagine alternative developments of the earlier practice and reflecting that we cannot say that such developments are impossible.

Can we combine acknowledgement of this shadowy presence of other 'possible developments' with any kind of modal realism? Can we thus have our cake and eat it? And what has happened to the distinction between valid and invalid proofs? These questions now become pressing. We need, if we can, to show that modal realism of some sort is an element of the Wittgensteinian position.

Let us remind ourselves of how these questions are linked with some we have already discussed. In section 6.3 I claimed that Wittgenstein's position was significantly different from that of thoroughgoing pragmatism. Wittgenstein does not think that we can make sense of the idea of every fundamental principle being chosen in the light of supporting reasons. There are certain things which we just take for granted, in the sense of relying on them unhesitatingly while not knowing how to argue for them. We may become aware of their pivotal status. But we do not justify our adherence to them (in the light of this or any other considerations) in the sense of comparing them with some alternative and seeing their superiority.

At that earlier stage in the discussion we had not considered Wittgenstein's rejection of mirroring realism and all that flows from this. So the conclusions there were supported on different grounds from the ones (about the imponderability of questions about different forms of life) which we have just considered. But there is no conflict in the upshot of the two discussions. Both lines of thought draw our attention to the fact that certain principles are ones that we rely on unhesitatingly and that the idea of not so doing can be allowed no more than the most shadowy verbal status by us.

We also carry forward from earlier discussion in chapter 6, and from the end of section 8.1, the idea that minimal realism is bound up with these principles. Minimal realism has to do with incompatibles. And the fundamental principles we are talking of include articulations of what we find incompatible, of those rules in thinking and speech which we must not violate on pain of stultifying ourselves.

An implication of these earlier moves is that if, at the end of the day, modal realism is found to be an illusion which needs outright rejection, then the whole Wittgensteinian realist edifice begins to totter again. Let us imagine that we accept the remarks about the centrality to us of certain principles and we accept also their role in sustaining minimal realist practices. Suppose also that we take the view that it is definitely wrong to construe these principles as themselves records of facts to be realistically construed – then we shall need an alternative characterization of their status. What could this be other than the announcement that they are projections of the way our minds work or of ways we have (somehow, at some level) decided to make them work? And if we say this, then the practices that arise from acceptance of the principles and the things in the world which those practices have us talking of, all inherit this non-realist status.

So returning to the discussion of Wittgenstein's views on proof, validity and the like, the problem is to reconcile, if we can, the emphasis on proof as introducing new concepts with a realist treatment of modality. We have to remember here that allowing the notion of valid proof to be defensible in a (minimal) realist fashion will bring *some* notions of 'unfolding' and 'same concept' riding piggyback with it.

The only way of effecting the reconciliation is to see talk of new concepts as aimed at undermining a particular metaphysical picture of what valid proof is, rather than at undermining our ordinary (and rightly realist) use of that notion. Can we make any sense of this? An extremely important fact, to which we have not hitherto given its proper place, is that our way of life is one in which enunciation of certain truths as necessary, together with formal techniques of manipulating and extending them, play an important part. We are trained to look at things in a certain way, by pictures being exhibited, by people saying 'But seven and four *must* make eleven' and by being put through routines. But we are also trained to construct further pictures and patterns for ourselves, to put ourselves through routines and to say to ourselves 'Ah! Such and such *must* be the case'. For example, someone who has learnt how to add has learnt how to put him or herself through a procedure which will result in firm acceptance of some formula like '25 + 47 = 72' and in confident performance of the kind of actions that flow from that, even when he or she has never been confronted with that sum before.

We take it for granted that most human beings will cotton on to these procedures and will agree in the verdicts and actions they produce. Even if we have come, by philosophical reflection, to the awareness of endless shadowy possibilities for alternative responses branching off at every stage of every proof, this does nothing to weaken the conviction with which we put our children through the training or the confidence with which we ourselves perform calculations, seek proofs and use the results. Those alternative responses, as we have seen, are not live options for us; whereas the enunciation of these familiar necessities and their extension by the familiar techniques are not only actually livable by us but entirely compelling.

It is in this context, of everyday training in and use of formal procedures that the concept of valid proof has its home. It is because we live the kind of life in which we calculate and train each other in proof procedures – and because it all works out satisfactorily as it does – that we have the concepts of validity and invalidity. So from one perfectly proper point of view, it is absurd to say that someone performing the usual sort of calculation shifts to a new way of life or adopts new concepts; doing this sort of thing – and adapting our practices in the way that goes with it – is a normal part of our (one) way of life; moreover we may perfectly properly say, from this point of view, that a person is, for example, getting a better understanding of numbers. But the Wittgensteinian remarks which seem to conflict with these come from another point of view, or are appropriate at another stage in discussion, when we are trying to combat a mistaken philosophical account of what such activity involves.

The temptation we must resist is to try for some kind of further account of what makes use of concepts like validity the proper thing in particular cases. There are, broadly speaking, two kinds of account available – something in the 'realist' and Platonist style or something in the projectivist, speech act or pragmatist style. On the first we try to explain talk of validity in terms of discerning more of the structure of the totality of possibilities by unpacking what was hitherto inexplicit in our grasp of it. On the second we say that when someone says 'seven and four must equal eleven' or 'If this is true then that must be true as well', what he or she is really doing is expressing some state of psychological conviction or performing a speech act of enjoining everyone to behave in a certain way.

We asked above whether it was possible to have our cake and eat it – to be, in the minimal sense, modal realists while rejecting

Platonism. The answer is that it is – but that there is a price to be paid. And the price is that we abandon as misguided (and, at bottom, unintelligible) the ambition to give a metaphysical account of modality in any such way as those mentioned above. If someone wants to know what makes it right to say that seven and four make eleven or that such and such a proof is valid the only answer to be given is that it is that seven and four do make eleven or that the proof is indeed valid. And if our questioner doubts these things we might attempt to convince him in the usual ways – by showing the pictures, running through the proofs and so forth. This is what quietist realism, as opposed to the mirroring or pragmatist variety, enjoins. All this should not come as a surprise. There should be, from a strategic perspective, a place in a Wittgensteinian outlook for modal realism without Platonism, if there is a place for realism in general without the mirroring view. Indeed the former will be just a particular case of the latter.

The natural objection here will be that we are going round in circles. The project we set ourselves was that of defending modal realism, in order to prevent its failure ramifying through the system and undermining the defence of minimal realism that we had attempted to put in place for other areas of our thought. But all we have been given is the same story over again! And it was just the acceptability of that story which was at issue.

What this protest amounts to, however, from the non-mirroring point of view, is yet another manifestation of the same impulse which all along we have been trying to combat. It is yet another attempt to get (as its proponents suppose) our concepts firmly and properly grounded by linking them to something quite outside our practices and responses. But right across the board we need to be coaxed out of the impulse to metaphysical speculation, to be persuaded that we can and should be content with that understanding of our concepts which comes from seeing how judgements using them are placed in a context of actions, interests and other judgements, so that together they constitute the only sort of life that we have any idea how to live. 'Necessity', 'possibility', 'validity' and the like are just as much deserving of this treatment as any other of our concepts. It is not the case that they alone are inseparable from the mirroring/Platonist picture and so must fall into disrepute with it. The challenge to any objector who wishes for something other than what has been offered, is to give some coherent account of what it is that he wants. The claim is that any such attempt will run into the problems outlined in section 7.1 – those of demanding the self-extrapolating series or the self-interpreting sign.

9.5 FACTS ABOUT MEANING

In this final section we turn at last to the question of whether there are facts about meaning, how we are to understand the claim that there are and how such claims should be made defensible. The key ideas we need have already been introduced. It remains to assemble them in order and to indicate how they enable us to avoid the disastrous paradoxes explored in chapter 6.

In order that we should be realists about meaning, in the minimal sense, we need to show two things: One is that there is a practice of making judgements about meaning which fits the minimal realist pattern. The second is that the practice is proper or legitimate. The second task is likely to be more difficult, but let us start with something about the first.

The requirement is that we should make statements about our own and other people's meanings which we recognize to be subject to the law of non-contradiction. We take it, in other words, that there are incompatible meaning ascriptions and that incompatible ones cannot both be fully defensible. The well-nigh intolerable paradoxicality and bizarreness of Quinean scepticism is strong evidence that we do operate such a practice.

But what are the incompatibles in the case of meaning? It is worth remarking that incompatibility of meaning ascription, where 'means that X' and 'means that Y' are an incompatible pair, includes but also extends far beyond cases where 'X' and 'Y' themselves are incompatible moves in the language. In Kripke's case of the 'plus' and 'quus' functions, the two functions yield the same answer in application to certain numbers and hence are not incompatibles.[20] Nevertheless, on a realist view, the related meaning ascriptions do exhibit incompatibility. One important feature underlying the intuition of incompatibility here is that the 'plus' and 'quus' functions do or clearly could diverge, and that this is linked with our grasp of them as different concepts.

We should note at this point that the realist about meaning is not committed to the idea that people are never muddled, never have vague ideas, or never have ideas which fail to tally exactly with ours. It may be, for example, that we possess two concepts which we distinguish because we know they can diverge, while another person operates some notion which does not equip him or her to deal with the cases where, as we see it, the notions come apart. This is not a case where ascription of both of our concepts to the other person is justified, but rather a case where either might do for some purposes but, in other contexts, neither would be entirely happy.

Another thing the meaning realist is not committed to is the idea that there is some one thing which is 'the' meaning of any given remark. For different purposes, in different contexts and so forth, different meaning ascriptions may be in order. The point is only this: given a particular question in a particular context, there will be a range of answers; some of these answers will be incompatible; and we properly take it that not more than one of the incompatibles can be fully defensible.

Someone might object that we conceded in chapter 2 that it was possible for a person to make contradictory judgements – to think that both p and not p. Indeed, in section 2.1, that claim played an important role in linking together the various strands characteristic of minimal realism. But if this is so, the objection continues, how can one claim that meaning that p and meaning that not p (for example) are incompatible?

But let us make some careful distinctions here. We may have a person who says that p and also says (in another, distinguishable, remark) that not p and we may take it that both remarks are sincere. We may even have a person who produces one utterance which means that p and not p. But these are not cases which would threaten the claim of the existence of incompatibilities in meaning ascription. For that we need a case in which a person can rightly be claimed to say, in a given remark to a given audience, that p and also rightly be claimed to say, in that very same remark and to that very same audience, that not p, where each of these, that p and that not p, is represented as the full content of what is said and is thought of as conveyed by the very same features of what is uttered. This is the sort of case which the meaning realist will reject as incoherent. The important difference from the other cases is that in them we had two remarks to interpret or some relevant complexity within one remark, so that the meaning that p and the meaning that not p got attached to different vehicles. In these circumstances what leads to the interpretation and what we expect in virtue of it can be intelligibly set out. But what we are now asked to imagine is that one and the same vehicle be rightly given two opposed inter-pretations. The problem for the realist is not that we make the person we are interpreting out to be so confused that one can hardly suppose that anyone could be that muddled. The problem rather is that *we*, the interpreters, cannot give any sensible account of what we think we are up to. But the non-realist about meaning, a believer in the indeterminacy of interpretation for example, sup-poses on the contrary that when we reflect on how we proceed in meaning ascription we will see that this is exactly the kind of thing the possibility of which (even if it does not happen in practice) is built into the notion of meaning. For the non-realist the realist aspects of our practice of meaning ascription are mere superficial appearances.

Let us turn now to the second of the two conditions which I mentioned at the start of the section. It is here that all the serious problems arise. We need to show that our realist practice does not need re-interpretation or rejection but is properly taken at face value. Some flaw must be found in those sceptical arguments which purport to show that our practice of meaning ascription is, by its own lights, not realistic. The sceptic undertakes to show us, by examining the working of our notion of meaning, that the realistic seeming practices with meaning are at best temporarily advan-tageous ploys and at worst plain mistakes.

The sceptical move that we have examined in chapter 5 pin-points the crucial source for the difficulties with realism about meaning. These difficulties arise from the acknowledgement of the fact that possession of meaning by any item presupposes the existence of an immense and intricate pattern of other meaning-bearing items, stretching out over time, including the future, and also of the fact that the particular meaning which an item has is bound up with its role or place in the pattern. Whatever the exact account we give of the kinds of item in the pattern, or of the nature of the organizing relations, the central problem in defending realism about meaning remains. It is to see how, if possession of a particular meaning is bound up with place in the pattern, anyone could be justified in attributing a given meaning to a particular item unless he or she had some independent access to the rest of the pattern in which the item occurs. But how could such independent access be made sense of? Large parts of the pattern are in practice or principle unobservable. And, worse, even if we suppose that problem overcome and ourselves supplied with all imaginable data about other utterances and behaviour, it seems that the evidence may still be inadequate and we may be faced with the indeterminacy problem explored in chapter 5. We do indeed make confident judgements about meaning, as though the limited part of the array of utterances we are confronted with allowed us to be certain of the existence and nature of a unique best pattern into which those utterances, and others made by our subject, will fit. It is as though, having picked up just a handful pieces from an immense and difficult jigsaw we immediately and confidently assigned roles to them. But how can we maintain such confidence in the light of our inability to show that an alternative interpretation of our subject's utterances does not exist? This is the crucial question to which we must now address ourselves.

Wittgenstein's interlocutor at one point asks 'But if you are *certain*, isn't it that you are shutting your eyes in the face of doubt?' And Wittgenstein replies 'They are shut'.[21] My contention, to put it provocatively, is that, with Wittgenstein, we should keep our eyes shut. To vindicate our realism about meaning we do not have to attack directly the contentions of chapter 5; we do not have to deny that meanings ascriptions are answerable to placement in a coherent pattern or to show the existence of some strategy for discerning patterns which yields a guarantee that utterances fit together in only one way. The mistake rather is in the sceptical conclusion that is drawn from these observations about the holistic nature of the concept of meaning. To avoid the sceptical upshot all we have to do is keep our eyes shut, to ignore the possibility of alternative interpretation which the sceptic thrusts at us. And we are not to be criticized for so doing.

The sceptic, or any philosopher who wishes to see justice done to him, will find this quite outrageous. It will seem to him to be a blatant example of the advantages of theft over honest toil. How can all that intricate and laborious argument about holistic methodology and its implications be swept away as irrelevant? How can keeping one's eyes shut be other than irresponsible?

There are indeed circumstances in which a person might irresponsibly shut his eyes and refuse to admit a doubt which should have been admitted and should perhaps have influenced behaviour. Imagine that I am confronted with a row of boxes in one of which, I am told, there is a diamond. I am given some clues as to which box the diamond is in – it is in an intricately carved box, made of oak and having corners bound with brass. I see a box which answers all elements of the description and leap to the conclusion that the diamond is in it. It is then pointed out to me that another box also fits the requirements. But I remain entirely convinced that the original box is the one containing the diamond and refuse to take out any insurance policies to cover error. I am, however, wrong. The diamond is in the other box. Clearly I have been foolish and am in for a nasty shock. I should have hedged my bets. And even if we tell the story differently and imagine me to have been right, it is still clear that I was foolish and my confidence misplaced; I have been saved from disaster only by luck.

The structure of this situation closely parallels that in which traditional sceptical problems arise in the context of mirroring realism. I have emphasized at several earlier points how mirroring realism goes naturally together with the idea of a given totality of metaphysical possibilities or ways that things might be. Let us equate these with the boxes and let us equate being actual with containing the diamond. Then the sceptic imagines that we are supplied with some information about the actual world (by being in it and having it impinge on us) and we also have some information about the range of possibilities (from some of the real properties of the universe having revealed their nature and fitness for combination to us). On this basis we try to find out more about the actual world, i.e. to identify which of the possibles is the one we actually inhabit.

Material object scepticism, for example, emerges like this: The sceptic admits that we know of the actual world that it contains sensory experience of a certain character. But, he says, among the range of possible ways things might be are not only ones in which such experiences are explained by material objects but also ones in which they are the outcome of malicious demons, chance, scientists manipulating brains in vats and the like. How are we to justify our confidence that our situation answers to the first description? One might suppose that going out to have a further look at our actual world, interacting with it some more, would supply relevant evidence. But, of course, the problem has been set up precisely to make this inefficacious, since all it could supply us with (the sceptic urges) is more of the same stuff, i.e. sensory experience, the explanation of which is what is in question.

Matters are comparable in the case of meaning. It is supposed that we are aware of (supplied with information about) uninterpreted utterances. Our problem is to show the legitimacy of our confidence in the linkage of those utterances with particular features of the world, in the face of the possibility that they could be arranged in such a way as to display different linkages.

There are, however, some interesting differences between the two cases. In the case of material objects the desired upshot of the sceptical reflection is not (at least in the case I have imagined) the undermining of the concept of material object. The notion remains usable and we continue to admit that in some possible situations there is experience explained by such objects. What is supposed to have evaporated is our confidence that there are any such objects in our world. In the case of meaning however the upshot is more drastic. We are accepting, at this stage in the argument, the important negative thesis which is in common between Quine and Wittgenstein, namely that to hold that an utterance means so and so is not to take it that some item lies behind or causally explains that utterance – rather it is to take it that the item has a certain place in a pattern of items. The effect then of countenancing the possibility of another arrangement, of discerning another pattern in which the utterance means something quite different, is to under-mine the viability of meaning as a realistically intended descriptive tool. We do not just say 'We cannot be sure that people mean what we earlier took them to mean – although they might mean that, since in some possible situation they do mean it.' We say rather that in no possible situation does anyone really mean anything – that talk of meaning is not any part of saying how things really are.

This now casts an odd light backwards on the moves by which the conclusion was reached. The claim was that there is a possible situation in which the utterances I am confronted with are differ-ently arranged from the way in which I arrange them. To talk in this way seems to admit that I do indeed arrange them one way, even if someone else does it another way. But my arranging utterances (i.e. my interpreting them) consists, given the non-existence of meanings outside patterns of utterance, merely in my producing certain utterances of my own which in turn may be formed into a pattern. It is as though all one could to towards assembling a jigsaw was to throw down another handful of jigsaw pieces – while allowing that this second lot themselves could be built into more than one picture of the assembling of the first lot. But then no single arrangement has been imposed on the first lot by the appearance of the second lot and the whole notion of an arrangement begins to crumble on us. This head-spinning outcome is not, however, a difficulty that we can wheel up against the non-realist about meaning. His point is that the notion of meaning undermines itself; his will therefore be happy to deploy it *ad hominem* at certain stages of the argument.

Let us pause to assess matters here. One might remark that the sceptical arguments presented above proceeded on the assumption that we know that it is (metaphysically) possible that sensory experience like ours should be explained by something other than material objects, or that utterances like the ones we hear should be differently interpreted. But this is very arguably too strong, too much of a concession to the sceptic. The meaning-sceptical argu-ments considered by us have not claimed to show that other arrangements can for certain be produced or to suggest an algor-ithm for producing them, only that we do not know that they cannot.[22] Similarly one might argue that it is not clear that sensory experiences like ours could occur in the absence of physical objects. How confident we are in the existence of either of these possibilities will depend on how confident we are that we now correctly grasp the nature and relations of the real characteristics which define the world. Perhaps the supposed possibilities of other arrangements of utterances or other explanations of sensory experience are merely epistemic and not real?

Unfortunately this thought, in the context of the current picture, cannot help us. Consider a slightly different situation with boxes and a diamond. This time I am told there is among these boxes (and my informant gestures vaguely at a group) just one box which contains a diamond and I am given clues as before on what the box is like. On this occasion however I am not so foolish as in the previous case. I look carefully at all the boxes I can see and I make sure that I select the only one which fits the description. But then the thought strikes me that there might be other boxes which I have not seen but which were included in the group. Are there some under the floorboards or behind the curtains? I realize that I do not know whether or not the ones I can see are the only ones I need bother about and my original informant is no longer at hand to help. Should my confidence that the selected box contains the diamond be undermined? It seems that it ought. (It might be sensible, for example, to take out an insurance policy on its not containing the diamond, if a lot hangs on the question and the policy is cheap.) And this is so irrespective of whether I am right or wrong in my supposition that there are more boxes.

The analogue in the possible situations case is clear enough. I realize that I do not know whether or not there are possible situations in which sensory experiences like ours is to be explained by something other than material objects or in which utterances are intelligibly interpreted differently. So my confidence in the existence of material objects or the coherence of the notion of meaning ought, it seems, to be correspondingly undermined. Whether I am right or not in my supposition about possibilities is irrelevant.

As a matter of psychology, it seems likely that in some actual versions of the box and diamond story the guesser's confidence might well be shaken by the reflection that he had no clear information on what boxes were included in the relevant group. By contrast it is notorious that sceptical arguments do not in fact shake our beliefs about material objects or meanings (to say nothing of the past, the sensations of others, the sun's rising tomorrow etc.). We may adjure ourselves 'Face up to the (possible) facts! Open your mind to the thought that there is no such thing as determinate meaning!' But we find that, like Gloucester trying to jump off the cliff, we come down exactly where we were before. The sceptic, however, may not be impressed by this. He may suppose it to be merely force of habit or immensely strong natural propensity.

The key question then is what we are to make of propositions like 'Sensory experience such as ours is explained by something other than material objects' and 'Utterances like these are arranged in a different pattern'. On the mirroring realist view either they describe possibilities or they do not. We may admit ignorance of the nature of the full range of possibilities, but in so far as we have a grasp on it, it may seem to us (epistemically) more likely than not that the sentences do describe real possibilities. And even if we are not prepared to attach a probability to the judgement that they describe possibilities, the mere fact that, as we conceive things, we do not know that the situations are impossible ought to make us adjust our confidence in the existence of material objects or the defensibility of minimal realism about meaning. Thus it is irresponsible and improper to ignore that (epistemic) possibility that these things are (metaphysical) possibilities. But on what I suggest is the Wittgensteinian view we are entitled to ignore them, to shut our eyes to them. How can this come about?

It is clear that if we reject mirroring realism then we may also reject the idea of the given totality of possibilities defined by combinations of real properties. But this thought alone is not enough to give us what we need. Why should we not suppose that any conceptual scheme brings with it its own set of possibilities in connection with which honest accounting must be done when assessing the degree of confidence to be reposed in various judgements? The assumption behind the question is, in a sense, right. For example, in our conceptual scheme we may describe situations like the box and diamond one, and such a situation brings with it relevant ranges of possibilities of which participants should take account. And sometimes participants fail, through inadequate reflection, to notice some of the possibilities which are relevant. The possibilities are thus given and are independent of the epistemological state of the participants. Why is it not the same for the philosophically controversial 'possibilities' which interest us?

The answer is that in abandoning mirroring realism we cease to be in a position where we can insist on saying of every (in some sense) intelligible sentence 'Either it describes a possibility or it does not'. What has been emphasized again and again is that our concepts do not come isolated. To understand a concept is to see it at work in its setting. As I tried to suggest in the last section, possibility is a notion (or better a family of notions) of which this is true, just as much as of any other. And the fact is that we are not trained in, we have in our lives no role for, assessing the possibility of every kind of conceptual combination. We talk of possibility in a variety of contexts – some having to do with derivations in formal systems, some with whether men can swim rivers, pegs fit into holes or diamonds are to be found in boxes.[23] In these contexts we know what to do with the notion of possibility – how to go about establishing whether or not something is possible and what accepting the judgement might lead to. But in connection with the sentences the sceptic or non-realist thrusts at us we are at a loss on all these fronts. In particular we are completely stymied on, so to speak, how to proceed with thinking (how to do it, how to conceive of it, how to feel about it) if the indeterminacy, and hence non-reality, of meaning were to be accepted. The thesis that meaning is indeterminate presents itself as immensely important, as concerning the fundamental matter of what we and the world are really like. Surely then even entertaining it, let alone accepting it, ought to produce some kind of upheaval – as with considering that the Earth is not the centre of the universe or that God does not exist. But in fact nothing of the kind occurs. The most strenuous attempts to get to grips with the idea may produce a sense of gloom, allied with images of being tied up alone in a cold dark place. But these do not persist; and if they did, or if they came to dominate one's thoughts, it would be evidence not of deep philosophical insight but of madness.

From the point of view of mirroring realism, this all looks like a paradoxical impasse. We have, it seems, excellent arguments that meaning is or might be indeterminate. The difficulty in doing anything with the thought seems a kind of limitation or blinkeredness in us. But from a stance which rejects mirroring realism, the sceptic's impasse takes on quite another appearance; now it presents itself as an indication to us of what our form of life is.

Let us come at this from another angle, linking it in to the reflections about stage setting which were introduced in section 8.1. What we are doing in attributing meaning looks to the sceptic like picking up jigsaw pieces and straightaway assigning them roles in a picture, on the basis merely of the shape, colour etc., without what he conceives to be proper attention to the other utterances (for example future ones) or to the possibility of quite different strategies of picture construction. When someone utters a remark to us in a familiar language we hear it as a saying that so and so. We do not concern ourselves either with the possibility that the future utterances will go against our expectations and force us to reinterpret, nor yet with the possibility that alternative construals of the whole lot might strike someone. Instead we carry on as though the meaning of an utterance, its place in the pattern, could be directly discerned in the individual item. The sceptic will admit this as a phenomenological description but insists that it masks the underlying epistemological situation, which is one of perceiving uninterpreted utterances and arriving at hypotheses about the nature of other such utterances and their possible arrangements. He will protest vigorously at the idea that we can perceive an utterance as having such and such a meaning, that its place in the pattern could be for us present at an instant.

What fuels the protest is the idea that in hearing meaning in an utterance we are going beyond what we are entitled to. The burden, however, of the earlier discussion, in section 8.1 and again with the example of numbers earlier in this chapter, is that there is a way of regarding the application of any concept on which it appears risky. To use any concept is to make a move in one sort of life rather than another. When we reflect we see that the livability of that life, and hence the usefulness and defensibility of that concept, presupposes a whole ramifying set of circumstances – that results of various sets of procedures will coincide, that projects will develop and give rise to other projects and so forth. And the idea of discharging all these presuppositions is quite fantastical. There are so many of them, each one spawns more, and we soon lose even the feeblest grip on how we could set about investigating them. The hope of finding a set of concepts free of any such entanglement with things which present themselves, when we become aware of them, as contingencies, concepts the use of which carries only the risk of falsehood and not the risk of having the concepts themselves turn out misguided, is a will o' the wisp. It is the illusory ambition of discovering the real joints at which the world is to be sliced.

The implication of the illusoriness of that ambition is that the application of any concept involves a risk of 'going beyond what is supplied'. But this is not quite the right way of putting it. There is no such thing as 'not going beyond what one is entitled to' if this is conceived as making a judgement the propriety of which requires nothing beyond the moment. This is not to say that there are no things which occur all in an instant – jabs of pain, flashes of lightning. It is to say that their occurring all in an instant is bound up with those other happenings at other times which make it possible for talk of lightning or pain to be appropriate.

So use of any concept carries the risk brought by involvement, without external guarantee of success, in living the life of which its use is a part. To point out that someone runs this risk is thus, in itself, no criticism of his concepts. It is simply to remark on an aspect of what it is to live and to think. Whether we take ourselves to be confronted with a flash of lightning, a pen resting on a table or a person saying that dinner is ready the commitments and the risks are there. They are importantly different in the different cases. This is what we have tried to mark with the talk of holism and so forth. But the use of a concept is not to be criticized unless the critic can indicate a livable, real alternative in which that concept is not employed. And this, as we have seen, is what the sceptic in the case of meaning is unable to do.

'Following according to the rule is FUNDAMENTAL to our language game. It characterizes what we call description.'[24] We act spontaneously, in a way which is not to be explained by pointing to something outside us which makes us behave that way, and yet quite unhesitatingly, with no sense of choice or arbitrariness. What it is that we thus do and say, and the way that it all hangs together with the things about which we do deliberate, make the notions both of meaning and of reality available to us.

Notes

CHAPTER 1   INTRODUCTION

1 Quine, *Word and Object* (1960), p. 77.
2 S. Kripke, *Wittgenstein on Rules and Private Language* (1982), pp. 55–8;
   R. Rorty, *Philosophy and the Mirror of Nature* (1980), pp. 169, 265; C.
   Hookway, *Quine* (1988), p. 47; C. Wright, *Wittgenstein on the Foundations
   of Mathematics* (1980), pp. 358ff.
3 Wittgenstein, *On Certainty*, 96–99.
4 Quine, 'Two Dogmas of Empiricism', in his *From a Logical Point of View*
   (1953).
5 E.g. *Word and Object*, pp. 218–21; *From a Logical Point of View*, pp. 138;
   The Ways of Paradox, pp. 193–4.
6 James C. Edwards, *Ethics without Philosophy: Wittgenstein and the Moral
   Life* (1982).

CHAPTER 2   VARIETIES OF REALISM

1 The ideas pursued in this section, and also in section 2.4, have been
   stimulated by the thought of B. A. O. Williams (in 'Consistency and
   Realism' (1973) and 'The Truth in Relativism' (1981)) and David
   Wiggins (in 'What would be a Substantial Theory of Truth?' (1980)).
2 This is not to say that they do not have other things with which they
   are incompatible, for example 'This is pure white' or 'This is pale
   blue'. The existence of other incompatibles is enough to enable us to
   defend minimal realism with respect to colour ascriptions, in terms of
   the account of realism offered below.
3 To say this is not to deny that imperatives have a dimension of 'fit
   with the world', in some ways analogous to truth and falsity. They do;
   it is fulfilment and non-fulfilment. Neither is it to deny that fulfilment,
   or the likelihood of it, is important in the assessment of an imperative.
   And it is not to say that the issuing of an imperative can carry no

implications about the facts. The claim is simply that when I say of the dinosaur 'Paint it green' I am not thereby making a claim about how it is with the world, a claim which would be contradicted by 'Paint it orange'.

4 Compare here Crispin Wright's 'Does *Philosophical Investigations* I 258–60 Suggest a Cogent Argument against Private Language?' (1986), esp. pp. 227ff.

5 See R. Kirk, *Translation Determined* (1986), pp. 61ff for such a proposal in connection with Quine.

6 R. Rorty, *Philosophy and the Mirror of Nature* (1980).

7 This is, of course, Descartes' view.

8 This is how B. A. O. Williams uses the word, for example in his 'Wittgenstein and Idealism' (1981).

9 Similar thoughts are found in Davidson 'On the Very Idea of a Conceptual Scheme', in *Inquiries into Truth and Interpretation* (1984).

10 There may be a link between this thought and the whole tangle of considerations known as 'the private language argument'. But I shall not explore this issue here.

Chapter 3   Instrumentalism and Meaning Scepticism

1 See for example Quine, *Ontological Relativity and Other Essays*, (1966), pp. 26, 97–8, 126–7; *Theories and Things* (1981), pp. 21, 72, 85.

2 H. Field, 'Quine and the Correspondence Theory' (1974); C. Hookway *Quine* (1988).

3 Quine, 'Facts of the Matter' (1979), p. 166.

4 Quine, *Theories and Things*, p. 98.

5 'Facts of the Matter', esp. p. 165.

6 Quine, 'On the Reasons for the Indeterminacy of Translation' (1970), p. 178. See also his 'Epistemology Naturalised', in *Ontological Relativity*.

7 For more about the notion of 'observation statement' invoked here, see Quine, *Word and Object* (1960), ch. 2 and also section 3.2 below.

8 'Facts of the Matter', p. 158.

9 *Ontological Relativity*, p. 81.

10 Let us note also Quine's approval of Follesdal's remark, in 'Indeterminacy of Translation and Underdetermination of the Theory of Nature' (1973), that indeterminacy of translation can be derived from holism and the verification theory of meaning. See Hahn and Schilipp, pp. 155–6.

11 'On the Reasons for Indeterminacy of Translation'; *Ontological Relativity*, pp. 80–1; *Theories and Things*, p. 70.

12 *Theories and Things*, pp. 24–30; Schilpp and Hahn, p. 427; *Ontological Relativity*, pp. 79–80.

13 This seems to be Dancy's view in *An Introduction to Contemporary Epistemology* (1985), pp. 93–4, although at other points he expresses a view closer to the one I suggest.

14 D. K. Lewis, 'General Semantics', in *Collected Papers I* (1983), pp. 189–90; D. Davidson, *Inquiries into Truth and Interpretation* (1984), pp. 129–30, 175, 220–1; G. Evans, 'Identity and Predication', in *Collected Papers* (1985), pp. 25–7.

15 *Word and Object*, p. 78.

16 Many commentators have found this difficult to fathom: e.g. N. Chomsky, 'Quine's Empirical Assumptions' (1969); R. Rorty, 'Indeterminacy of Translation and of Truth' (1972). See also the useful article by Roger F. Gibson Jr, 'Translation, Physics and Facts of the Matter', in Hahn and Schilpp, *Philosophy of W. V. Quine* (1986).

17 Quine, 'Two Dogmas of Empiricism', in *From a Logical Point of View* (1953), and *Philosophy of Logic* (1970), ch. 6.

CHAPTER 4   QUINE'S NATURALIZED EMPIRICISM

1 Quine, 'Two Dogmas of Empiricism', in *From a Logical Point of View* (1953), pp. 44, 42.

2 Quine, *Theories and Things* (1981), pp. 39–40.

3 Ibid., p. 1.

4 Quine, *Word and Object* (1960), pp. 2–3.

5 Ibid.

6 Ibid., p. 3.

7 Ibid., p. 10.

8 Quine, 'Facts of the Matter' in *Essays on the Philosophy of W. V. Quine*, ed. R. W. Shahan and C. Swoyer (1979), p. 155.

9 *Word and Object*, pp. 40ff. *Ontological Relativity and other Essays* (1969), pp. 85–9.

10 *Ontological Relativity*, pp. 86–7.

11 *Word and Object*, p. 9.

12 Ibid., p. 76.

13 Hahn and Schilpp, *The Philosophy of W. V. Quine* (1986), pp. 336, 364, 428.

14 *Word and Object*, p. 9.

15 Hahn and Schilpp, *Philosophy of W. V. Quine*, p. 336. (The emphases are mine.) See also *Theories and Things*, pp. 29–30.

16 *Theories and Things*, pp. 1–2.

17 Ibid., p. 72.

18 'Facts of the Matter', p. 167.

19 S. Kripke, *Wittgenstein on Rules and Private Language* (1982).

20 For example 'Notes on the Theory of Reference', in *From a Logical Point of View*, pp. 130ff.

21 *Ontological Relativity*, p. 50.

22 *Word and Object*, pp. 68ff.

23 *Ontological Relativity*, p. 49.

24 H. Field, 'Quine and the Correspondence Theory' (1974).

25 *Ontological Relativity*, p. 49.

26 Field, 'Quine and the Correspondence Theory', p. 208n.

27 It is worth bearing in mind here Quine's downplaying of the import-ance of ontology; according to him, effectively systematising the holophrastically construed observation sentences is the important matter; ontology is a mere by product of this. E.g. Hahn and Schilpp, *Philosophy of W. V. Quine*, p. 115; 'Facts of the Matter', pp. 164–5.

28 *Word and Object*, p. 24.

29 For the line of thought in this section I am much indebted to C. Hookway's discussion in his *Quine* (1988), esp. ch. 12.3.

30 Quine *Philosophy of Logic* (1970), p. 1.

31 *Ontological Relativity*, p. 81.

32 Quoted by R. F. Gibson in Hahn and Schilpp, *Philosophy of W. V. Quine*, p. 153. In the context of this discussion it is also worth noting that Davidson clearly reads Quine as endorsing some thesis of the quoted kind. See his 'On the Very Idea of a Conceptual Scheme', in *Inquiries into Truth and Interpretation* (1984). Quine rejects Davidson's interpretation ('On the Very Idea of a Third Dogma', in *Theories and Things*) in the same spirit as he reformulates the passage quoted by Gibson. But my suggestion is that the rejection, when closely exam-ined, preserves the spirit if not the letter of the instrumentalism charged.

33 Hahn and Schilpp, *Philosophy of W. V. Quine*, p. 153.

34 *Theories and Things*, pp. 21–2.

35 Hahn and Schilpp, *Philosophy of W. V. Quine*, p. 157.

36 *Word and Object*, pp. 24–5.

37 *Word and Object*, p. 76.

38 Hahn and Schilpp, *Philosophy of W. V. Quine*, p. 12.

39 For an illuminating discussion of this, to which I am indebted, see Hookway's *Quine*, esp. chs 2 and 3.

40 See also 'Truth by Convention' (1935), 'Carnap and Logical Truth'

(1954), 'On Carnap's Views on Ontology' (1951), all in *The Ways of Paradox and Other Essays* (1966).

41 'Five Milestones of Empiricism', in *Theories and Things*.

42 See, for example, R. Gregory, *Eye and Brain* (1972) and J. Fodor, *Modularity of Mind* (1983).

CHAPTER 5   THE MONA LISA MOSAIC

1 I shall not here pursue exegetical questions about Davidson's views. The papers of particular relevance are 'Radical Interpretation', 'Belief and the Basis of Meaning', 'On the Very Idea of a Conceptual Scheme' (all in his *Inquiries into Truth and Interpretation* (1984)), and 'Mental Events' (in his *Essays on Actions and Events* (1980)).

2 See the discussion of 'seeing in' in R. Wollheim, *Art and Its Objects* (1970).

3 G. Ryle, *Concept of Mind* (1949), pp. 130–1.

4 J. Fodor, *Psychosemantics* (1975) p. 56.

5 Ibid., pp. 88, 89.

6 Quine and Davidson differ in what they take to be offered at this level. Quine thinks that the descriptions are purely behavioural, Davidson that they will involve the minimally intentional notion of 'holding true'. (See Davidson's 'Radical Interpretation' and also 'The Inscrutability of Reference', both in *Inquiries into Truth and Interpretation*). But the difference is not relevant to the structure of the particular argument we are considering.

7 Acceptance of this sort of holism does not rule out allowing for some useful distinction between observational and theoretical sentences, couched for example in terms of things that we tend to agree on, that we do not arrive at by explicit inference and the preservation of which is agreed to be an important aim in a world view. But this rough and ready idea of the 'observational' is far from Quine's. Neither does this holism entail insistence on the idea that all 'observational' concepts are 'theory laden'. That a judgement may be rejected in the light of theoretical considerations does not (without a link of epistemological to semantic which I reject) imply that the concepts in the first are theoretical. For some recent work on the idea of 'observations' see C. Wright, 'Scientific Realism, Observation and the Verification Principle', in *Fact, Science and Morality* (1986), ed. MacDonald and Wright.

8 As Fodor remarks, *Psychosemantics*, 62ff.

9 Related worries are expressed in my 'Replication and Functionalism',

in *Language, Mind and Logic* (1986), ed. Butterfield. See also J. McDowell, 'Functionalism and Anomalous Monism', in *The Philosophy of Donald Davidson* (1986), ed. Lepore and McLaughlin .

10 This constitutes yet another difficulty for simplistic inference from cause to intentional content. The rest of a background view will need to be taken into account in determining what an item is seen as. And it is not clear that there must be a determinate way of so doing.

CHAPTER 6   THE SLIDE INTO THE ABYSS

1 *Zettel*, sections 135, 170, 172, 173, 175, 176, 534; compare also *Philosophical Investigations*, Part II, p. 174; *Blue and Brown Books*, 5; *Remarks on the Foundations of Mathematics*, 334, 335, 345–7, 390.

2 C. Wright expresses similar views in 'Kripke's Account of the Argument against Private Language' (1984), pp. 769–70.

3 This seems to be Rorty's position, as expounded in his *Philosophy and the Mirror of Nature* (1980) and *Consequences of Pragmatism* (1982) and some have seen it as the logical outcome of the position Quine urges in 'Two Dogmas of Empiricism', in *From a Logical Point of View* (1953).

4 C. Wright, 'Inventing Logical Necessity', in *Language, Mind and Logic* (1986), ed. Butterfield, pp. 192–3.

5 Ibid., pp. 193–4.

6 Ibid., p. 194.

7 S. Blackburn proposes some view of this sort. See his *Spreading the Word* (1984) section 6.5. Wright also makes remarks suggesting sympathy with some such outlook in 'Inventing Logical Necessity', pp. 204–5. But it may well be that they both intend something subtler than the crude view I address. The suspicion however will be that the less crudely psychological the view, the less it will have any power to demystify ontological and epistemological questions about necessity.

8 Wright, 'Inventing logical necessity', p. 194.

9 For more on this theme see Bob Hale's discussion, in *Abstract Objects* ch. 6 of Philip Kitcher's *The Nature of Mathematical Knowledge* (1984).

10 Wright is attracted to such a conventionalist view and thinks that Wittgenstein held it. (See his 'Facts and Certainty' (1985), pp. 451–3) And he also thinks that Naturalism is more defensible in conjunction with some kind of conventionalism (i.e. in the context of the thought 'I've got to choose some rule or other; but I can't conceive of any one but this; so I'll choose this') than simply in the context of remarking that we do not, in fact, doubt such and such things (see 'Facts and Certainty' pp. 467–8). At the same place he criticizes

Strawson for inappropriately invoking Naturalism as a response to scepticism (in *Scepticism and Naturalism: Some Varieties* (1985), pp. 10–29) in the form of a merely descriptive remark that we do not doubt. It will be clear that my sympathies are with Strawson. We may remark also that Wright's interpretation of Wittgenstein does not make sense of those passages where Wittgenstein speaks of our search for justification coming to an end in description, on our discovering the propositions that stand firm for us (e.g. *On Certainty* 152, 189; *Philosophical Investigations* 124ff).

11 *On Certainty*, sections 56, 83, 88, 89, 94, 95, 96, 98, 105, 109, 110, 117, 119, 120, 130–1, 144, 150, 152, 189, 210, 321, 337, 343, 375, 411, 421–2. Wittgenstein in some of these passages toys with the idea that 'everything speaks for' some of our framework or scaffolding beliefs (*On Certainty*, sections 89, 117, 119). But he clearly finds this an unsatisfactory this view of things and emphasizes instead our awareness of inability to do without them (*On Certainty*, sections 94, 105, 110, 117, 120, 144, 150, 152). Wittgenstein is, in *On Certainty*, discussing most of the time certain empirical propositions which he takes to have this interesting status, while we have been concerned here mainly with conceptual ones. But we shall need to return to the fundamental 'empirical' propositions at the end of ch. 9 below.

12 A. J. Ayer, *Language Truth and Logic* (1971), pp. 113–15. For another similar positivist view see Hans Hahn's 'Logic, Mathematics and the Knowledge of Nature', in *Logical Positivism* (1959), ed. Ayer, pp. 156–7.

13 M. Dummett, 'Wittgenstein's Philosophy of Mathematics', in *Wittgenstein, Critical Essays* (1968), ed. Pitcher, pp. 424ff.

14 This argument is urged in ibid., and elaborated in C. Wright, *Wittgenstein on the Foundation of Mathematics* (1980), esp. ch. 5.

15 See J. McDowell, 'Anti-Realism and the Epistemology of Understanding' in *Meaning and Understanding* (1981), ed. Parrett and Bouveresse, and also 'Wittgenstein on Following a Rule' (1984) for more on this theme.

16 D. Davidson, *Inquiries into Truth and Interpretation* (1984), p. 230.

CHAPTER 7   THE DISSOLVING MIRROR

1 *Philosophical Investigations*, Part II, p. 230.
2 *Zettel*, 331.
3 Ibid., 352.
4 Ibid., 357–8.

5 Ibid., 364.

6 Ibid., 387–8.

7 S. Kripke, *Wittgenstein on Rules and Private Language* (1982). See also the useful discussion by C. McGinn in *Wittgenstein on Meaning* (1984).

8 Williams, *Ethics and the Limits of Philosophy* (1985), pp. 138–9.

9 Williams, *Descartes: The Project of Pure Enquiry* (1978), pp. 64–5.

10 *Ethics and the Limits of Philosophy*, pp. 138–9.

11 Ibid., pp. 139–40.

12 For more on this theme see my 'The Disinterested Search for Truth' (1987–8).

13 His idea would, on this reading, fit in with the programme of giving naturalized accounts of mind and meaning, and so defending mirroring realism, which was mentioned at the end of ch. 6 above.

14 Williams, *Descartes*, pp. 297–9.

15 J. McDowell, 'Non-Cognitivism and Rule Following' in *Wittgenstein: to Follow a Rule* (1981), ed. Holtzman and Leich; Williams, *Ethics and the Limits of Philosophy*, 141–2.

16 Williams, *Descartes*, pp. 64–5.

17 Williams, *Ethics and the Limits of Philosophy*, pp. 111–12, 138–40.

18 Williams, *Descartes*, p. 64.

19 Ibid., p. 243.

20 It may be that Williams includes also other phenomena under the heading of 'perspectivalness', for example indexicality or the use of special vocabulary which marks one out as having some particular social position. And it may be that he is right to say that we must be able to make sense of a language from which these have been eliminated. But my objection will have force as long as the kind of perspectivalness I have indicated is one of the things Williams means.

21 *Philosophical Investigations*, sections 70, 71, 97–107.

22 Ibid., 80.

23 For further remarks to this effect see G. P. Baker and P. M. S. Hacker, *Wittgenstein: Meaning and Understanding* (1983), ch. 11.

24 In S. A. Kripke, *Wittgenstein on Rules and Private Language* (1982).

25 E.g. S. Blackburn, 'The Individual Strikes Back' (1984), p. 287.

26 Kripke, *Wittgenstein on Rules and Private Language*, pp. 8ff.

27 Ibid., p. 37.

28 See, for example, McGinn, *Wittgenstein on Meaning*, chs 2 and 4. For some further discussion see my critical notice of McGinn, in the *Philosophical Quarterly* (1986), pp. 412–19.

29 David Hume, *Treatise of Human Nature*, Part III; *Enquiry Concerning the Principles of Morals*, Appendix I.

30 S. Blackburn, *Spreading the Word* (1984), ch. 6; 'Truth, Realism and the Regulation of Theory', in *Midwest Studies in Philosophy* (1980), ed. French, Uehling and Wettstein.

31 Kripke, *Wittgenstein on Rules and Private Language*, pp. 89–92.

32 J. McDowell, 'Wittgenstein on Following a Rule' (1984); McGinn, *Wittgenstein on Meaning*.

33 Heal, 'The Disinterested Search for Truth' (1987–8).

CHAPTER 8   INTERPRETATIONS AND MISINTERPRETATIONS

1 It is possible to see this idea in D. Wiggins 'On Singling out an Object Determinately' in *Subject, Thought and Context* (1986), ed. Pettit and McDowell, esp. pp. 179–80, and *Sameness and Substance* (1980), chs 4 and 5. Another possible expression of it is P. M. S. Hacker 'Are Secondary Qualities Relative?' (1986).

2 *Philosophical Investigations*, section 1.

3 J. L. Austin, *How to do Things with Words* (1962).

4 'Can Analytic Philosophy be Systematic and Ought it to Be?', pp. 452–4.

5 *Philosophical Investigations*, sections 127, 415.

6 The literature here is immense but some central items are M. Dummett, 'Wittgenstein's Philosophy of Mathematics' in *Wittgenstein, Critical Essays* (1968), ed. Pitcher, and 'The Philosophical Basis of Intuitionistic Logic', S. Kripke, *Wittgenstein on Rules and Private Language* (1982). C. Wright's papers are collected and usefully introduced by him in *Realism, Meaning and Truth* (1986).

7 Dummett, 'Can Analytic Philosophy be Systematic and Ought it to Be?'

8 C. Wright, 'Anti-realist Semantics: The Role of Criteria' in *Idealism Past and Present* (1982), ed. Vesey.

9 Introduction to Wright's *Realism, Meaning and Truth*.

There is also a line of argument mentioned by Wright centring on the interpretation of Wittgenstein's rule-following considerations. On Wright's view these considerations are designed to show the untenability of 'objectivity' about meaning (roughly, minimal realism) and hence the untenability of Dummettian realism. I shall not discuss this line of thought explicitly. The objectivity of meaning is what the whole discussion is about and, on the general view I wish to propose, the rule-following considerations connect with Wittgenstein's rejection of mirroring realism (as sketched in section 7.1 above) and so play an important role in defusing anti-realist pressure and making objectivity about meaning defensible. What I would wish to oppose to Wright's rule-following argument in favour of anti-realism is thus implicit in section 7.1, in the latter part of this section and in ch. 9.

10 Wright, *Realism, Meaning and Truth*, p. 26.

11 Ibid., pp. 16–17.

12 For more on the difficult topic of criteria see S. Cavell, *The Claim of Reason* (1979), esp. Part I, and J. McDowell, 'Criteria, Defeasibility and Knowledge' (1982).

13 The argument of this section owes a great deal to J. McDowell 'Anti-Realism and the Epistemology of Understanding' in *Meaning and Understanding* (1981), ed. Parrett and Bouveresse.

14 This is a point pressed by E. J. Craig in 'Meaning, Use and Privacy', and by S. Blackburn in *Spreading the Word* (1984), pp. 64–6.

15 Wright, *Realism, Meaning and Truth*, pp. 20–2.

16 Wittgenstein's interlocutor asks 'But how can human understanding outstrip reality and itself *think* the unverifiable?' He answers himself, 'Why should we not say the unverifiable? For we ourselves made it unverifiable' (*Zettel*, section 259).

17 It is worth noting that Wright is attached to the mirroring idea and to the reality representing/non-reality representing distinction to which it gives rise. He explicitly remarks on the mirroring idea as an element in 'realism' – but he does not seem to think it likely to be one which will cause difficulties. See, for example, Wright's *Realism, Meaning and Truth*, pp. 6–7 and 'Inventing Logical Necessity' in *Language, Mind and Logic* (1986), ed. Butterfield, pp. 195ff.

18 For more on this issue see D. Edgington 'The Paradox of Knowability' (1985) and 'Verification and the Manifestation of Meaning' (1985); T. Williamson, 'Intuitionism Disproved' (1982); and Wright, *Realism, Meaning and Truth*, pp. 309–16.

19 H. Putnam, *Reason, Truth and History* (1981), ch. 2; *Meaning and the Moral Sciences* (1978), p. 125.

CHAPTER 9   INTERESTS, ACTIVITIES AND MEANINGS

1 See for example *Remarks on the Foundations of Mathematics*, III 31ff, III 41, V 45, VII 45.

2 Ibid., I 168, III 27, IV 23, VI 8, 24.

3 M. Dummett, 'Wittgenstein's Philosophy of Mathematics' in *Wittgenstein, Critical Essays* (1968), ed. Pitcher; C. Wright, *Wittgenstein on the Foundations of Mathematics* (1980).

4 *Philosophical Investigations*, 186, my italics.

5 *Remarks on the Foundations of Mathematics*, III 28.

6 Ibid., VII 47, VI 24.

7 Ibid., IV 29, VI 23, VII 21.

8 C. Wright, *Wittgenstein on the Foundations of Mathematics* (1980), pp. 45ff.

9 Cf. ibid., pp. 42–3.

10 Ibid., pp. 43ff.

11 For some other interesting cases of conceptual development see T. S. Kuhn 'A Function for Thought Experiments' in *Scientific Revolutions* (1981), ed. Hacking.

12 Compare the possibilities discussed by J. Fodor in *The Language of Thought* (1975), pp. 79–84.

13 D. Davidson, 'On the Very Idea of a Conceptual Scheme', in his *Inquiries into Truth and Interpretation* (1984).

14 Wittgenstein is interested in these kinds of differences. See *Remarks on the Foundations of Mathematics*, I 42–50, 58, 68, 69.

15 Wright, *Wittgenstein on the Foundations of Mathematics*, pp. 43, 96, 442ff.

16 Compare *Remarks on the Foundations of Mathematics*, VI 22.

17 As imagined by E. J. Craig in 'The Problem of Necessary Truth' in *Meaning, Reference and Necessity* (1975), ed. Blackburn.

18 Compare an illuminating attempt to do just this in connection with Wittgenstein's remarks about measuring in S. Cavell, *The Claim of Reason* (1979), pp. 115–18.

19 This is a line of Wittgensteinian interpretation explored by B. A. O. Williams in 'Wittgenstein and Idealism' (1981); see also J. Lear 'Leaving the World Alone' (1982) and 'The Disappearing "We"' (1984).

20 S. Kripke, *Wittgenstein on Rules and Private Language* (1982), pp. 8ff.

21 *Philosophical Investigations*, Part II, p. 224.

22 There are arguments which do aim to suggest the existence of just such algorithms. Quine's discussion of rabbit and rabbit parts (*Word and Object* (1960), ch. 2) and in *Ontological Relativity and Other Essays* (1969) may be regarded as such. See also J. Wallace 'Only in the Context of a Sentence do Words Have Any Meaning' 1977; D. Davidson 'The Inscrutability of Reference' in *Inquiries into Truth and Interpretation* (1984); H. Putnam *Reason, Truth and History* (1981), ch. 2. These arguments deserve consideration which I cannot give them here.

23 See the *Brown Book*, Part I, 44–9, 60–9, for some of Wittgenstein's examples.

24 *Remarks on the Foundations of Mathematics*, VI, 28.

Bibliography

Anscombe, G. E. M., 'The Question of Linguistic Idealism', in her *From Parmenides to Wittgenstein*, Collected Philosophical Papers, vol. I (Oxford: Basil Blackwell, 1981).

Austin, J. L., *How to do Things with Words* (Oxford: Clarendon Press, 1962).

Ayer, A. J., *Language Truth and Logic* (Harmondsworth, Middx: Penguin Books, 1971).

Baker, G. P., and Hacker, P. M. S., *Wittgenstein, Meaning and Understanding* (Oxford: Basil Blackwell, 1983).

Blackburn, S., *Spreading the Word* (Oxford: Clarendon Press, 1984).

——'The Individual Strikes Back', *Synthese* (1984), pp. 281–301.

——'Truth, Realism and the Regulation of Theory', in *Midwest Studies in Philosophy*, vol. V, ed. P. A. French, T. E. Uehling and H. Wettstein (Minnesota: University of Minnesota Press, 1980).

Cavell, S., *The Claim of Reason* (Oxford: Oxford University Press, 1979).

Chomsky, N., 'Quine's Empirical Assumptions', in *Words and Objections*, ed. D. Davidson and J. Hintikka, (Dordrecht, Holland: Reidel, 1969).

Craig, E. J., 'Meaning, Use and Privacy', *Mind* (1982), pp. 541–64.

——'The Problem of Necessary Truth', in *Meaning, Reference and Necessity*, ed. S. Blackburn (Cambridge: Cambridge University Press, 1975), pp. 1–31.

Dancy, J., *An Introduction to Contemporary Epistemology* (Oxford: Basil Blackwell, 1985).

Davidson, D., *Essays on Actions and Events* (Oxford: Clarendon Press, 1980).

——Inquiries into Truth and Interpretation, (Oxford: Clarendon Press, 1984).

Dummett, M., 'Wittgenstein's Philosophy of Mathematics', in *Wittgenstein, Critical Essays* ed. G. Pitcher, (London: Macmillan, 1968).

——'Can Analytic Philosophy be Systematic and Ought it to be' and 'The Philosophical Basis of Intuitionistic Logic', in *Truth and Other Enigmas* (London: Duckworth, 1978).

Edgington, D., 'The Paradox of Knowability', *Mind* (1985), pp. 557–68.

——'Verification and the Manifestation of Meaning', *Aristotelian Society Supplementary Volume* (1985), pp. 33–52.

Edwards, James C., *Ethics without Philosophy, Wittgenstein and the Moral Life*, (University Presses of Florida, 1982).

Evans, G., 'Identity and Predication', *Journal of Philosophy* (1975) pp. 343–63. Also in his *Collected Papers* (Oxford: Clarendon Press, 1985).

Field, H., 'Quine and the Correspondence Theory', *Philosophical Review* (1974), pp. 200–28.

Fodor, J., *The Language of Thought* (New York: Thomas Y. Crowell, 1975).

——*Modularity of Mind* (Cambridge, Mass.: MIT Press, 1983).

——*Psychosemantics* (Cambridge, Mass.: MIT Press, 1987).

Follesdal, D., 'Indeterminacy of Translation and Underdetermination of the Theory of Nature', *Dialectica* (1973), pp. 289–301.

Gibson Jr, Roger F., 'Translation, Physics and Facts of the Matter', in *The Philosophy of W. V. Quine*, ed. H. Hans and S. Schilpp, (La Salle, Illinois: Open Court, 1986).

Gregory, R. L., *Eye and Brain* (London: Weidenfeld and Nicholson, 1972).

Hacker, P. M. S., 'Are Secondary Qualities Relative?', *Mind* (1986), pp. 180–97.

Hale, B., *Abstract Objects* (Oxford: Basil Blackwell, 1987).

Hahn, H., 'Logic, Mathematics and the Knowledge of Nature' in *Logical Positivism*, ed. A. J. Ayer (London: Allen and Unwin, 1959).

Hahn, L. E., and Schilpp, P. A., (ed.), *The Philosophy of W. V. Quine* (La Salle, Illinois: Open Court, 1986).

Heal, J., 'The Disinterested Search for Truth', *Proceedings of the Aristotelian Society* (1987–8), pp. 97–108.

——'Replication and Functionalism', in *Language, Mind and Logic* ed. J. Butterfield (Cambridge: Cambridge University Press, 1986), pp. 135–50.

Hookway, C., *Quine* (Cambridge: Polity Press, 1988).

Hume, D., *A Treatise of Human Nature* (Oxford: Clarendon Press, 1978).

——*Enquiries Concerning Human Understanding and Concerning the Principles of Morals* (Oxford: Clarendon Press, 1975).

Kirk, R., *Translation Determined* (Oxford: Clarendon Press, 1986).

Kitcher, P., *The Nature of Mathematical Knowledge* (Oxford: Oxford University Press, 1984).

Kripke, Saul A., *Wittgenstein on Rules and Private Language* (Oxford: Basil Blackwell, 1982).

Kuhn, T. S., 'A Function for Thought Experiments', in *Scientific Revolutions*, ed. I. Hacking (Oxford: Oxford University Press, 1981).

Lear, J., 'Leaving the World Alone', *Journal of Philosophy* (1982), pp. 382–403.

——'The Disappearing "We"', *Aristotelian Society Supplementary Volume* (1984), pp. 219–42.

Lewis, D. K., 'General Semantics', *Synthese* (1970), pp. 18–67. Also in his *Collected Papers*, vol. I (Oxford: Oxford University Press, 1983).

McGinn, C., *Wittgenstein on Meaning* (Oxford: Basil Blackwell, 1984).

McDowell, J., 'Anti-Realism and the Epistemology of Understanding', in *Meaning and Understanding*, ed. Herman Parrett and Jacques Bouveresse (New York: Walter de Gruyter, 1981), pp. 225–48.

——'Non Cognitivism and Rule Following', in *Wittgenstein: to Follow a Rule*, ed. S. H. Holtzman and C. M. Leich (London: Routledge and Kegan Paul, 1981), pp. 141–62.

——'Criteria, Defeasibility and Knowledge', *Proceedings of the British Academy*, vol. LXVIII (Oxford: Oxford University Press, 1982), pp. 455–79.

——'Wittgenstein on Following a Rule', *Synthese* (1984), pp. 325–63.

——'Functionalism and Anomalous Monism' in *The Philosophy of Donald Davidson: Perspectives on Actions and Events*, ed. E. Lepore and B. McLaughlin (Oxford: Basil Blackwell, 1986), pp. 385–98.

Putnam, H., *Meaning and the Moral Sciences* (London: Routledge and Kegan Paul, 1978).

——*Reason, Truth and History* (Cambridge: Cambridge University Press, 1981).

Quine, W. V., *From a Logical Point of View* (New York: Harper and Row, 1953).

——*Word and Object* (Cambridge, Mass.: MIT Press, 1960).

——*The Ways of Paradox and Other Essays* (Cambridge, Mass.: Harvard University Press, 1966).

——*Ontological Relativity and Other Essays* (New York: Columbia University Press, 1969).

——*Philosophy of Logic* (Englewood Cliffs, NJ: Prentice Hall, 1970).

——*Theories and Things* (Cambridge, Mass.: Harvard University Press, 1981).

——'On the Reasons for Indeterminacy of Translation', *Journal of Philosophy* (1970), pp. 178–83.

——'Facts of the Matter', in *Essays on the Philosophy of W. V. Quine*, ed. R. W. Shahan and C. Swoyer (Hassocks, Sussex: Harvester Press, 1979).

R. Rorty, 'Indeterminacy of Translation and of Truth', *Synthese* (1972), pp. 443–62.

——*Philosophy and the Mirror of Nature* (Oxford: Basil Blackwell, 1980).

——*Consequences of Pragmatism* (Brighton, Sussex: Harvester Press, 1982).

Ryle, G., *The Concept of Mind* (London: Hutchinson, 1949).

Strawson, P. F., *Scepticism and Naturalism: Some Varieties* (London: Methuen, 1985).

Wallace, J., 'Only in the Context of a Sentence do Words Have Any Meaning', *Midwest Studies in Philosophy*, vol. II (University of Minnesota Press, 1977), ed. P. A. French, T. E. Uehling and H. K. Wettstein.

Wiggins, D., On Singling out an Object Determinately', in *Subject, Thought and Context* ed. P. Pettit and J. McDowell (Oxford: Clarendon Press, 1986).

——*Sameness and Substance* (Oxford: Basil Blackwell, 1980).

——'What Would be a Substantial Theory of Truth?' in *Philosophical Subjects: Essays Presented to P. F. Strawson*, ed. Z. van Straaten (Oxford: Clarendon Press, 1980).

Williams, B. A. O., 'Consistency and Realism' in *Problems of the Self* (Cambridge: Cambridge University Press, 1973), pp. 187–206.

——'The Truth in Relativism' and 'Wittgenstein and Idealism', in *Moral Luck* (Cambridge: Cambridge University Press, 1981).

——*Descartes: The Project of Pure Enquiry*, (Harmondsworth, Middx: Penguin Books, 1978).

——*Ethics and the Limits of Philosophy* (London: Fontana Press/Collins, 1985).

Williamson, T., 'Intuitionism Disproved', *Analysis* (1982), pp. 203–7.

Wittgenstein, L., *Philosophical Investigations*, 2nd edn (Oxford: Basil Blackwell, 1958).

——*The Blue and Brown Books* (Oxford: Basil Blackwell, 1958).

——*Zettel* (Oxford: Basil Blackwell, 1967).

——*On Certainty* (Oxford: Basil Blackwell, 1969).

——*Remarks on the Foundations of Mathematics*, 3rd edn, (Oxford: Basil Blackwell, 1978).

Wollheim, R., *Art and Its Objects* (Harmondsworth, Middx: Penguin Books, 1970).

Wright, C., *Wittgenstein on the Foundations of Mathematics*, (London: Duckworth, 1980).

——'Anti-realist Semantics: The Role of *Criteria*', in *Idealism Past and Present*, ed. G. Vesey (Cambridge: Cambridge University Press, 1982), pp. 225–48.

——'Kripke's Account of the Argument against Private Language', *Journal of Philosophy* (1984), pp. 759–78.

——*Realism Meaning and Truth* (Oxford: Basil Blackwell, 1986).

——'Facts and Certainty', *Proceedings of the British Academy*, vol. LXXI (1985), Oxford University Press, pp. 429–72.

——Inventing Logical Necessity' in *Language, Mind and Logic*, ed. J. Butterfield (Cambridge: Cambridge University Press, 1986), pp. 187–210.

——'Does *Philosophical Investigations* I 258–60 Suggest a Cogent Argument against Private Language?' in *Subject, Thought and Context*, ed. P. Pettit and J. McDowell (Oxford: Clarendon Press, 1986), pp. 209–66.

——'Scientific Realism, Observation and the Verification Principle', in *Fact, Science and Morality*, ed. G MacDonald and C. Wright (Oxford: Basil Blackwell, 1986) pp. 247–74.

Index

absolute conception 33–4, 149–60
abstract pattern of demands 95–6,
    100–2
analytic truth 54, 63–4, 83
analytical hypotheses 65, 71–2, 79
anti-realism 178–91
'assembling reminders' 176–7, 210
Austin, J. L. 170, 172
Ayer, A. J. 136

Blackburn, S. 163, 234

candid babbler 98, 105, 109
Carnap, R. 83
causal theory of meaning 90–1,
    104–11, 140, 145–6, 161, 162,
    165–6
colours 197–8, 200–3
conceptual change 192, 194–5,
    196–206, 211, 213
conceptual schemes 30, 31, 32,
    132–3, 196–7, 198–9, 210, 224
conventionalism 133, 136–7, 193,
    206, 208
convergence in judgement 18–19
criteria 184–7, 197–8, 201–2,
    203–4

Davidson, D. 5–6, 49, 86, 98, 141,
    153, 199, 232, 233
determinacy of sense 159, 196, 207
Duhem's thesis 46–7, 64
Dummett, M. A. E. 8, 136, 178,
    179, 180, 191

empiricism 4, 5, 27, 35, 40–1,
    45–6, 136–9, 150, 179, 193

fact, factual statement see realism
fact/value distinction 162–3
Field, H. 72–3
Fodor, J. 90–1
Follesdal, D. 230
forms of life 9, 206–10, 213–15
Frege, G. 196
functionalism 7, 8, 140–1, 152–3

Gibson, R. F. 78

holism 2, 5, 46
    epistemological 5, 97, 105–9, 123
    functional 46–7, 86–7
    semantic 5, 6, 8, 86–91, 99–100,
        107–8, 141, 218–19
holistic constraints 91, 96–7,
    100–2, 103–4, 140, 219
Hookway, C. 232
Hume, D. 162, 165

idealism 26, 27, 28
imperatives 12, 14–15, 18, 20, 229–30
incommensurability 30, 31
incompatibility of linguistic
    moves 12–14, 15, 18–20,
        29–30, 32, 126, 138–9, 155, 212,
        216–18
indeterminacy 20, 93–5
    of function 48, 50, 51, 52–3
    of meaning and translation 37, 47,
        51–2, 54, 68–9, 71–2, 75–6,
        77, 78, 91–2, 101–2, 115–21,
        129, 135
    see also meaning scepticism
inscrutability of reference see
    ontological relativity

instrumentalism 4, 35, 41–2, 46, 47, 54, 55, 66–9, 120
intelligibility 99–100, 148–9, 159–60
  see also semantic holism
intention 12, 181
interests as connected with
    meaning 8, 113, 144–5, 148–9, 151–2, 158–9, 160, 165–6, 168–9, 174–7, 203–6, 208–10, 215–16, 226–8
interpretation *see* translation
intersubjectivity 33–4

James, H. 134

Kripke, S. 8, 69, 112, 145, 160–6, 178, 216

language games 169–70
Leibniz, G. W. 72, 73
Lewis, D. K. 49

McDowell, J. 153
manifestation argument 180, 181–90
meaning and use 180, 182, 183–4
meaning scepticism 4, 5–6, 9–10, 20–1, 69, 111, 112–21, 194, 218–19, 221–2, 224, 227
  see also indeterminacy of meaning and translation
measuring 169, 171, 173–4
metaphysical realism 16, 191
mind independence 16–18, 24, 26–8
modal realism 54, 133–4, 135–9, 211–16
moral realism 16, 162–3
mosaic construction 92–8, 102–4

naturalism 35–6, 66–7, 79, 82–5, 133, 234
Neurath, O. 124
normativity of meaning 69, 161, 162, 180–1

observation statement 35, 37, 39, 41, 61, 63–5, 75, 84, 110–11, 122

ontological relativity 71–4, 78, 239

P-predicates 95, 96–7, 99, 101, 111
perspectival representation 150, 151, 153–4, 156–7, 158, 159, 236
philosophy of mathematics 9, 192–6, 210–16
physicalism 36–7, 38, 39, 68–9, 75–6
pictorial representation 88, 92–8
Platonism 1, 3, 135–9, 192–3, 194, 195–6, 207, 208, 209, 214–15
pragmatism 2, 6, 22, 54, 120, 121–9, 130–2, 137, 140, 173, 177
predictive sentence machine 42
  function of parts in 46–54
  self-modifying 56–9
  setting up 42–5
principle of non-contradiction 15, 16, 17, 18, 20, 91–2, 111, 115–18, 123, 177–8, 217–18
private language argument 230
proof 192, 194–5, 199–200, 205–6, 206–7, 210–16
projectivism
  about meaning 163–5
  about necessity 125–6, 214–15
  about value 162–3
Putnam, H. 191

Quine, W. V. O. 1, 2, 3, 4, 5, 7, 8, 20, 25, 35, 36–40, 47, 49–50, 51, 54, 55, 60–85, 87, 98, 105, 109, 112, 120, 153, 221

realism 3, 9, 12, 25, 26, 70, 77, 115, 177–8, 179
  minimal 3, 12–20, 21–5, 32, 33, 115–21, 133–4, 139, 148, 149, 212, 214
  mirroring 4, 6, 8, 9, 23–4, 27, 28, 32–3, 35, 70, 82–4, 135, 140–2, 143, 167, 174, 179, 188, 190, 210, 225–6
  pragmatist 4, 6, 9, 22, 120–1, 123, 127–9
  quietist 4, 9, 24, 176–7, 214–15
recalcitrant experience 122–3, 124–9

relativism 9, 30–4, 148–9, 210
revisability of logic 55–9, 124–9
rule following 145–9, 193, 194, 227–8, 237
Ryle, G. 89

secondary qualities 20
self-stultification 12, 13, 17, 29
sense data 27, 40–1, 47, 60, 61–3, 64
speech acts 169–75, 178
stage setting for meaning 170–1, 226–8
Strawson, P. F. 235

'taking for granted' 129–34, 157, 212
'taking seriously' 79, 80–1
theoretical statements 38, 39, 41, 110–11, 122
totality of possibilities 135, 139–40, 141, 159, 196–7, 207, 208, 211, 214, 220–1, 223–5
translation 38, 51, 68–9, 74, 98–9, 141–2

see also indeterminacy of translation and meaning
truth 18, 22, 151–2, 162, 164, 177
disquotational theory of 74, 77, 80, 81, 140

U-predicates 95, 96, 99, 101, 111
underdetermination of theory by data 46, 51, 52, 75, 77–8

verification transcendence 26, 178, 180, 183–4, 188–90, 190–1

Wiggins, D. 229
Williams, B. A. O. 8, 149–60, 229, 230, 236
Wittgenstein, L. 1, 2, 3, 7, 8, 10, 62, 69, 84, 112–13, 130–4, 139, 141–9, 159, 164, 167, 169, 170, 172, 178, 179, 180, 183, 185–7, 196, 199, 206–10, 211–16, 221
Wright, C. 8, 122, 124, 125, 126–7, 128, 130, 178, 180, 181, 183, 184, 194, 195, 239